JETS UNDERGROUND

Wahoo, Joe Willie, and the Swingin', Swaggerin' World of Gang Green

Jeff Freier

TRIUMPH
B O O K S

Library of Congress Cataloging-in-Publication Data

Freier, Jeff.
   Jets underground : Wahoo, Joe Willie, and the swingin' swaggerin' world of gang green / Jeff Freier.
      p. cm.
   ISBN 978-1-60078-607-5
   1. New York Jets (Football team) I. Title.
   GV956.N37F74 2011
   796.332'64097471—dc23

                                              2011025591

This book is available in quantity at special discounts for your group or organization. For further information, contact:

Triumph Books
542 South Dearborn Street
Suite 750
Chicago, Illinois 60605
(312) 939-3330
Fax (312) 663-3557
www.triumphbooks.com

Printed in U.S.A.
ISBN: 978-1-60078-607-5
Design by Patricia Frey

CONTENTS

ACKNOWLEDGMENTS

I'D LIKE TO THANK Michael Emmerich, Don Gulbrandsen, and Noah Amstadter of Triumph Books for their trust and faith; Monta Derden, Nikki Rowe, Wesley Walker, Raul Allegre, and Steve Serby, for their time and graciousness; Rob Kowal of 1240 WGBB Sports Radio New York, Ed Valentine of SB Nation New York, and Jeff Zachowski of Hot Stove New York, for hiring me to write for their respective websites (and Rob for his assistance with this book); the triumvirate of Leslie Ryan, Steve Greene, and Joe Giannella, for their Jets expertise, memories, and wisecracks; Michele Martin, for her detective skills; my father, Van, and brothers, Greg and Eric, for digging up old books and their knowledge of the Jets, football in general, and *The Odd Couple*; and special thanks to my wife, Janmarie, for letting me commandeer the computer and having full faith in me ("I don't care if you don't know how to write a book, if somebody's paying you, you'd be an idiot not to do it."), and young daughter, Tracey, for putting everything in perspective. After asking me how I knew so much about the Jets, I answered that I had to research the team's history, read old newspaper and magazine articles, and conduct interviews. To which she replied, "Oh, so you're cheating."

INTRODUCTION

THE JETS WERE BORN WILD. They came into the world leaning against a brick wall while coolly smoking a cigarette. When the old-fashioned, good-citizen NFL posed the question, "What are you rebelling against?" New York's newly formed franchise answered, "Whaddya got?" The Jets came from a rebel league and were instantly cast as the incorrigible little brother to the staid New York Giants. The franchise was a juvenile delinquent. They were the red-headed stepchild, if the red-headed stepchild pilfered money from your wallet and guzzled from a bottle of Wild Turkey. They were so bad they even had to change their name from the Titans to the Jets.

As the NFL lived its careful, stable life, the AFL and the Titans blew into town, bringing the Wild West with them. They were gunslingers. They were banditos who didn't need no stinkin' badges. And they were all rejects. The eight new teams of the fledgling league were built with castoffs, throwaways, stowaways, and orphans. The Titans were the Dirty Dozen. Quarterback Al Dorow was Lee Marvin. Don Maynard was Charles Bronson. Art Powell was Jim Brown. Larry Grantham was John Cassavetes. And Bill Mathis was Donald Sutherland.

While the tradition-filled NFL franchises descended from

legendary paternalistic families that went by names such as Halas, Mara, and Rooney, the Titans stumbled into the world with broadcaster, skinflint, hustler, and storied hyperbolist Harry Wismer as their founding father. Has their long, colorful, and checkered history been due to nature or nurture? Maybe they never had a chance. No wonder they were about to be sent to juvie before Sonny Werblin came to their rescue in 1963.

The Titans could barely draw 10,000 fans a game for their first three seasons. But that didn't stop them. They often didn't pay their own players. But that didn't stop them. They played in a crumbling, decaying stadium. But that didn't stop them. They ran out of money. But that didn't stop them. The local media treated them with disdain, when they bothered to acknowledge them at all. Even that didn't stop them. They just couldn't take a hint.

On the field, the Jets have only won one Super Bowl. But they were the insurgents, the agitators, the anarchists—they took no prisoners as they introduced the old NFL to their swashbuckling personality, defeating the crew-cutted Baltimore Colts while boastfully announcing they would do so beforehand. And with that one championship victory, professional football was never the same again.

Gang Green has authored miracle comebacks and exhilarating overtime victories, but the word heartbreak lies near the top of every Jets fan's lexicon. The battle cry "J-E-T-S, Jets! Jets! Jets!" can quickly be followed by the often-uttered sad lament of "Same old Jets." They're one big roller-coaster ride. Or maybe the fun house is more like it. After the team's humble beginnings as the Titans and meteoric rise as kings of the world, the Jets crashed in the 1970s, with Namath's knees as fragile as New York City's financial situation ("Ford to Broadway Joe's Knees: Drop Dead"). The '80s were a wild ride of a party. The '90s were middling to rock bottom and then up again. The Aughts saw success with five playoff appearances. And now the team is in the booming, boisterous Rex Ryan era, swaggerin' rebels once again.

What follows isn't a history of the New York Jets. Nor is it a police blotter. It's more of an epic poem, an ode to the team's mirthful, carefree, wild side, a rhapsody to the colorful, flaky, rambunctious, and just plain odd personalities that have graced the Jets' roster over the years. And to a few of their rocking, rolling, and rollicking games on the field (not to mention movies and TV shows). It's a snapshot of the franchise. While the picture was being taken, however, a handful of players were starting a fracas. They were flipping off the photographer. They were mooning the camera. They were being rogues and knaves. They were being the New York Jets—but they were having the time of their lives.

The Jets may not be a model franchise. They may not have won multiple championships. They may not be America's Team or even all of New York's team. But to the loyal, die-hard fans of Jets Nation who live and die with every play and embrace the talented player and not-so-talented alike, they're the *only* team. And that's all that matters.

CHAPTER 1

HUSTLIN' HARRY, SLINGIN' SAMMY, AND THE BIRTH OF THE TITANS

LET'S START AT THE BEGINNING. Before the Jets (or Titans) were even a gleam in anybody's eye, there was Lamar Hunt, the George Washington of the AFL. "In January of '59...the thought just occurred to me.... Why wouldn't it be possible to form a second league?... It was like the lightbulb coming on over your head," Hunt said. And from that revelation sprung the AFL. And from the AFL sprung the New York Titans.

Gotham's virgin team crawled out of the primordial ooze an outcast, an underdog, a vagabond. Its first home was the Polo Grounds, which technically was in Manhattan, but the Titans were not Park Avenue or the Upper East Side—they were the outer boroughs, the hustling street corners, the palookaville section of the City. They were a Ralph Kramden get-rich scheme, with a dash of Ricky Ricardo's Tropicana Club style and panache thrown in but with Lucy always right around the corner, sporting a mustache and disguise, trying to finagle her way into the show bringing an amateur-hour aspect to the proceedings. While the Titans' fraternal

1

twin, the New York Mets, replaced the Brooklyn Dodgers and New York (baseball) Giants in a century-old league, thus having a built-in fan base, the infant AFLers were a brand-new concept. They were a crapshoot, only one poker game away from ceasing to exist.

When Lamar Hunt said, "Let there be an American Football League," Harry Wismer declared, "Deal me in." Wismer was a man of many feuds and cooked-up concoctions, and he never met an exaggeration he didn't like. He was a name-dropper of the highest order. He was a drinker. He was mercurial. He was unconventional. He was idiosyncratic. But he was also enthusiastic, a people person, and a visionary. If there were a brisk, CliffsNotes, 1940s-newsreel version of The Harry Wismer Story, it would go something like this:

Born in 1913 in Port Huron, Michigan, Wismer was a top-flight high school athlete. He played football at both the University of Florida and Michigan State University. But a knee injury foiled his dreams of gridiron stardom. Moving into the broadcast booth, he became the voice of Michigan State football and moonlighted as the public address announcer for the NFL's Detroit Lions. He continued his career behind the microphone as a freelancer, working collegiate games before moving up to the pro ranks with the Washington Redskins. He became synonymous with the D.C. fighting 11 and even purchased 25 percent of the team. After a bitter feud that resulted in litigation with Redskins founder George Preston Marshall (partly over Marshall's refusal to sign African-American players), Wismer moved on again.

Wismer was one of the first to imagine football games shown on television at night when he broadcast edited reruns of Notre Dame contests on Sunday evenings. He was also in the broadcast booth when the NFL briefly scheduled a Saturday night game each week to be aired over the old DuMont TV network in the 1950s. Wismer bought the New York Titans in 1959 and sold them in 1963. By the mid-'60s, he was broke, depressed, an alcoholic, and in failing

2

Original New York Titans owner Harry Wismer (center) meets with AFL Commissioner Joe Foss (left) and Houston Oilers owner Bud Adams after the Oilers' victory in the 1960 AFL Championship Game. (Lou Witt/Getty Images)

health. In 1967, while drunk, he fell down a flight of stairs in a New York City restaurant and died the next day. So the Harry Wismer Story was not necessarily a happy one.

Getting back to 1960, one thing Wismer did have was a fertile imagination. And out of that imagination came an idea that was so brilliant, presumptuous, and forward-looking that it lives on to this day. And it has made many men rich beyond their wildest dreams. Even though he owned the New York franchise of the neophyte AFL, which one would think would be the most prosperous and have the most money-making potential out of the eight AFL teams, he hatched the idea of television revenue sharing. Each team would split the profits from the rights to broadcast their games. A league needed each team to be strong and profitable, not just one or two powerhouses.

"The whole difference in this league is the sale of television, and your old buddy here sold it. The American Football League is the league of the future," Wismer proudly declared. That concept has been the lynchpin of success for the NFL going on 50 years now. Today's team owners can thank Wismer for his vision and forethought.

Next on Wismer's to-do list was to hire a coach. And for that he reached back to his Redskins days and enlisted one of the greatest quarterbacks in pro football history, Slingin' Sammy Baugh, who had spent his entire 16-year career with the 'Skins.

Baugh was born and raised in Texas and played baseball and football for Sweetwater High School. Baseball was his first love. In fact, he picked up his nickname while playing third base for Texas Christian University's Horned Frogs. He was also a two-time All-American quarterback while attending college. Baugh signed with baseball's St. Louis Cardinals, but dissatisfied with playing in the low minor leagues he decided to devote his full attention to football and the Redskins. An immediate success, he led Washington to the 1937 NFL Championship in his rookie season. He won a second title in 1942.

There were many two-way players in Baugh's era, but Slingin' Sammy was a three-way threat: quarterback, defensive back, and punter. And he was one of the best ever at all three positions. His signature season came in 1943, when he led the NFL in passing,

4

punting, and interceptions (caught, not thrown). He threw four touchdown passes and snared four picks in one game alone.

Baugh is credited with modernizing the quarterback position as the forefather of the forward pass. When he retired he held 13 different NFL records spanning three positions, was named to the All-NFL team seven times, and led the league in passing six times and punting five times. He was elected to the Pro Football Hall of Fame with the inaugural class of 1963. Baugh spent two years at the helm of the Titans. He coached the Oilers for one season in 1964 but left professional football for good after that short stint in Houston. He went on to live a long life, married to his high school sweetheart, and died at the age of 94. Unlike Wismer's, his was a happy story.

On the field, the Titans weren't great but they weren't awful. "We had a poor football team when we left training camp. Right now we've got a very ordinary team," Baugh said around opening day in 1960. But when queried if his measuring stick was the NFL or AFL, he went on to say, "By this league's standards, a pretty good team." Titans defensive tackle Sid Youngelman added, "In the NFL there are no weak spots. Here, while you don't relax, you are better able to pace yourself."

Let's face it, with eight teams filled with players who had never met each other, much less played together before, the quality of play in those early days suffered. The games resembled something out of *Horse Feathers*, minus Harpo and the horse. The Titans (and every other team) were strangers thrown together to construct a cohesive unit, to build chemistry with unfamiliar, disparate parts. And they had to do it in the decomposing Polo Grounds without knowing if they would actually get paid for their services from week to week. It wasn't as easy as it looked—especially in those blue-and-yellow Titan uniforms.

In their inaugural season of 1960, New York came in second place to the AFL Champion Oilers in the East Division with a 7–7

Al Dorow (12), New York's quarterback during the Titans' inaugural AFL season, is sacked by Houston defensive end Dan Lamphear (73) as Don Floyd (75) closes in during the Oilers' 27–21 win over the Titans in 1960. New York finished 7–7 in its first season. (Lou Witt/Getty Images)

record. They led the league in scoring, averaging 27.3 points per game, reflecting Baugh's chuck-it-down-the-field-and-see-who-catches-it offensive philosophy. Unfortunately, they were last in defense, reflecting a complete lack of any philosophy. They repeated their performance in 1961, again finishing 7–7. And in Wismer's final season, the last with the franchise calling itself the Titans, the team dropped to 5–9.

Off the field was where the fun could be found, though. When Harry Wismer was around, fun was a constant companion. Well, maybe fun is not the right word. Antics, high jinks, capers, shenanigans, stunts, and larks may be better descriptors. And add infuriation, stinginess, pettiness, puffery, and drunkenness for good measure. We're talking about a man who would occasionally claim to have spotted celebrities and public figures in the crowd back in his radio announcing days, when those persons of renown were nowhere near the football stadium and might possibly not even have been in the same country. "I plug my friends. I say, 'Dean Acheson is here. President Eisenhower just walked in. There goes Dick Nixon.'" The truth never stopped Harry Wismer.

And when he bumped into an old acquaintance, he'd excitedly exclaim, "Congratulations!" "I always say congratulations," Wismer said. "It makes people feel good. 'Congratulations!' Congratulations can mean anything! It rings a note! It's wonderful! And it's a great opening line! 'Congratulations!' And they say, 'How do you know?' And I say, 'I keep pace.'" On top of that, he wasn't shy about spreading false rumors just for kicks. A favorite was, "So they shot Castro!" "You get a lot of emotional reaction from people," he said. And let's not forget the self-promoting hucksterism of Wismer. After soliciting team pictures from the Titans to promote an upcoming game, the Chargers received a dozen photos of... Harry Wismer.

The First Touchdown

On Sunday, September 11, 1960, the Titans made their debut. Two games had already been played in the new AFL, as the Denver Broncos and Boston Patriots opened the proceedings on Friday night (with Denver being the answer to the trivia question of who won the first AFL game) and the Los Angeles Chargers taking on the Dallas Texans on Saturday.

The Titans hosted the Buffalo Bills in a downpour and watched as their opponent opened up the scoring in the first quarter with a 35-yard Darrell Harper field goal. Since the "Same old Jets" sentiment hadn't yet bubbled to the surface (there would be plenty of time for that later), there was no need to worry, as that field goal was the sum of Buffalo's offensive output for the afternoon. The Titans scored their first points in the second quarter on a 15-yard Bill Shockley field goal.

With the Titans unable to muster up much offense in the early going, Coach Sammy Baugh yanked starting quarterback Dick Jamieson and replaced him with Al Dorow, a wily, tough-as-nails 30-year-old who never shied away from scrambling and improvising. In fact, he led the Titans in rushing in 1960, gaining 453 yards. He had previously spent three seasons with the Redskins, one with the Eagles, and two in the Canadian Football League before being handpicked by Wismer to join the newly formed Titans. In that inaugural season, Dorow would lead all AFL quarterbacks with 26 touchdowns, and the following year he was atop the leader board in completions, attempts, and interceptions. Before the 1962 season Dorow was traded to Buffalo, but he injured his arm in Week 4 and eventually had to retire.

In the second quarter, after a poor Bills punt, the Titans started a drive in golden position on Buffalo's 43-yard line. The key play that would set up the first franchise touchdown was appropriately made by Don Maynard, the team's most prolific receiver. Maynard reeled in a 20-yard pass from Dorow. With only two yards to go, Dorow's running skills would be put to good use. Taking the snap, he followed a perfect block by Maynard and waltzed around the left side of the line untouched into the end zone for six points.

Dorow went on to rush for another touchdown that afternoon, Shockley kicked a 39-yard field goal, and Art Powell caught a 13-yard touchdown pass from Jamieson to finish the scoring, as the Titans rolled to a 27–3 victory.

The Titans owner was a complex man. He could be grating, he could be charming, he could be profane, he could be miserly, and he could be exuberant—all on the same day. All in the same hour. A friend once said of him, "If you knew Harry for a month or two, you'd hate him. After a year, you'd begin to reverse yourself. If Harry would only let his accomplishments speak for themselves instead of letting himself speak for his accomplishments, he'd be much better off. There are so many compensating qualities to the man."

In his brief tenure in the AFL, Wismer grew to resent his fellow owners. He had, after all, acquired his money through years of working his way up in the sports world. He didn't inherit a fortune. He was a self-made man. His humble background was a constant source of motivation. His father managed a clothing store, and one of Wismer's four siblings died of diphtheria only weeks before the future Titans owner was born, with his mother also coming down with the disease.

"I think I was born to keep driving," Wismer said. "My mother often said that she was so determined to have me born that it helped her live, and I think some of the strength and determination might have crossed over." He went on to say, "I used to read extensively when I was a kid. Those Horatio Alger and Merriwell books. They used to send a chill up and down me! I'd read every book about this man's success, that man's success. I'd wipe the dishes for my mother and I'd say, 'Don't worry. Someday you won't have to worry about all those bills. I'll take care of everything.'"

The majority of his seven comrades on the other hand, particularly Dallas Texans/Kansas City Chiefs owner Hunt and fellow AFL founder and Oilers owner Bud Adams, made their money the old-fashioned way—through their fathers. In the eyes of the streetwise Wismer, who was still broadcasting Notre Dame games while running the Titans, they were little rich kids playing with their new toys. "I've gambled everything. I'm not getting a dime," he said of his investment in his team. "I don't have an H.L. Hunt, a Boots Adams, or a Conrad Hilton to back me up." Wismer even went so far as to hire a private investigator to have Hunt and Adams tailed when he discovered they were meeting with the NFL to ensure there were no back-room deals going on to undermine Wismer's stake in the league.

And Wismer's animosity toward AFL commissioner Joe Foss reached Hatfield vs. McCoy feud levels when the powers that be tried to force Wismer out of the league in 1962. Wismer used pranks, crank phone calls, and other assorted tomfoolery to stick it to his foe. And Foss was no lightweight or fool. He was a World War II flying ace and Medal of Honor winner, after all. He was an actual real-life American hero who brought legitimacy and dignity to the new league.

While Foss was traveling around on the road, engaged in his commissioner duties, Wismer would find out where he was staying and order room service for 10 to be delivered to Foss' room before the crack of dawn. Wismer would somehow cancel Foss' plane travel arrangements, with Foss not discovering the ruse until he was already at the airport. Wismer would even make crank phone calls to sportswriters, anonymously badmouthing the Titans and the AFL. Were those escapades childish? Petty? Unbecoming of an adult? Especially one in position of power? Yes, they were. But that was Harry Wismer.

After the Titans' first two seasons, Wismer soured on Baugh, which presented a problem. The coach had signed a three-year contract before the 1960 season, so he was still owed his $20,000 salary for 1962. Now if you owned a football team and wanted to fire your coach with one year left on his contract but didn't want to pay him, what would you do? Bite the bullet, fire him, and eat the money? Suffer through one more year of him on the sidelines? Try to work out a deal with another team, hoping to unload his contract and accept a pittance in return? That trio of scenarios makes perfect sense, of course. Now what about these outrageous ideas? All of the following are ridiculous and aren't based in reality at all, right? Well, here's a pop quiz—one of these brainstorms is the course of action that Wismer took with Baugh. See if you can guess which one the Titans owner chose:

1. Tell the coach that the team has folded, apologize, trick him into submitting his resignation ("Just a legal formality"), and wish him luck in his further endeavors while crossing your fingers he doesn't notice when the new season begins play.
2. Pretend like the team never existed in the first place while slyly getting him to sign a letter of resignation as you sell him insurance.
3. Demote the coach while moving training camp to an undisclosed location without divulging to him where it's being held in the hopes that he'll just never show up.

If you selected option number three, you're the grand winner. Baugh learned of his demotion to kicking coach and the hiring of new head coach Bulldog Turner in the newspaper. He unearthed the double-secret location of the Titans' training camp through his players (it helps to be a players' coach) and showed up on schedule. Knowing exactly what Wismer was up to, Baugh gladly accepted $20,000 to be a low-rung assistant. He stayed out of Turner's way as much as possible, while doing a minimal amount of coaching and hung around for the ride. Once Wismer realized Baugh wasn't going to storm off and quit, a compromise was reached. Baugh would get his money in monthly installments and stay on as something of a consultant to the team. Baugh received a portion of his money but went to his grave waiting for the rest.

In the Titans' debut season, the team drew 114,682 fans in seven home games. By 1962 that number had shriveled all the way down to 36,161 total attendees for the season. Before a game at the Polo Grounds against the Boston Patriots, the Titans ran onto the field for pregame warm-ups and noticed that the clanking of their cleats on the concrete ramp sounded slightly peculiar. When they looked up into the stands, they discovered why. There weren't enough fans to drown out a handful of chirping crickets. The players' cleats were echoing in a near-empty stadium. Linebacker Larry Grantham came up with an inspiring idea: "Instead of running through the goalposts for introductions, let's just go up and shake hands with everybody," Grantham said. "It would be faster. It won't take more than one or two minutes."

With the result of a dwindling fan base came a stark and ominous fact: Harry Wismer and the Titans were running out of money. To make it appear that the team was drawing a larger crowd than it was, they started letting in the neighborhood kids for free. While those lucky tykes were sitting at the 50-yard line, the players' wives were banished to the corner of the upper deck. The team wouldn't splurge for better seats. On many occasions, Wismer just fabricated attendance figures anyway. He counted eyeballs instead of people, joked one wiseacre. If he didn't blush at telling fans that Dick Nixon was enjoying front-row seats when he was 2,000 miles away in his vice presidential office, why not claim 15,000 attended a Titans game when the actual figure was less than 5,000?

Another cost-cutting measure included cutting down the team's film projector inventory. Down to only one, the offense and defense had to take turns viewing game film of the opposing team, which, of course, now took twice as long, reducing their practice time. While preparing for a game against Houston, the projector broke, and the players and coaches were on their own in scouting the Oilers' tendencies, plays, and players. A defensive coach queried his team about Houston's offense, and one Titan cracked, "It's like ours, only better." With that scouting report in hand, they lost 56–17. A bulb was magically replaced in the projector before the next game with Dallas, which helped them immensely as the Titans only lost 20–17.

The Titan players spent every road trip in 1962 never knowing if the team bus would show up to take them to and from practice or even to the game. After a practice before the second game of the year in the torrid, scalding heat of San Diego, the bus never arrived to chauffeur them back to their hotel, which was 45 minutes away from the field. Even their coach abandoned them when he jumped into a car with a sportswriter. A few players hitched rides with some nearby high school kids, but most of the team slogged back to the hotel, dragging pads and equipment with them.

Later in the season, in Boston, the team was packed onto the bus ready to head to Nickerson Field, but there was one glitch in the procedure. The bus driver refused to move until he got paid. He was good-hearted and charitable enough to only insist on the one-way fare, though. After the game, the team could find their way back to the hotel on their own. General Manager George Sauer went off to cash a check, returning with money in hand before the bus driver shifted the bus into drive. But Harry Wismer appeared with his new bride. The two climbed aboard just long enough for the owner, who appeared to be in his cups, to inspire his charges. "Fellas, this has been a rotten season," the owner told the team. "It's been a rotten season, but it's not over yet. But today is my wife's birthday. And I want you to win this one for her." The two walked back into the hotel. His team lost 24–17.

Wismer had recently wed the widow of reputed mobster Abner "Longy" Zwillman. Known as "the Al Capone of New Jersey," Zwillman had hanged himself in the basement of his West Orange, New Jersey, home a few years earlier. In a sign of letting bygones be bygones, Wismer's best man was Joe Foss. Wismer could start feuds with the best of them, but he could also end them. Wismer had previously been married to Henry Ford's niece. Apparently a high profile was one of the attributes he was looking for in a wife.

The players were hoping their owner's latest bride's money would save the team. Instead, Wismer named her team president. It was just another case of Harry Wismer being Harry Wismer. The owner instructed reporters that she would be the spokesperson for the team going forward. When a journalist posed a question and she began to respond, Wismer butted in, "Honey, *after* this story you can talk all the time."

In the meantime, players never knew if there was enough money to cover the payroll. Grantham said, "I was living at the Concourse Plaza Hotel in the Bronx. I used to cash my checks at a bank near there where I was pretty well known. It was always the same story. 'We can't give you immediate credit. We have to see if the check will clear.' Of course a lot of times it wouldn't. So I'd call Wismer or his secretary and they'd tell me, 'Oh, we've changed banks,' or something like that. I was a young naïve kid that didn't know any better, and I believed them." His advice to one of his teammates became the team slogan: "Don't cash it with anybody you like."

Sometimes there were no paychecks at all. A league rule stated that teams must pay their players within 24 hours after a game. When guard Bob Mischak declared, "Our paychecks are now 194 hours overdue," the players went on strike, refusing to practice or play in that week's game. The players eventually practiced on their own—the infuriated Wismer wouldn't allow his coaching staff to coach them—and the owner reluctantly paid the players before that weekend's game. It was the best set of practices the players had all year, they claimed.

Finally, the players were told they could only cash their paychecks at one certain bank and by one designated teller. Which day would actually be payday was a weekly mystery. If the players were on the field for practice but the coaches had suddenly disappeared, they knew that paychecks were being doled out. They would bolt back inside, grab their checks, and race each other to the bank. The coaches already had a head start, of course. A handful of the more hygienic players would shower first, but most would throw on a coat over their practice sweats and hotfoot it to the bank. It was a first-come-first-served, you-snooze-you-lose situation. If the teller ran out of money, the players at the end of the line were just plain out of luck.

The other league owners were running out of patience with Wismer and were wholly exasperated with him. Bud Adams flatly stated, "Frankly, I'd like to see a change in ownership in New York. Harry Wismer is likely to lose $400,000 to $500,000 this year, and I don't know how much longer he can go on. But as long as Harry is fulfilling his obligation to the league, there's nothing we can do."

Wismer didn't go on much longer, though, as the league seized control of the Titans' finances. The team was sold to a group headed by Sonny Werblin after the season. With the players about to take the field for the last game of the 1962 season against the Oilers, Coach Turner imparted a few pearls of wisdom to his crew. In his attempt to out–Knute Rockne Wismer, Turner sent his troops out to their final battle with this speech: "This is the final game of the season. There probably won't even be any New York Titans next year. So most of you are playing in your last pro game. Most of you aren't good enough to play anywhere else."

They promptly lost 44–10. And thus ended the era of Harry Wismer and the New York Titans.

CHAPTER 2

PORTRAIT OF A COWBOY IN A STRANGE LAND

SEASON THREE'S 17TH EPISODE OF *The Simpsons* was titled "Homer at the Bat." The premise involved the usually inept Springfield Nuclear Power Plant's softball team, which was producing a surprisingly successful year. The majority of the credit was due to Homer's magical "Wonder Bat," which led them to an undefeated regular season.

With Springfield meeting Shelbyville Nuclear Power Plant for the league championship, the nefarious Montgomery Burns, owner of the Springfield plant, places a huge wager on the game. To ensure victory for his team, he rounds up a group of major league ringers to replace his employees. After being informed by his subordinate, Smithers, that his original selections—Honus Wagner, Cap Anson, Mordecai "Three-Finger" Brown—were either long retired or dead, Mr. Burns settles on present-day players such as Darryl Strawberry, Wade Boggs, and Don Mattingly.

Mr. Burns, crotchety and old school to the end, walks by a shaggy Mattingly and demands that the first baseman shave off his sideburns. Mattingly, confused, insists that he doesn't sport sideburns. Mr. Burns sternly repeats his order. And on it went with more ultimatums. Finally, Mattingly completely shaves the sides of

With his trademark sideburns, Don Maynard looks on during a 1971 loss in San Diego. Maynard starred at receiver for the Jets for more than a decade. (Richard Stagg/Getty Images)

his head, leaving himself with a wisp of front hair and a Mohawk-like back mane, which still doesn't appease Mr. Burns, who rebukes the Yankee: "Mattingly, I thought I told you to trim those sideburns. Go home! You're off the team, for good!" Mattingly replies, "Fine...I still like him better than Steinbrenner."

An incident eerily similar occurred some three decades prior to the airing of that cartoon, when New York Giants head coach Jim Lee Howell took the same no-nonsense approach to one of his players' lack of clean-cut grooming habits. "Shave those sideburns off," Howell demanded of Don Maynard on the first day of training camp in 1958. But the young soon-to-be-ex-Giant was an iconoclast and wouldn't bow to his boss's mandate. When he arrived at practice the following day, his sideburns were one day longer. "I thought I told you to shave those sideburns off," growled Howell again. A year later, on his first day on the job, new offensive coordinator Allie Sherman took one look at Maynard and snapped, "We don't wear sideburns in New York." "Well, I do," was Maynard's retort. The sideburns stayed, but Don Maynard's time with the New York Giants would be fleeting.

It wasn't just Maynard's sideburns that made an impression on people, as teammate Larry Grantham explained when he arrived at the first New York Titans training camp in 1960. "Don was the first guy I saw. He had those long sideburns and he was sitting on one of those old New England stone walls wearing cowboy boots, Levi's, a big Western hat, and a belt with a huge brass buckle. The belt had No. 13 on each side where it rode the hip and the word 'shine' across the back of it. The whole thing was unreal. I mean, where was the rodeo?"

When attempting to analyze Don Maynard, three themes rise above all others: His outward appearance, which acts as a conduit to his rugged, stubborn individualism; his unique style of play on the football field; and his almost mythical frugality.

Maynard wasn't a cowboy in the truest sense of the word, but he was a cowboy in spirit. He was born on January 25, 1935, in tiny Crosbyton, Texas, the son of a cotton gin manager. The fortitude and hard-working life of 1940s Texas was instilled in him from an early age. He once said, "I was 12 years old before I realized my name wasn't 'Git Wood.'" Because of his father's itinerant work life, the Maynard family moved from town to town. A drifting rebel from the beginning, Don attended eight grade schools, five high schools, and briefly Rice University before enrolling in Texas Western College, where he starred on the football team as a running back.

Though he was a small-town Southern kid, Maynard had no fear of New York City. Titans/Jets teammate Bill Mathis once said, "I was kind of shy with my Southern accent and all. But not Don. He would hitch up his pants, pull on his boots, polish his buckle, and march downtown." Picturing Maynard fitting into the Big City would be similar to watching an old rerun of *McCloud*. It's all too easy envisioning the Jets great atop a horse, riding down Fifth Avenue as Dennis Weaver occasionally did while solving a crime. Maynard did ride a mule named Kate to school as a child, after all. How much of a stretch would it be to have him galloping his way to Shea Stadium?

So it's no wonder that Maynard's teammates called him "Country." He was a man of many nicknames, though, as he was also known as "Sunshine" going all the way back to his Texas days, and it wasn't uncommon for his Jets cronies to refer to him as Barney—as in Barney Fife. *The Andy Griffith Show* was his favorite television program, and Maynard identified with the scrawny, bumbling, small-town deputy, though the Jets receiver held onto passes with more security and poise than Mayberry's second-in-command handled a gun.

And then there were the boots. Oh, how Don Maynard loved his cowboy boots. His No. 13 was etched into his Western footwear, and he even had golf spikes fitted onto a pair so he could hit the links Texas-style. An old Jet roommate once recalled, "It's a heck of a sight waking up in the morning and seeing a guy cook eggs in his pajamas and boots." Linus had his blanket, and Maynard had his boots. If there were a Cowboy-Boot-Wearers Hall of Fame, Maynard would surely be inducted with the inaugural class. And we also must give Maynard his due and put him in the Muttonchops Hall of Fame alongside legends such as Martin Van Buren, Elvis Presley, 1972 Joe Torre, and *Beverly Hills, 90210's* Dylan McKay.

Maybe there's just something about Jets receivers and cowboy boots. Another famous Jets pass catcher, Wesley Walker, also liked to don western wear. Walker has nothing but praise for his pass-catching predecessor. "He's just a funny guy. What we have in common, I used to wear cowboy hats all the time and cowboy boots. He loves his cowboy boots, but I wear cowboy boots all the time. He's a piece of work, very funny, entertaining. Just a nice, down-to-earth guy, and I love him."

The Texan was also stubborn when it came to wearing his signature No. 13. An injured teammate on his high school football team wore the unlucky number, and when he was shelved for the season, Maynard decided to take it over because he felt it was a "challenge." When he joined the NFL, he once said if the Giants wouldn't give him the number, he wouldn't have played for them. And he was just as particular about his football cleats as he was about his everyday footwear and jersey number—they had to be white with exactly 24 spikes on the bottom.

Maynard's sideburns weren't the only thing the Giants didn't like about him. Mainly used as a kick returner in his rookie season of 1958, Maynard fumbled a punt in a playoff game against Cleveland, which the team and its fans never let him forget. The Giants won the game despite the muff, but Maynard was stuck with the "bad hands" label. The last straw came during training camp in the summer of '59 when Sherman, aside from taking offense to his whiskers, didn't care for the way Maynard ran. He had the long, loping strides of a track runner, and when Sherman shouted at him to run like a football player and stop with the track-meet stuff, Maynard answered back, "Dang it, I can cover more ground with one stride than anybody else here can with three."

Sherman, who had it in for Maynard from the beginning, sent the future Jet to stand under the goalpost for the remainder of practice, and a few days later he was cut from the team, ostensibly to make room for rookie Joe Morrison. Long sideburns, funny way of running, Southern cowboy—Don Maynard just wasn't New York

Giants material. They were Madison Avenue, and he was Mayberry R.F.D. He wasn't about to change for them—or anyone else for that matter.

Maynard's unorthodox running style coupled with his improvisational method of running pass routes would dog him the rest of his career. "When I first joined the Jets, I was a little leery of Don," Joe Namath said. "I'd heard rumors that he broke pass patterns pretty often, that he didn't run the paths he was supposed to run. Well, hell, that was ridiculous. In my first four years with the Jets, I can remember Don breaking only one pattern he didn't have the right to break."

The Originals:
Bill Mathis and Larry Grantham

Don Maynard wasn't the only original Titan to play as a Jet in Super Bowl III. There were two others: fullback Bill Mathis and outside linebacker Larry Grantham. Punter Curley Johnson was the other Titan to face the Colts in Miami, but he joined New York in 1961 after spending a year with the Dallas Texans.

Mathis and Grantham had much in common. They were both born in 1938, they were both rookies in 1960, they both played their whole career with the Titans/Jets franchise, they were both as tough as a pickup truck, and they were both immensely popular with their teammates.

Mathis—a Rocky Mount, North Carolina, native—was a two-time All-Star (1961, '63) and a First-Team All-AFL selection in 1961, playing with a broken collarbone for much of the season. By the mid-'60s, he was part of the successful three-headed Jets backfield with Matt Snell and Emerson Boozer. In Super Bowl III, Mathis was one of Joe Namath's outlets in thwarting the Baltimore blitz, catching three passes for 20 yards. He played 10 seasons with the team, and by the time Namath arrived, Mathis was entrenched as a leader.

"When I first joined the Jets, everybody was talking about 'The Birdman'... The Birdman's coming in soon, and I kept wondering who in the hell's the

Later in his career Namath went on to state, "I had trouble with Don my first year. But I know him now and sense what he can do. He doesn't run a pass pattern with the perfect precision of a George Sauer. Sometimes Don will run a square-out that looks more like a round-out. But he's usually there, just where he is supposed to be. He reads defenses so well that he'll signal me with his hand when he's breaking the pattern. Then I look for him somewhere else."

While riding the bench in his one season with the Giants, Maynard was taking notes, watching how the veterans went about their business on the field. He learned his "rounded" way of

Birdman?" Namath recalled. "Mathis showed up at training camp a week late—in those days, I couldn't imagine anyone coming to camp a week late—and everybody was so damn happy to see him. I took one look at his legs, and I knew why he was called the Birdman. Mathis'll tell you he doesn't have skinny legs, but he's lying."

From Crystal Springs, Missouri, Grantham was drafted as a wide receiver/tight end, but he was switched to safety and then finally to linebacker when he joined the Titans. Though undersized, he was one of the franchise's greatest tacklers, and he finished his career with 24 interceptions. He was a five-time All-Star, a five-time First-Team All-AFL pick, and was named to the All-Time All-AFL second team. He was the leader of the defense and was responsible for calling the plays in Super Bowl III, holding the Colts' No. 1–ranked offense to a mere late-game touchdown. When the final whistle blew, Grantham grabbed the game ball and literally jumped for joy as he propelled himself high into the air.

Like Maynard, Mathis and Grantham were part of the group of 20 players to play all 10 years in the AFL and part of a gang of seven to do it with the same team. After suffering through those lean early days of the AFL, and the rocky road that was the New York Titans, surely winning the Super Bowl on January 12, 1969, meant just a little bit more to these three than the rest of their Jets teammates. They formed an exclusive club: The Originals.

running pass patterns from Frank Gifford and Kyle Rote. His flailing arms and off-kilter legs while sprinting were all natural, though. He became the first New York Titan when he phoned just-named head coach Sammy Baugh, who gladly accepted Maynard onto his team. They were fellow laid-back Texans, so sideburns, Levi's, and an awkward running style were not an issue.

Maynard's future New York coaches were also sympathetic and more understanding of his mode of pass catching. Assistant Walt Michaels said, "He's one of the fastest receivers I've ever seen. And he's got good hands. But the biggest thing is his change of pace. When many guys come down the field, they're going all out. But while they're going all out, Maynard is going at three-quarter speed. When you think he's going all out, he turns it on. Fast, slow, fast, slow. Then he makes his moves."

Weeb Ewbank, the Jets head coach for most of Maynard's career, added, "He's deceptive. He has a gait that makes him look like he's coasting, and then he turns it on, goes into overdrive, and leaves you there. He just explodes." Ewbank also admired his stamina. "Maynard is one of those lean and hungry Texans who can run forever."

When Maynard broke Raymond Berry's all-time record for pass receptions with his 632nd catch near the end of the 1972 season against Oakland, Sherman must have looked on from afar with regret. Maynard himself reflected on his long journey, "I hadn't thought about the record too much that night because we were trying real hard to win a football game, but as I lay on the ground with the ball it sort of jumped in my head about how many things had to go right all down the line, through the years, to make that one catch possible."

One aspect to Maynard that everyone agreed on was his tightfisted ways with a dollar. He worked every offseason as a plumber or teacher and started keeping his eye on his pennies as

Don Maynard runs upfield during Super Bowl III against the Baltimore Colts. Playing with an injured hamstring, Maynard was used as a decoy. Although he had no receptions in the game, his presence on the field created opportunities for quarterback Joe Namath to connect with other receivers. (Vernon Biever/Getty Images)

a teenager. "I'd been saving $2 a week since I was 15 years old. My mother always told us to save a little bit, so it all carried over."

One could probably fill an edition of *Bartlett's Quotations* with quotes about Maynard's frugality alone. Here are a few:

"He used to write down everything he spent in a little notebook, like 'Newspaper, 5 ¢; subway token, 15 ¢.'" —Bill Mathis

"Once we sent Don to the grocery store. We thought he would bring back some steaks. He brought back a couple of cans of beans." —A Jets roommate

"Don is closer than nine is to ten; he just doesn't believe in spending money." —Joe Namath

"Of course, sometimes when Don throws up his hand [while running a pass pattern], I'm not sure whether he's breaking a pattern or asking for room money." —Joe Namath

"The Super Bowl was, to me, just another game. If we showed up, we were going to get the loser's share. If we played a little harder, we could possibly get the winner's share." —Don Maynard

"Save your receipts from the Triborough Bridge." —Advice from Don Maynard to rookie Joe Namath

It wasn't a surprise to find Maynard holding up a celebrity golf tournament while he waded around a pond—after taking his boots off of course—because he discovered a treasure-trove of free golf balls sitting on the bottom. He once tricked out his Ford coupe to run on the cheaper butane instead of gasoline. And he even took the time to procure a few extra bucks from his teammates the day before the *Heidi* game in 1968.

A number of Jets were relaxing around a pool in Oakland after dinner. The beautiful, calm water looked so nice that one

Jet remarked somebody should dive right in. The water may have looked tempting for a leisurely dip, but the reality of the November temperatures made it a freezing proposition. A voice called out in the night, "Put up some money, and I'll do it." If money was involved, it must have been the utterance of Don Maynard. Wanting to see their flaky teammate put on a spectacle, the Jets players passed around a hat and collected a goodly sum of dough. But they had two stipulations: Maynard had to dive in with his clothes on, and he had to jump off the diving board. The clothes and diving board aspects of the dare were not a problem for No. 13, but there was no way he was going into the water with his boots on. He wasn't going to destroy his pride and joy. "They're mighty expensive, and I could ruin 'em."

Agreed that the boots could be taken off, the players watched as Maynard climbed onto the diving board in his brown slacks and tan shirt. Looking like a man who was either engaged in shenanigans caused by inebriation or one who would go to extremes just for a couple extra bucks, he bounced off the diving board, soared into the air, and descended perfectly into the icy water. The Jets hooted as a streak of brown swam to the other side of the pool and shinnied out. Maynard scooped up the money and his boots, laughed, and headed back to his room to change into some dry clothes. Yes, Don Maynard would do just about anything for a dollar—except spoil a perfectly good pair of cowboy boots. And the frigid water only helped his pass catching, as he had one of the best days of his career the following afternoon.

Like his childhood, when he roamed from town to town and school to school, Maynard's football career was a wandering odyssey. Before his 13 seasons with the Jets franchise, he spent one year in the NFL and one in the Canadian Football League, and when his Jets days were over, he was briefly a St. Louis Cardinal followed by time in yet another league, the short-lived World Football League.

After leaving the Giants because of facial hair, an un-football-like running manner, and good old-fashioned Texan stubbornness, Maynard was forced to travel north to play for Canada's Hamilton Tiger-Cats, where he began his career as a receiver after being a backup running back and kick returner for the Giants. Catching passes suited him just fine, and splitting out wide was a better spot for the rawboned, swift Texan.

His time in Canada was so enjoyable that when Vince Lombardi, his former offensive backfield coach in his one season with the Giants, phoned to inform him that Green Bay had claimed him off the waiver wire, Maynard turned down the offer to join the Packers and finished out the year in Canada. His Tiger-Cats made it all the way to the championship game, playing for the Grey Cup. And in a bout of foreshadowing, Hamilton's coach, Jim Trimble, made a Namath-like guarantee when he insisted his team would come out victorious. "We'll waffle 'em," he boasted, Canadian-style. Unfortunately, that was all Trimble had in common with Broadway Joe, as Hamilton lost to the Winnipeg Blue Bombers 21–7.

Maynard ended his NFL career in St. Louis. But he was only a tiny footnote in Cardinals history as he was activated for just two games and caught only one pass for 18 yards. His football career came to an end in 1974 as a member of the WFL's Shreveport Steamer, which had begun the year as the Houston Texans but moved to Louisiana a few months into the season. The WFL only lasted a season and a half, but it made headlines when the new league began poaching stars from the NFL, such as Larry Csonka, Jim Kiick, and Paul Warfield of the Miami Dolphins.

It was no surprise that Maynard ended up in the fledgling league. He was a real-life, football-playing Zelig. There's Maynard in the Greatest Game Ever Played. There he is in the Grey Cup in Canada. There he is on the first Sunday in the new American Football League. There he is in the greatest upset that ever took place, Super Bowl III. There he is on TV in the debut of *Monday Night Football* in 1970. There he is in the newfangled World Football League. Wherever history was being made on a football field, Maynard was sure to be there.

Don Maynard was elected to the Pro Football Hall of Fame in 1987. His 633 receptions and 11,834 yards were both pro football records at the time of his retirement. In the 1968 AFL Championship Game, he caught the game-winning touchdown pass. He was named to the All-Time All-AFL Team, as well as being a four-time AFL All-Star. He was one of only 20 players to play in all 10 years of the AFL's existence and one of seven to do it for the same team.

But the maverick receiver wasn't just an original Titan (actually *the* original Titan), he was just plain original. "Do something different to get yourself noticed. You've got to be a little different," he once advised an acquaintance. Maynard was more than statistics, wins, and accolades. He was someone who couldn't be reined in. He was an untamed bronco. He was an urban cowboy. He was a gridiron Hud. He was a concrete rustler. He was a boot-wearin', belt-bucklin' free spirit from the heart of wide-open America who somehow became a legendary New Yorker.

Don Maynard went from NFL reject to the Canadian wilderness to the AFL to the Pro Football Hall of Fame, and he did it on his terms—and he did it all with his stylish sideburns and trademark cowboy boots.

CHAPTER 3

JUST WATCH *HEIDI*, BABY

THE RAIDERS ARE BADASS ASSASSINS. At least they used to be back in the primitive, barbarous days of the AFL, the anything-goes, reckless 1970s and the riotous, debauched '80s. Their slogan, "Just win, baby," could just as easily have been, "Just bludgeon and decapitate your opponent, baby." Over the decades, they've sent a rogues' gallery of criminals, sinners, ogres, and a giant named Otis Sistrunk, professing to have gone to the University of Mars out onto the field to do battle every Sunday afternoon.

The Jets, of course, have not always filled their rosters with church-going puritans themselves. They did once claim madmen like Johnny Sample and Mark Gastineau as their own, along with the booze-tippling chick-magnet Joe Namath. The difference between the two teams is obvious, though: While the Raiders are out in a dark alley beating you up (with their friends holding you down, getting in their own cheap shots), the Jets are back in the bar swilling scotch and stealing your girlfriend.

The Jets and Raiders have played many games against each other. And they've been played with animosity, ferocity, and a loathing that didn't just border on repugnance but flew past it and went straight to abhorrence. In the 21st century, Gang Green's biggest rivals are the Patriots and Dolphins, but in the prehistoric

31

days, their enmity was saved for Oakland (and briefly Los Angeles). And for Al Davis. So let's drift back in time and take a peek at a slice of what once was—three games in the Jets-Raiders rivalry.

From 1960 through '67, the head-to-head matchup between New York and Oakland was fairly even, with the Jets winning eight, losing six, and two games ending in a tie. But Oakland dominated in the Namath era, going 3–1–2. After not much success in the early days of the AFL, both squads were hitting their stride by the time 1968 rolled around. The Raiders were coming off a Super Bowl II loss to the Packers, while the Jets managed their first winning season in '67. They only met once in the '68 regular season, but it was one of the most memorable games in pro football history. It was the *Heidi* game.

The first thing we need to do is ask ourselves, what is a *Heidi*? *Heidi* began long ago, so long ago in fact that George Blanda wasn't even born yet. It was originally a novel written in 1880 by Johanna Spyri. The first instance of the tale being turned into a movie was in 1937, when a big-screen version starring Shirley Temple was released. It was a made-for-TV remake, though—featuring Jennifer Edwards (the daughter of Blake Edwards and stepdaughter of Julie Andrews), Maximilian Schell, and Michael Redgrave—that was broadcast by NBC on that fateful night in 1968.

And what is this children's story about? Well, a five-year-old orphan's aunt takes her to live in the Swiss Alps for a few years with the girl's curmudgeonly grandfather, who refuses to go into the village due to his distaste for the locals. While living there, Heidi meets a boy named Peter, who becomes her best friend. Heidi's aunt then sells her to a wealthy family in Frankfurt to be the companion of a disabled child named Clara. Heidi learns to read and write but becomes sickly and sleepwalks a lot, so she goes back to live with her grandfather, who previously became nice because of Heidi. Clara visits Heidi, and the disabled girl magically starts getting better because of Heidi's good-natured camaraderie, a steady diet of goat's milk, and the clean mountain air. But Peter becomes jealous of the girls' friendship and pushes Clara's wheelchair down the mountain. Without her wheelchair to rely on, Clara learns to walk. Her family is amazed, and they open up their home to Heidi, insisting that she'll always have a place to live if she so desires.

A number of questions instantly come to mind. Was the aunt a well-known child-slave trafficker? Have Social Services or the FBI knocked on her door lately? Is Heidi a miracle worker? What would she have been able to accomplish with the gang from *Cocoon*? Should we all start drinking goat's milk? Should we hurl all wheelchairs down a mountainside and stop coddling the disabled?

But before that whirlwind of a story appeared on television screens across America on November 17, 1968, a football game was played at the Oakland-Alameda County Coliseum. And it was a typical madcap AFL affair. Namath threw for 381 yards (and one touchdown), while Raiders quarterback Daryle Lamonica aired it out for 311 yards of his own, including four touchdown passes. And it was a typical Jets-Raiders contest, as well, with numerous penalties and skirmishes.

The Jets opened up the scoring with a pair of Jim Turner field goals in the first quarter. But Oakland's Warren Wells caught a 9-yard touchdown pass from Lamonica to take the lead. In the second quarter, the two teams traded touchdowns. Oakland's came on another throw by Lamonica, this time to Billy Cannon. The Jets reached the end zone on one of Namath's seven career rushing touchdowns, but missed a two-point conversion try. The Raiders took a 14–12 lead into halftime. So far, so good. NBC was still broadcasting the game. Announcers Curt Gowdy and Al DeRogatis could still be heard.

The game continued on its back-and-forth path in the second half. A Bill Mathis touchdown run was followed by Raider Charlie Smith's 3-yard scoring rush. The fourth quarter saw the first points scored on a 97-yard drive by the Jets. But it wasn't one of those clock-chewing, 12-play drives. Namath and Don Maynard only needed two plays on this one. Raiders rookie defensive back George Atkinson had been covering Maynard all afternoon, and Maynard was having his way with him. Starting at the Jets' 3-yard line, Namath heaved the ball to No. 13, who was brought down at midfield. On the next play, the two connected again for a 50-yard touchdown. For the day, Maynard caught 10 passes for 228 yards.

Turner kicked his third field goal, Fred Biletnikoff caught a 22-yard touchdown pass, and Turner booted another one through the uprights. The score was Jets 32, Raiders 29, with 1:05 left to play and the time closing in on 7 PM.

Charlie Smith returned Turner's kickoff to the Raiders' 22-yard line. A Lamonica quick strike to Smith resulted in a 20-yard gain, but a facemask penalty against New York moved the ball all the way to the Jets' 43-yard line. NBC cut to a commercial, which was followed by the beginning of *Heidi*. Dick Cline, broadcast operations control supervisor for the network, was just following orders. "I didn't do anything wrong," he said. "I'm not guilty. I did what I was supposed to do. Joe Namath & Co. didn't get the game over in time, so I went to *Heidi*." While all hell was breaking loose on the phone lines, and all hell was breaking loose on the football field.

As poor, innocent little Heidi headed to her grandfather's house, Lamonica tossed a 43-yard pass to Smith for a touchdown. The Jets were now down by four points, but they still had time to move the ball down the field. They did have Namath and Maynard, after all, who had just traveled 97 yards on two throws. But Earl Christy never gave them a chance.

On the ensuing kickoff, Christy fumbled the ball near the 10-yard line, scooped it up, and promptly fumbled again. Half a dozen Raiders descended on the ball, with Preston Ridlehuber being the lucky player to recover it as he dove into the end zone for the final points, making the score 43–32 Raiders. After the kickoff the Jets only had time for one more play. Emerson Boozer dropped a handoff, picked up the ball, but was tackled for a loss. Game over.

By this time, Heidi was most likely on her way to Frankfurt. And angry fans had already been flooding the phone lines with calls to NBC, the phone company, the police, radio stations, even *The New York Times*. As writer Art Buchwald wrote at the time, "Men who wouldn't get out of their chairs during an earthquake rushed to the phones to scream obscenities." But the phone lines were already dead around a six-block radius of NBC's headquarters.

Fans had wasted no time and had started calling while the game was still being broadcast. They were imploring NBC not to cut off the thriller they were witnessing. If those rabid fans didn't jump the gun and take to the phones, they just might have gotten their wish. NBC president Julian Goodman tried to send word to Cline to stick with the game, but the phone lines were dead, and Cline adhered to his original order. The phone lines weren't dead in Oakland, though, as Weeb Ewbank's wife congratulated her husband on his team's victory.

The public outcry was staggering. Goodman even issued a public apology. "It was a forgivable error committed by humans who were concerned about the children who were expecting to see *Heidi*. I missed the game as much as anybody else." As the evening progressed, NBC couldn't get out of its own way and kept committing one blunder after another. The full game was broadcast on the West Coast, but Smith's touchdown in the last minute of play was missed because NBC was stuck in a commercial. And east of the Rockies, in a glaring example of bad timing, NBC ran a crawl with the final score just as Clara was dramatically walking without the use of her wheelchair. Clara walks, Jets lose, highlights at 11:00.

If anything, the incident proved how popular pro football had become, including the AFL, and how its stock as a television commodity had risen. Nobody could have predicted the clamorous hullabaloo that took place. Because of the fiasco, broadcast rules and regulations were soon changed, which ensured games would be shown in their entirety in home markets—even if a viewing of *Chitty Chitty Bang Bang* was scheduled to be shown afterward.

Would there have been the same uproar if instead of a children's movie, NBC had interrupted the game for a program more palatable to a football fan's taste, or at least one that didn't feature a spunky, pigtailed child? Was part of the problem *Heidi* itself?

The person who suffered the most was likely actress Jennifer Edwards, the portrayer of Heidi. She received supportive fan mail and hate mail alike. "But it was bizarre in the sense that you were either loved or hated," she recalled. "I remember clippings from newspapers calling me things like, 'The little brat in white stockings.' Like I had something to do with it. And I couldn't quite fathom that. I couldn't quite understand why I was being personally attacked."

Heidi is now synonymous with sports, the New York Jets, and the Oakland Raiders. Edwards was once at a pool party, and her friend Howie Mandel exclaimed, "You're on TV. You're a great moment in sports." The moment has cemented its place in American popular culture, with even the producers of *The Love Boat* once contemplating an episode featuring Edwards and Namath lampooning the famous game.

We'll let Edwards have the last word: "That's the thing that blows my mind. I live with a devout Lakers fan, and I know for a fact that if anything like that happened during a Laker game, our television sets would be hurled from the nearest window—and not

Don Maynard (13) falls into the end zone to score the game-winning touchdown against the Oakland Raiders in the 1968 AFL Championship Game. (Bruce Bennett Studios/ Getty Images)

being involved in sports myself, that's an unusual emotion for me to understand. But, then again, if you did it to *ER,* I would probably have the same reaction."

Six weeks later, New York and Oakland would meet again, this time with more at stake than the happiness of an orphan in the Swiss Alps. The AFL Championship was up for grabs, and the Jets had revenge on their minds.

The Super Bowl was two weeks away, but in some ways that was a piece of cake compared to what the Jets would be facing in the Silver and Black, who would do whatever it took—a forearm to the back of the head, a punch in the neck—to make their opponent black and blue. And they especially liked to beat up Namath, as the Raiders constantly targeted the star quarterback when it came to their infamous torture treatments. But out of all the tough guys, behemoths, and derelicts on the field that day, it was skinny, speedy Don Maynard who triumphed as the hero.

Oakland was the defending AFL Champion, finishing tied for the best record in '68 at 12–2, and they had pummeled Kansas City 41–6 in a tie-breaker playoff game. They boasted the No. 1 offense and No. 2 defense in the AFL, but it was the Jets (11–3, second in offense, fourth in defense) who had home-field advantage, which meant playing the game in a swirling wind–filled, cold-as-ice Shea Stadium. And the field itself was not in the greatest shape. The outskirts were littered with mud puddles, while the middle was hard and slick—except for the baseball-infield portion, which resembled the slop of Woodstock.

Despite the conditions, both teams took to the air. And the wind didn't dampen either team's efforts as Namath and Lamonica would each go on to break the AFL playoff record for pass attempts. (Namath went 19 for 49, and Lamonica went 20 for 47, with a record 401 yards.)

One reason for the Jets' aerial inclinations was the effective blocking of Dave Herman, who switched from right guard to tackle in an attempt to stop Raider defensive end Ike Lassiter, who had terrorized the Jets in their previous meeting. "I had never played tackle in my life except a little bit against Oakland out on the Coast. I looked upon it as a challenge because Ike is big, strong, and tough. He beat me to the inside a couple of times early in the game, so I moved in a little and steered him outside when he charged. One time he told me to quit holding him. I said, 'Ike, you know I don't hold people.'"

It was a 14-yard Namath-to-Maynard touchdown pass that broke the ice. The receiver's quick move caused defensive back George Atkinson to stumble, and Namath found a wide-open Maynard in the end zone. This would be an ongoing theme, as Maynard schooled the rookie cornerback all afternoon. When the day was done, the Hall of Fame receiver finished with six catches for 118 yards, which shouldn't have surprised anyone after what he did to Atkinson back in November in Oakland.

The Jets jumped out to a 10–0 lead by the end of the first quarter, but a Fred Biletnikoff touchdown closed the gap. By the time the first half wound down, with the Jets holding a slim 13–10 edge, the Raiders defense had done a number on Namath. It was the usual routine by the Neanderthals from Oakland. They dislocated Namath's left ring finger. His already painful right thumb and contused coccyx became even more painful and contused. The mammoth Ben Davison, twirling his sinister mustache, gave the Jets quarterback a concussion with a knee to the head. And getting by Herman this once, Lassiter slammed Namath to the ground as if he were a ragdoll. Joe Willie was so dizzy and out of sorts, he was seeing stars—well, he's Broadway Joe, so he was probably having visions of Ann-Margret.

George Blanda, a young 41 years old at the time, opened the second-half scoring with a 9-yard field goal. The Raiders did everything within the rules, outside of the rules, and even utilized tricks that would get the average person sent to prison in trying to knock Namath out of the game, but No. 12 hung in there and followed up Blanda's field goal with a 20-yard touchdown pass to Pete Lammons. Oakland answered back when Blanda booted another one through the uprights, cutting the Jets lead to four points.

After a full game and three quarters of getting burned by Namath and Maynard, Atkinson finally had his one bright moment in the sun. Namath, known for throwing risky passes throughout his career, did just that. Atkinson picked it off and almost ran it back for a touchdown, but he was brought down by Namath at the Jets' 4-yard line, which set up Oakland's last score, a Pete Banaszak run. "Hell, if I'd known they were going to do that, I wouldn't have bothered tackling him," cracked Namath. Wisecracks aside, Oakland was now ahead 23–20.

When the Jets got the ball back on their own 32-yard line with eight minutes left in the game, Namath went to work to atone for his interception. And it took all of 68 seconds. He started with a quick 10-yard pass to George Sauer to the left side of the field, where he was wide open, as defensive back Willie Brown was laying back guarding against a potential bomb.

On the second play of the drive, with Atkinson isolated on Maynard, Namath heaved a long pass toward the right sideline. Maynard looked over his left shoulder and spotted the ball flying through the gray Queens sky, but the wind sent the ball toward the sideline. He turned to his right and, mimicking Willie Mays catching Vic Wertz's fly ball in the 1954 World Series, hauled in the pass over his head as he and Atkinson toppled in the mud at the Raiders' 6-yard line. Maynard bobbled the ball and fumbled it out of bounds, but he had possession long enough for it to be ruled a catch.

The final blow started with a play-action fake to Matt Snell, who then made a key block as Namath rolled out to his left. The Jets' quarterback looked for Bill Mathis, who was covered, and then for Sauer, who was in the left side of the end zone, but he was blanketed by two Raider defenders. Lammons wasn't open, either.

Namath momentarily lost his footing in the sludgy Shea turf but quickly recovered his balance and spotted Maynard cutting toward the middle. He turned right and threw a low bullet to his favorite receiver, who made a diving catch in the end zone for the go-ahead points. And who was one step behind on the play once again? Poor George Atkinson.

"I was all ready to throw the ball away, to throw it over everybody's head and out of the end zone. But then I saw that Maynard had a step on Atkinson and I knew, instinctively, without measuring the pros and cons, that I could get the ball to him," Namath later said. "Once I made the decision to try to hit Maynard, I knew I had to throw hard. I must have gone up a little more than three-quarters overhand, a little higher than usual, but still, just like my brother taught me, I threw from my ear. I threw the ball as hard as I've ever thrown a ball in my life."

The drive was so quick in the making that the Raiders still had two more chances to take the lead. Oakland made it all the way to the Jets' 26- and 24-yard lines, but both times they eschewed the field-goal attempt on fourth down and went for it but couldn't come up with the necessary yards. The game was over, and payback for the brutal loss earlier in the season was complete. Even Heidi's cantankerous grandfather might have flashed a smile and surely would have agreed with Namath: "I just felt perfect after that Oakland game. I was really worried about Oakland, more than I was about Baltimore in the Super Bowl, and I just about exploded inside when we won that game."

The Jets were crowned AFL Champions in a thriller thanks to Maynard's amazing day. The only thing left to do was celebrate. "Ok Weeb, where'd you hide the champagne?" a happy Namath wanted to know. Told that there were 25 cases in the back room, Broadway Joe answered in true Broadway Joe fashion: "Twenty-five ought to be enough."

And now it's on to the third and final game of our trilogy. The names may have changed, but the seething hatred remained the same.

The Jets and Raiders hadn't met in the playoffs in 14 years, but on January 15, 1983, they picked up right where they left off back in the 1968 AFL Championship Game.

Instead of Ben Davidson and Co. doling out the eye gouges, kidney punches, and foot stomps, it was Ted Hendricks and Lyle Alzado keeping the cheap-shot tradition alive. Alzado went so far as to rip off the helmet of Jets tackle Chris Ward and hurl it at him. "We tried to intimidate them, they tried to intimidate us; it's part of the game. We felt whoever wins the game wins the whole thing," Alzado reasoned.

When the Jets took a knee for the final play of the contentious contest, even that didn't put an end to the high jinks, as a brawl broke out. But what do you expect from Al Davis' minions when the picture exemplifying all things Raiders in the team's home office is one of Davidson pummeling Namath? So it may be an understatement to say the Jets and Raiders did not care for each other, even after all these years.

Coming off of a playoff appearance the previous year, Gang Green finished the 1982 season (shortened due to a labor dispute) with a 6–3 mark, which was good enough for a wild card berth. They whipped the Bengals 44–17 in the first round of the postseason, setting up their meeting with Los Angeles at the Coliseum. The Raiders may have moved south, but they were the same punishing gang as always. Between the opening kickoff and closing brouhaha, the game was jam-packed with penalties, fumbles, and interceptions.

It was the not-to-be-intimidated Jets who jumped out to a 10–0 lead at halftime, though, thanks to a Wesley Walker 20-yard touchdown catch and a 30-yard Pat Leahy field goal. But it was quarterback Richard Todd who had to face the stiffest test. His guts and mettle were on display all afternoon, as he refused to shrivel up in the face of the savage, frenzied L.A. defense. It was 1968 all over again, with the Raiders going after Todd like he was Joe Namath. The Silver and Black just didn't like quarterbacks that wore green and white. Todd spearheaded the offense, going 15-for-24 for 277 yards, while his two main offensive weapons—running back Freeman McNeil (101 yards) and Walker (seven catches, good for 169 yards)—also withstood L.A.'s defensive *blitzkrieg* and shined in the game.

The Jets were in front, but the Raiders certainly would not go gentle into that good night. On back-to-back possessions in the

Jets tackle Chris Ward (72) loses his helmet while having heated words with the Raiders' Lyle Alzado during the Jets 17–14 victory over the Raiders in the 1982 AFC Divisional Playoffs. (MPS/Getty Images)

third quarter, the Raiders took the lead. A Marcus Allen 3-yard touchdown run capped off a 14-play, 77-yard drive that took chunks of time off the clock. Their next seven points were obtained in swifter fashion, though, when Jim Plunkett's 57-yard bomb to Malcolm Barnwell put the score at 14–10.

The Crank Call

The roots to the January 1983 playoff game go all the way back to 1962. Walt Michaels, the Jets coach in '83, spent that year as the defensive backs coach for the Raiders in their third year of existence, but he was unceremoniously given the heave-ho by Al Davis. And Michaels never forgave him for it. Michaels moved on to the Jets, where he was the defensive mastermind of the Super Bowl III–winning team. He was named the Jets' head coach in 1977 after spending a few years in Philadelphia.

In this playoff game against his old employer, as Michaels was walking off the field at halftime, he was informed that Jets owner Leon Hess was waiting on the phone for him. When Michaels picked up the receiver, a voice on the other end rambled on about Mark Gastineau's sack-dance antics and how the Jets needed to play harder. Michaels, realizing the voice didn't belong to his boss, promptly hung up. After the game, he had no problem speculating on who was to blame. "I just want to say that whatever member of the Raiders organization called me on the phone at halftime and said my owner wanted to talk to me is a sick s.o.b.," he said. "It's a sick, rotten way to try to disrupt our team. His initials are A.D., and I don't care who knows it or not."

It was a good educated guess, but it turned out to be wrong. The real caller was Larry Hammond, a bartender at the Winfield Inn, in Woodside, Queens. "I told Coach Michaels to tell his team to fight harder in the second half, to go out and kick hell out of the Raiders," Hammond said. The bartender had a bet on the game and used Hess' name in order to get through to the coach. Davis was hardly amused himself. "Oh, geez, that stuff. It's just so stupid, but that's Walt. Crazy and stupid, both. I was sitting upstairs in my box at halftime. It doesn't even have a phone in it. I don't have enough to worry about at halftime, right? I've got to start making phone calls. Crazy and stupid." Just another chapter in Jets-Raiders lore.

And according to Plunkett, that's how the game should have ended. "When it was 14–10, that's when we should have put the game away. We had the game, we had the damn thing right here, and we let it slip away." The Raiders quarterback himself was one of the main culprits ensuring the Jets would come out on top, though.

With 43 seconds left in the third frame, Raiders defensive back Lester Hayes picked off a Todd pass, meaning the depleted, injury-riddled Jets defense which was already running on fumes (Joe Klecko, Marty Lyons, Abdul Salaam, and Darrol Ray were all banged up or missing altogether) had to come back on the field, giving L.A. all the momentum. But they gave it right back to the Jets when Klecko recovered an Allen fumble. Of course nothing came easy in this game of giveaways, as Todd tossed another interception on the ensuing possession. But soon after, the Jets would finally go ahead for good after Todd completed a 45-yard missile to Walker, setting up a 1-yard touchdown run by Scott Dierking.

Enter linebacker Lance Mehl. The Penn State graduate and Ohio native would make two game-saving plays, the second one nearly an instant replay of the first. With the Raiders backed up in their own territory and time ticking off the clock in the fourth quarter, Plunkett tried to whistle a pass to Cliff Branch on a down-and-in pattern, but Mehl stepped in front of the Raiders receiver for his first pick. Mehl's the hero, the game is over, and NBC can cue up a rerun of *Heidi*, right? Of course not, as McNeil fumbled the ball right back to L.A., giving them one more shot to win the game.

Plunkett moved his offense to the Jets' 42-yard line with less than 2 minutes remaining. As he dropped back to pass for the final time that afternoon, he looked for Branch again, running the exact same route as the previous drive, but there was Mehl once more, this time saving the game for good. "The exact same thing. Branch curled in, I curled in with him. I was surprised Plunkett threw the ball there." But he did throw the ball, and Mehl was in the right place at the right time once again.

All that was left was for Todd to take a knee, and the Jets would be victors for the second consecutive time over the Raiders in the playoffs. But this is Jets-Raiders we're talking about, so of course one last donnybrook would break out before the players would retire to their respective locker rooms. Raiders linebacker Matt Millen explained, "Ted Hendricks grabbed their center, Joe Fields. I was trying to break it up. Then someone took a shot at me." Richard Todd is no dummy, though. "I looked around for Plunkett, someone my own size."

Just like the exhilaration Namath felt after topping Oakland for the AFL Championship, one of his descendants experienced similar jubilation in defeating the Big Bad Raiders, as Mark Gastineau was beyond elated. "I was jumping up and down and I tripped and fell," he said. "Did you see that? That's how excited I was out there. I've never been so excited in a football game in my life."

Sure, there were many other memorable games played between the Jets and Raiders, including the final game of the 2001 season when John Hall booted a 53-yard field goal to send the Jets to the playoffs, the Jets' first win in Oakland in almost 30 years. The Raiders defeated the Jets six days later in the first round of the playoffs, though, and Gang Green would fall to their arch nemesis again in the postseason the following season, evening the playoff tally at two victories apiece. But you just can't beat the originals, the first two-plus decades of the black-eye-inducing, broken-boned, brawling rivalry between the Jets and the Raiders.

CHAPTER 4

CHIEF WAHOO

ED "WAHOO" McDANIEL NEVER MET a challenge he didn't accept. Whether it involved the game of football, where he played offense, defense, and special teams; the sport of wrestling; out on the golf course; or even guzzling viscous liquids that were not meant for human digestion, he never backed down from a dare. While in college, McDaniel was once goaded into drinking a quart of motor oil. Sure, it was dangerous and hazardous to his health, and most right-minded people would laugh off the challenge as a joke, but most people aren't Wahoo McDaniel. The gauntlet had been thrown down, and he took on the challenge. Unfortunately (or maybe fortunately is more like it), he could only quaff the equivalent of a few spoonfuls. "That oil made me sick," he said. "For months every time I'd sweat, I could feel that stuff oozing out. I smelled like an old pickup truck. In those days I'd do anything on a bet. Eat a gallon of jalapeño peppers. Didn't matter."

Wahoo was an original. He was one of those characters who seemed more like a spirit than the flesh and blood that he was. He was so much larger than life, so witty, so wild, so tough, so funny, so ferocious, so charismatic, so uncontrollable, so one of a kind—so Wahoo—that he begs the question: Was he real? He had to be born out of someone's wild imagination, didn't he? He was, of course, real. But if there were a mold anywhere near him when he entered the world, he would have smashed it with a two-by-four, swung a chair at it, and body-slammed it to pieces. And God himself would have looked on and chanted, "Wa-hoo! Wa-hoo! Wa-hoo!"

McDaniel's story is made for the cinema. From humble Southern/Native American beginnings to local athletic standout to pro football fan favorite to wrestling legend—not to mention five marriages, parking lot brawls, and being gored by the horns of a Viking helmet—there's an Oscar waiting to be polished by some brave soul savvy enough to create and produce *Chief Wahoo: The Ed McDaniel Story.* We already have *The Wrestler,* but did that movie have wild AFL action? Did it feature a colorful, charismatic Native American who had fans chanting his name at Shea Stadium? Jim Thorpe may have been the greatest Native American—or how about just American—athlete, but Wahoo played middle linebacker for the New York Jets, goddammit, and starred on television and all across the country as a "rasslin'" hero. He may not have been an All-American or All-Pro, but he was All-Wahoo.

McDaniel was born on June 19, 1938, in Bernice, Louisiana, to Hugh and Catherine McDaniel. His father, Big Wahoo, was part Choctow and part Chickasaw Native American, while his mother was of German heritage with a little Native American thrown in. But Little Wahoo was all hurricane. He was a force of nature, and there was only one person on earth who could control the tornado that went by the name of Wahoo. "He was a mama's boy," his daughter Nikki once said of him. "She was the only one who could keep him in line. She would hit him with a folding chair."

The family moved to Texas while Wahoo was a youngster, and after moving from town to town, they eventually settled in Midland. Little Wahoo learned the value of hard work at an early age by working for his father at his welding company. And the unruly youth soon stood out on the athletic field, as well. He was the catcher on a successful Pony League team that made it all the way to the state tournament in San Antonio. His baseball coach was none other than George Herbert Walker Bush, future president of the United States. "I remember Wahoo McDaniel well," the 41st president said of his catcher. "He was a good kid and a pretty fair baseball player. He had his ups and downs, but I'll always remember him as a wonderful kid who captured the imagination of West Texas in the 1950s. He was idolized by everyone who knew him."

"Yeah, Bush was my baseball coach, and in high school Nixon coached me in track," Wahoo cracked years later. But he indeed was coached by Nixon—Ed Nixon, that is. Besides starring on the Midland High School football team as a running back, McDaniel participated on the track team, and Nixon attempted to turn him into the next Jim Thorpe.

"I could run and jump, finished second in the state in the shot put with a toss of 58-plus feet, and was third in the discus," McDaniel said. "I never met Jim Thorpe, but his times and distances in the 1912 Olympics were scarcely better than mine in high school. But Coach Nixon simply could not teach me to pole vault."

The rambunctious athlete never did become the next Jim Thorpe; instead he settled for being the first Wahoo McDaniel. After high school, he attended the University of Oklahoma, where he played a number of positions for Bud Wilkinson's powerhouse Sooners. The versatile McDaniel saw time as a halfback, fullback, defensive end, and punter. In 1958, he belted a 91-yard punt, which remains the school record to this day and was just another example of his all-around athletic prowess.

His off-the-field high jinks almost overshadowed his on-field talent, though. McDaniel was kicked off the team by Wilkinson when he was caught cutting classes and drinking at a private club.

But the coach allowed his players to take a vote on whether they wanted Wahoo back on the team. They did, and he was reinstated.

Part of his training for the college wrestling team had him running 10 miles a day. A group of his dorm-mates and fellow wrestlers, who witnessed the big Indian taking his daily jogs, issued a challenge that McDaniel couldn't pass up. They dared him to run from the front steps of their dorm in Norman to the faraway town of Chickasha. No problem, thought McDaniel. His gang of friends followed behind in a car as McDaniel endlessly chugged along. Wahoo won the $185 bet. All he did was run 36 miles in six hours. Without stopping.

The challenges kept coming, and the challenges were always accepted. Even later, while playing in the AFL, he would go back home to Midland in the offseason with everyone wanting to take a crack at the big football star. The locals soon learned that challenging him to arm wrestling matches was not a wise decision. In one contest Wahoo, of course, came out the victor. The loser came out of the match with a broken arm.

McDaniel graduated from college in 1960, which turned out to be impeccable timing, as the American Football League was just getting underway. He was drafted by the AFL's Los Angeles Chargers, but instead he went to the expansion Dallas Cowboys' training camp on a tryout basis. After receiving criticism for leaving Texas to attend Oklahoma, he felt the need to make good in the eyes of his fellow Texans. Though he was cut before opening day, he did make an impression with his toughness and hard-hitting attitude and style of play. Cowboy trainer Clint Houy said of McDaniel, "He has an Indian stoicism toward pain." Wahoo could dish it out, but he could take it, as well.

After failing to make the Cowboys (well, he was an Indian), McDaniel fortuitously hooked up with the Houston Oilers. He was back in Texas, and he was on a winner. He worked his way into the lineup in seven games as an offensive guard. Led by starting quarterback and kicker George Blanda, the Oilers finished in first place in the AFL East Division with a 10–4 record and then defeated the Chargers 24–16 to capture the first AFL Championship.

The following season, McDaniel moved on to Denver. And that's where he started becoming a little more Wahoo-like. He settled into his familiar middle linebacker position and wore his signature No. 54. He played in all 14 games, but the Broncos finished with a lowly 3–11 record. In 1962, McDaniel added punting to his professional résumé when he boomed five kicks for a 34.6 average. McDaniel's coach, Jack Faulkner, said of his player at the time, "He was a wild Indian." After improving to 7–7 and climbing up to second place in '62, Denver fell all the way down to the basement the next year, finishing at 2–11–1.

The 1963 season was McDaniel's last in Denver. He didn't miss a game in his three years with the Broncos, but he would be on the move once again; this time heading to the city that was made for Wahoo McDaniel. Faulkner shrewdly stated, "I told Wahoo if he went to New York and did a good job he could make a fortune. He has a great sense of timing both on and off the field." New York was where he went, and the city was barely big enough for him.

Wahoo McDaniel was traded to the New York Jets in a blockbuster nine-player deal. The team was just entering a new era. They had been bought by Sonny Werblin the previous year, and the successful Weeb Ewbank was now roaming the sidelines for the Jets. McDaniel's first season as a Jet also coincided with the team's move into Shea Stadium. Fans were finally coming out to see the Jets, and they were starved for a hero to call their own.

Another football transaction affected McDaniel's emergence into the city's limelight. Popular New York Giants middle linebacker Sam Huff was shipped off to the Washington Redskins that same offseason. The Giants, and Huff in particular, were the stars of

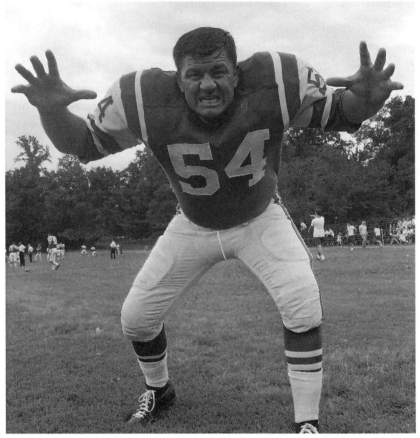

Edward "Wahoo" McDaniel of the New York Jets poses during Jets training camp in 1965. (AP Images)

Gotham. But Wahoo wouldn't take a back seat to anyone, not even a perennial Pro Bowler and Pro Football Hall of Famer. "This place ain't big enough for me and Huff," McDaniel bellowed. "It's lucky for him he moved."

After causing an uproar with that cocky statement, McDaniel tempered his boasting, but not by much, "When I said that about Huff, it was a rib. I sure didn't mean to be sarcastic. But everybody picked it up, and that was fine, too. Right away they knew I was out there." He was the original swaggering Jet, with Joe Namath, Rex Ryan, and all the others following in his footsteps.

He didn't waste any time making an impact on Jets fans, nor did the fans waste any time in showing their love for Wahoo. Let's face it, how could a hulking, hard-hitting Indian, built like a refrigerator with a magnetic personality and the nickname "Wahoo" not be a fan favorite? Football premiered at Shea Stadium on September 12, 1964, and the place was jammed with more than 60,000 spectators. The old apathetic days of the Titans were officially over, and Wahoo McDaniel helped usher in the modern era of the alluring, captivating, and yes, now-popular New York Jets.

McDaniel's former team, the Broncos, was the opponent, and the hometown Jets smoked them to the tune of 30–6. But the scoring—even the victory—was just a backdrop to Wahoo's coming-out party. When he recorded his first tackle as a Jet, and the public address announcer uttered the word "Wahoo," the packed house stirred with excitement. They sensed something special was happening with this oddly named newcomer to New York.

As he made a second tackle, and a third, the crowd got louder and louder, cheering harder for their new favorite. He didn't disappoint them, as he proved to be a tackling machine, and he batted down passes and blocked kicks left and right. Though his prowess on the field that night didn't need any embellishment, McDaniel was given credit for tackles he didn't make and for knocking down passes he didn't touch, which was all just an excuse for the public address announcer to say the word "Wahoo" and prod the crowd into a fresh batch of cheering for the linebacker. By the second half, instead of formally announcing which player made a tackle (and it was almost always McDaniel), the public address announcer began asking the fans, "Who made that tackle?!" "Wa-hoo!" was the response, and a legend was born.

McDaniel was credited with 23 tackles in that first game. *Sports Illustrated* wrote that McDaniel "plays middle linebacker as if it were the last wild charge at the Little Big Horn." Harry Farrar of the *Denver Post* added, "All the applause Wahoo got in three years at Denver wouldn't amount to half of what he gets in one yell in New York."

"I've played hard every year, but I've only had so-so recognition," McDaniel said at the time. "This year I'm playing harder than ever. But the way that crowd reacted the first night surprised me. I was anxious for the second game to see if it kept up." It did. Wahoo wasn't a one-game wonder. And for the second game, he had a new jersey. Instead of reading "McDaniel" over his No. 54, it simply said, "Wahoo." It marked the first time in professional football that a player had something other than his last name across the back of his shirt.

The fan reaction didn't go to his head, though. "He was very humbled," said his first wife, Monta. "There was no bragging or anything like that." There would soon be Wahoo t-shirts to go along with his fans' devotion, and the spotlight shone brighter on McDaniel than on any other Jet. "I don't think the other players resent the attention I'm getting," he said. "They know how I am. I'll play just as hard whether those people holler or not. But it sure does sound sweet." It was no surprise that he was voted the most popular Jet of 1964. For his accolade, he, Monta, and little Nikki starred in a television commercial for H-O Oatmeal.

After living across from Shea Stadium for six months, the McDaniels moved out to Long Beach, Long Island, to a high-rise apartment complex where a group of other Jets players and wives resided. They were all one big happy family, enjoying parties together without any jealousy directed toward Wahoo. Don Maynard, Larry Grantham, and Curley Johnson were all part of the gang. "We were real close-knit. That was just a fun time," Monta recalled.

McDaniel did have his critics, though, football-wise. He was strong on the blitz and could handle the run when it was coming up the middle right at him. But his passing responsibilities and outside ground coverage were questioned because of his husky physique. Wahoo did not agree with that assessment, though.

"My greatest assets are my size and strength," McDaniel said at the time. "I just don't get blocked. If I got blocked more than twice, I had a lousy game. I'm only 6'1", which is short for my weight, but I have tremendous shoulders and arms and can knock off blockers. I have regular pass responsibility. San Diego tried to throw on me six or seven times when we played them this season. They made me cover Paul Lowe. I don't have his speed, but I would stay in there and read whether the play was a run, draw, or screen, and then if Lowe came I went with him hard. I've seen the same backs in this league year after year for five years, and I know what they can do and where they're going. I can go with them. I knock down about three passes a game. I intercepted six in the last two seasons, and I'm 50 percent improved on pass defense this season. Nobody kills me passing."

The Jets finished with a mediocre 5–8–1 record in 1964, and they would repeat that performance the following season. But there would be another fan favorite to go along with McDaniel that year, when Joe Namath joined the Jets. And the rookie sensation noticed McDaniel immediately. "The Jets were human," Namath said. "Well, most of them were human. I'm not so sure about Wahoo McDaniel, a veteran linebacker from Texas. He jumped on my back once when we were running laps, and I wanted to kill him, but most of the time he just talked. If he'd spent as much time working on his linebacking as he spent shooting his mouth at me, Wahoo would have had a helluva year."

He may have occasionally leaped on the backs of rich quarterbacks, but he didn't touch a drop of motor oil anymore, as he was now a married man with a young daughter. "I'll admit I used to be wild," Wahoo said. "But that's behind me. I don't have time for all that cutting up." He may have been trying to convince himself more than anything with that statement. It wasn't uncommon for him to come home after having a drink or two, and if he had trouble locating his key, he would just break down the door. "He would just go crazy when he had too much to drink. A crazy Indian," Monta said. "He was wild, but everybody knew he was, and that was him."

During the 1965 season, he was still the people's choice, which was proven when his second daughter, Cindi, was born. A local paper published a big picture of the newest tiny Wahoo along with the beaming mother and father. So many flowers and plants were sent by adoring fans to Long Island Jewish Hospital that they couldn't all fit in the McDaniels' room. Nurses had to set up rows of flowers in the hallway.

No matter his popularity with the New York fans, his time in Queens would be short. He only lasted two years with the Jets before he was taken by the Miami Dolphins in the 1966 expansion draft. He played three seasons with the Dolphins, still wearing No. 54 with the name "Wahoo" over it, and he even picked up some of his old punting duties in the team's inaugural season, kicking 33 times for a 37-yard average. (He didn't boot so much as one kick with the Jets.) His tenure in Miami ended in 1968 due to a usual Wahoo antic. After having a little too much fun in a bar, he beat up three or four policemen when they tried to arrest him. The Dolphins let him go, and his football career came to an end.

He did get a chance to play with future Super Bowl winners Bob Griese, Larry Csonka, Jim Kiick, Manny Fernandez, and Dick Anderson, but playing in Miami just wasn't the same as New York. "Happiest years of my life," McDaniel said of his time with the Jets. "They take care of their athletes in New York." Wahoo played nine years in the AFL and finished with 13 interceptions, and he ran one back for a touchdown while with the Jets in 1964. He only appeared in two of the 51 seasons the Jets have played, he wasn't a member of the Super Bowl team, and he isn't atop of any franchise leader boards, but Wahoo was more than a footnote in the team's history; he was a shooting star, a once-in-a-lifetime player that the fans rallied around. Before there was "J-E-T-S, Jets! Jets! Jets!," there was "Wa-hoo! Wa-hoo! Wa-hoo!"

McDaniel's football career sounds like a fairly routine one. Sure, fans chanted his name wherever he went, but he wasn't a Pro Bowler, nor did he set any records. But starting back around 1961, McDaniel didn't just play football—he was a two-sport star. He was also a wrestler. Or as he would put it, a 'rassler. He began wrestling back in college at Oklahoma, and when his first season in the AFL came to an end, he turned pro when a promoter was searching for a large, colorful Indian. And Wahoo was nothing if not a large, colorful Indian. He fit the suit, if you will. "They were more interested in what I looked like than if I could wrestle."

He said at the time of his burgeoning career, "I wasn't a very good 'rassler in college, but the 'rasslers weren't very good football players, either. The guy in Indianapolis said don't worry, they would teach me. That was six weeks before the football season began, and I 'rassled every night. Last year from January 1 until training camp, I had 160 matches, sometimes two on Thursdays, all over Texas and in Albuquerque, Denver, Kansas City, places like that. I've gotten to be pretty good. I'm just now a main eventer. It takes five years to be a good pro football player and about that time to be a big-time 'rassler."

McDaniel wrestled under the name Chief Wahoo. At that time in American history, what most of the country knew about Native Americans came from John Wayne movies, *F Troop*, or the Cleveland Indians (who had their own Chief Wahoo). Newspapers and magazines couldn't restrain themselves from using phrases

Chief Wahoo McDaniel appears at a 1985 professional wrestling event in Houston. McDaniel wrestled professionally for parts of four decades. (AP Images)

such as "wampum," "warpath," or "firewater" when referring to Wahoo. Though McDaniel was fiercely proud of his Native American heritage, he did play it up as he nobly entered the ring in full Indian regalia, feathered headdress, tomahawk, and all. McDaniel was often compared to famous Native American wrestler Jay Strongbow, but many of his peers felt Wahoo was the better wrestler.

His Jets teammates would come and watch him at Madison Square Garden, and by the time he was playing for the Dolphins, he was earning more money in the wrestling ring than on the football field. After putting football behind him in 1968, Wahoo turned all his attention to grappling. And if he was popular in the stands of Shea Stadium, he made an even bigger splash in the world of wrestling.

Competing all over the country, in one region after another, McDaniel was a top draw and recognized name because of his football career, but he had his heyday in the National Wrestling Alliance's Mid-Atlantic region in the 1970s. He won dozens of titles spanning three decades, including the NWA Mid-Atlantic, Florida, and Texas Heavyweight Championships, as well as the NWA American Tag Team Championship, among many others. Wahoo had just as many feuds as he owned championship belts, and he was named *Pro Wrestling Illustrated*'s Most Popular Wrestler of the Year in 1976.

Chief Wahoo's signature move was the Tomahawk Chop, of course, and he was also the master of the Indian Strap Match, where two wrestlers are connected by the wrist with a leather strap. Just like on the football field, he was an intense hard hitter with strong chopping hands of fury. And also like his football days, he was usually a "good guy" in the ring. Later on in his career, he would occasionally stray into "bad guy" territory, but never for long.

Johnny Valentine, Greg Valentine, Ric Flair, Sgt. Slaughter, "Superstar" Billy Graham, Jesse Ventura, and Rowdy Roddy Piper were just a few of his arch enemies in the ring. Flair once hit Wahoo in the head with the leg of a freshly smashed table. Unbeknownst to both wrestlers, the leg had a nail sticking out of it. McDaniel was seriously injured, and Flair hurriedly pinned him to end the match. He also suffered a broken leg thanks to the rage of Greg Valentine. And he was gouged by the horns of an opponent's Viking helmet, which left him with a permanent scar on his stomach. But Wahoo handed out the punishment, as well. He once accidentally knocked Jack Brisco out cold with a head butt. When his opponent drifted back into consciousness, McDaniel apologized and then promptly belted him in the face.

Though much of his time was spent traveling around the country, he never forgot his family and tried to wrestle as close to home as possible. By the '70s, he was divorced from his first wife, but he lived nearby in Texas. When he had his daughters on a weekend, they would occasionally tag along with him to the matches. While he was in the ring busting heads, the doorman acted as babysitter for his two tykes.

"People can believe what they want, but what I experienced in the ring was as tough or tougher than anything I encountered on a football field," McDaniel once stated. "Rougher still was what wrestlers had to put up with outside the ring. I've been burned, stabbed."

One leisurely afternoon while still married to Monta, he was napping while his wrestling trunks were out back drying on a clothesline. A couple of neighborhood troublemakers snuck onto the property, grabbed his trunks, and began stomping on them. Monta alerted Wahoo to the goings-on. He bolted outside, threw the two trespassers over a 6' fence, and broke the nose of one of the agitators before they ran for their lives, escaping the wild man they just provoked. They might as well have poked a bear with a sharp stick to see what would happen. "And I know one time he was coming out of the wrestling match, and somebody said, 'Fake!'" Monta remembered. "Well, that guy went flying across the room, too." Wahoo also shot one of his fellow wrestlers, though unintentionally.

While hanging out in a bar with a few of his wrestling compadres, a drunk began making obnoxious remarks about the wife of one of Wahoo's cronies. Words were exchanged, and the kerfuffle moved out to the parking lot. The intoxicated lout pulled out a knife (or a baseball bat, as there are varying accounts of the story) and seeing the weapon, Wahoo grabbed a gun. As Andre the Giant and Dirty Dick Slater calmly watched McDaniel pistol-whip the drunkard, Wahoo's gun accidentally discharged and the bullet went through Slater's leg. Wahoo had to pay Slater's salary until he was well enough to get back in the ring, which was but a few weeks.

By his own count, McDaniel wrestled in approximately 10,000 matches and picked up 2,000 to 3,000 stitches, not to mention the aforementioned broken leg, nail in the head, and Viking goring. He finally retired for good in the mid-'90s. Though he never made it into the Pro Football Hall of Fame, in 1995, McDaniel was inducted into the World Championship Wrestling Hall of Fame, and in 2010, he was enshrined in the Professional Wrestling Hall of Fame.

As if McDaniel's athletic credentials weren't impressive enough, there was yet one more sport that he excelled in. And that was golf. Some thought he was actually a better golfer than football player or wrestler, though his exuberant, high-spirited brand of golf was seldom seen out on the course. He occasionally hit the links with Lee Trevino, who said of his buddy, "Old Wahoo used a hickory-shafted putter. One time he missed a high-dollar putt and smashed the thing against a fence post near the green. The putter snapped back and the clubhead split his lip open. That was the angriest man I have ever seen on a golf course."

The traveling and unorthodox lifestyle of the wrestling world took a toll on McDaniel's personal life. He was married five times to four women, with two daughters from his first marriage. "Fact is, when you wrestle for a living, you're never home, and that's hard on relationships. And, well, I never pretended to be an angel," he said.

His final years were filled with illness and family troubles, with the cheering fans but a distant memory. Sometime in the 1990s, McDaniel's health started deteriorating. For a few years, though, his teenage son from his last marriage came to live with him in Charlotte after the divorce. Though the boy turned out not to be his true flesh and blood, McDaniel raised him as his own. As Wahoo's condition worsened, and the money from professional sports

Ed Marinaro

Another former Jet who gained more fame after he left the team was Ed Marinaro. His time with the Jets was brief, as he only played in six games for the team in 1976, gaining 312 yards rushing, two touchdowns, and 21 receptions for 168 yards.

Born in New York but raised in New Milford, New Jersey, Marinaro became a legend in his time as a running back at Cornell, where he was the first college player to rush for more than 4,000 yards. By the time his collegiate career was over, he had set 16 NCAA records, including most career rushing yards (4,715), best career per-game rushing average (174.4), most single-season rushing yards (1,881), and best single-season per-game rushing average (209). He scored five touchdowns in a game twice, led the nation in rushing in 1970 and '71, and was the runner-up for the Heisman Trophy in '71. He also graced the cover of *Sports Illustrated* that year, and he was enshrined in the College Football Hall of Fame in 1991.

Marinaro was taken in the second round of the 1972 draft by the Vikings and spent four seasons in Minnesota, going to two Super Bowls with the team. Coming from the Ivy League, Marinaro faced some cynicism about his accomplishments. When he joined the Vikings, he was taunted, though good-naturedly. "Is that seven-man football you play out there in Cornell? Or is it was no longer flowing in, much of his family left him to fend for himself. It was a sad ending to a life jam-packed with mischievous adventure.

Ultimately, Nikki's husband flew to North Carolina and brought Wahoo back to live with them in Texas. "We were pretty tight," she said. "He and I have always been on the same page." They went hunting together when she was a child, and she moved in with her dad for a year, when, as a typical rebellious high school senior, her mother told her, "Go live with your dad." Now it was time for the rebellious father to live with the daughter who never turned her back on him, healthy or sick, wealthy or penniless.

---

touch?" But Marinaro accepted the ribbing with grace. "Cornell gave me the confidence to know I was more than just a football player."

The soon-to-be actor got a taste of the entertainment world in 1976 when he posed in nothing but a pair of underwear in a series of ads for Jockey, along with the likes of Lou Brock, Steve Garvey, and Brad Park. "It's just underwear. It was pretty good money and the exposure wasn't bad either, no pun intended," he said. It wasn't a hit with all fans, though, as a woman wrote a letter of complaint to the Vikings. "She said something about it being disgusting, disgraceful, and the work of the devil. She recommended that I read some book, but I don't remember which one."

After appearing in one game with Seattle in 1977, Marinaro retired from football and became a full-time actor. He really made a name for himself the following decade, starting off with a season on *Laverne & Shirley* as Sonny St. Jacques, the stars' building manager when the two wacky ladies moved from Milwaukee to California. But his most famous role was the portrayal of Joe Coffey in *Hill Street Blues* from 1981 to '86. Marinaro was also a regular on *Sisters*, and he now co-stars in *Blue Mountain State*.

Like Wahoo, he was a success in whatever career he chose. "In a lot of ways, what I've accomplished as an actor is greater than what I did as a football player."

While awaiting a kidney transplant, Wahoo McDaniel died on April 18, 2002, of diabetes and complications from renal failure. He was 63 years old. Calling him just another football player or just another wrestler doesn't do justice to Wahoo. He was more than what was seemingly possible for one man to be. He was a Native American, an American, a Texan, a Sooner, a Jet, a middle linebacker, a punter, a guard, a halfback, an end, a 'rassler, a golfer, a catcher, a track star, a daredevil, a ruffian, a husband, a father, a wiseacre—he was the original package. He was an off-the-beaten-path version of the American Dream.

McDaniel was a wild man who lived a wild life. But the mark of a man is how he is remembered by his loved ones. "He was very likable," Monta said. "He would give the shirt off his back to any of his friends. He was very protective of his family and his friends. Just a very likable person." And what did his eldest daughter think of him? "He was a good dad," Nikki said. Even 60,000 fans chanting his name can't top that.

CHAPTER 5

THEY MIGHT (NOT) BE GIANTS

THE NEW YORK GIANTS ENTRENCHED THEMSELVES in the area's consciousness with decades of history. Their fans were handed down through the generations. They won championships. They had a classy, family-run ownership. They were a model of all that was good. They were a paragon of professional sports. They were an emblem of American virtuosity. They were the mainstream. They were crisply combed hair. They were nicely pressed suits. They were Frank Gifford's classic handsome looks. They were the boy next door. They were wholesome. They were honorable. They were well-behaved. They were New York football.

But then the New York Titans showed up. And they were a ragtag, scraggly bunch if ever there was one. They were the Bowery Boys in shoulder pads. They weren't the Bad News Bears as much as just plain bad news. If the Giants were the ideal football model, the new AFL New Yorkers were setting the standard for hanging on by a thread. They had money problems, stadium problems, on-the-field-performance problems, and problem problems.

When the Titans climbed out of the sewer in 1960, the Giants, their fans, and the New York press looked down their noses at them and deemed these new ragamuffins unworthy to represent their fair city. *They call that AFL stuff football? The Giants play football. Who knows what the heck the Titans are doing.* While the Giants were going to three consecutive NFL Championship Games in 1961, '62, and '63, the Titans just shrugged their shoulders and went about their merry way. They might not have looked like Frank Gifford, but they were at least having a blast in their own unruly way.

As the decade went on and the Titans became the Jets, they got a little better on the field with every passing year. They got a little more popular, and they started looking a little more like a real football team. And over at Yankee Stadium, the Giants got a little bit older, a little less champion-like, and started looking a little less like a real football team. Things were beginning to even out. The Jets were going up. The Giants were going down. And they eyed each other warily from across the city.

Though their fortunes on the field had changed by the time the late-'60s came calling, the images of the two teams remained. The Giants were the clean-cut good guys, while the Jets were a collection of beatniks, hippies, cowboys, Indians, rejects, and rebels. They were the younger brother constantly getting into trouble and playing hooky. They were Kelly Leak tearing through Yankee Stadium in the middle of a Giants game on his dirt bike. Joe Namath was as renowned and lionized as any Giant had been, but he was an antihero—he was the epitome of the gambling, drinking, womanizing bad boy.

In 1969, *Sports Illustrated* described the Jets as "a band of mildly insane roughnecks." And the magazine painted this portrait of the Jets walking onto the practice field: "Clad in a motley of shredded sweatshirts, bloodstained foul-weather jackets, dirty wool caps, work-worn shoes, their noses and cheekbones scabbed and leaking pus, their mouths leaking gallows humor, the Jets came on like stragglers from the Eastern Front."

After giving each other the stink-eye for a decade, a rivalry between the two teams began to percolate. The antagonism between their leagues had been going on for years. A shaky truce was reached with the impending merger and the start of the Super Bowls, but as long as the Packers and the NFL were coming out on top, the old guard still felt superior. The AFL held a higher opinion of itself, but they would need to prove it on the field of play. The animosity reached a crescendo with Super Bowl III when the NFLers finally came toppling down. There was a new sheriff in town—and he had a Fu Manchu, filmed movies with Ann-Margret in his spare time, and caroused with a different chick every night.

The rancor the Jets and Giants felt for each other finally came to a boil, as well. On August 17, 1969, the first-ever showdown between New York's football teams was staged. It would be the biggest preseason game in the history of the world. Well, at least it seemed that way. And it was awfully personal.

Don Maynard had been cut by the Giants 10 summers earlier, and the man mainly responsible for the end of his tenure in the Bronx, Allie Sherman, was now the head coach of the team. Namath resented the Giants because they had passed on drafting him. Weeb Ewbank wanted to stick it to the NFL one more time to prove his team wasn't a second-rate outfit. Giants owner Wellington Mara viewed the Jets as a gang of dirty, long-haired hippies who should have been up in New York State at Woodstock, which would be taking place on the same day as the game, instead of playing on the football field. They were reprobates who shouldn't even come near his Giants. When Namath dropped back to pass, Mara might as well have been seeing Jim Morrison or Wavy Gravy as far as he was concerned. And to add insult to injury, Matt Snell, who was drafted by both New York teams, snubbed the Giants to join the Jets. With resentments and strong feelings of revenge piling up like a 10-car accident on the highway, both

Giants rookie Fred Dryer (89) rushes Jets quarterback Joe Namath (12) during the first meeting between New York's AFL and NFL teams, a preseason matchup on August 17, 1969. Dryer was called for roughing the passer. Namath completed 14 of 16 passes and threw three touchdown passes as the Jets won 37–14. (George Mattson/ NY Daily News Archive via Getty Images)

teams would play their starters for most of the game and go all out to win. It was an exhibition in name only.

The Giants and much of the NFL felt the Jets' Super Bowl victory over the Colts was merely a fluke. They were lucky to catch Baltimore on a bad day. It was nothing but happenstance, with the stars aligning for just that one afternoon. However, a Jets conquest over the Giants would make them indisputable champions. A win over their city rivals would be another win over the NFL. Their Super Bowl triumph would officially be sealed.

While hundreds of thousands of muddy, chemically altered kids were upstate listening to The Who, Jimi Hendrix, and Sly and the Family Stone, an overwhelming 70,000 New York football fans hit the road and traveled to the Yale Bowl in New Haven, Connecticut, the site of the Battle of New York. There wouldn't be any peace, love, or groovy vibes at this event. The only bit of violence at the rock festival—Keith Moon blowing up his drum set—was nothing compared to what the Jets would do to the Giants. If The Who's drummer thought he was a demolition expert, he could have taken notes watching the hippies of the AFL destroy the old fuddy-duddy Giants.

Ewbank's first bit of inspiration—not that his team needed any more ammunition to get riled up for the Giants than they already possessed—was to name the original Titans (Maynard, Bill Mathis, and Larry Grantham) as team captains for the game. Those three suffered through the indignity of the early years when they were treated like pariahs in the city. And now here they were, Super Bowl champions, with a chance to whip and humiliate their big brothers.

The game itself wouldn't be remembered as a battle for the ages. It wasn't a shootout, a gang war, or a slugfest. It wasn't a back-and-forth affair between two fierce rivals not giving an inch. It wasn't a struggle. It wasn't The Greatest Game Ever Played. It wasn't even The Second Greatest Game Ever Played. Instead it was a massacre. Hendrix's version of "The Star-Spangled Banner" lasted longer than the competitive nature of this preseason contest. It was almost over before the traffic jam could be untangled on Interstate 95.

On the opening drive, Namath and the Jets offense cut through the Giants defense like a Ginsu knife slicing through a tin can. It only took five plays for the Jets to jump out on top 7–0. George

Sauer hauled in a 28-yard touchdown pass, and Gang Green never relinquished the lead. Could it really be this easy? The Raiders put up more of a fight than this. Heck, the expansion Cincinnati Bengals were tougher than this.

The Jets soon added a field goal, which was promptly followed by a Giants fumble. The Jets recovered the ball and quickly scored another touchdown. Later in the second quarter, rookie Mike Battle returned a Giants punt 86 yards for another score. And just like that it was 24–0. The romp was on. Mara, Sherman, and the rest of the old boys' club from the Bronx had steam coming out of their ears watching these counterculture degenerates stomp all over their team. Maybe the Super Bowl win wasn't a fluke after all. Maybe the Jets could compete with the NFL. And maybe, just maybe, they were better than the NFL. They surely were better than the Giants.

Fran Tarkenton tried to make a game of it, leading two Giants scoring drives in the second half, but it wouldn't be close to good enough. The Jets were just toying with their opponent. Namath came right back with two touchdown throws of his own to put the game out of reach and show the world which quarterback owned New York City. While Tarkenton was a sloppy 9-for-21, with only 139 yards through the air, Broadway Joe, that depraved ne'er-do-well, went a machine-like 14-for-16, good for 188 yards, and threw three touchdown passes, to boot. The final score of the bloodbath: Jets 37, Giants 14.

Old Titan Mathis scored two touchdowns on the day, but the happiest person in New Haven that steamy afternoon was Maynard. He finally avenged his nemesis. Giants fans had been unhappy with Sherman for years by the time this game was played. The team had let assistants Vince Lombardi and Tom Landry get away, and that left them with Sherman to replace Jim Lee Howell in 1961. By the mid-'60s, choruses of "Good-bye, Allie" were heard throughout

Yankee Stadium with every wrong turn by the coach. And from the sidelines in New Haven in August 1969, Maynard himself conducted the choir of fans belting out the song that was music to his ears.

Sherman never made it to opening day, as Mara gave him the ax and replaced him with Alex Webster, completing the Revenge of Don Maynard. That day in Connecticut may have been a bitter one for the Giants, but it was one satisfying and joyous afternoon for the Jets as they were crowned Kings of New York.

The two teams would meet for real the following season on November 1, 1970, with the NFL/AFL merger now complete. Though the exhibition game the previous summer was real enough, this time it would count in the standings. The Giants came into Shea Stadium with a 3–3 record, while the Jets limped into the game at 1–5 and would finish with a lowly 4–10 mark. Namath, Snell, and Emerson Boozer were all out with injuries, and the season was a lost cause by the time these rivals took the field.

Namath or no Namath, things started out well for the Jets. The first half wasn't a scoring barrage like the last matchup. In fact, the game stood at 0–0 after the first quarter. Like the last game, the Jets got on the board first when backup quarterback Al Woodall completed an 8-yard touchdown pass to George Nock. Pete Gogolak booted a 25-yard field goal to start the scoring for the Giants, but in the third quarter Jim Turner kicked a 31-yarder to give the Jets a promising 10–3 lead.

Snell, Boozer, Namath—who needs them? Well, as it turned out, the Jets did. It was all Giants from that point on. Jets running back Chuck Mercein was tackled in the end zone for a safety. Tarkenton tossed touchdown passes to Bob Tucker and Clifton McNeil. And Gogolak added another field goal to finish the scoring as the Giants pulled away with a 22–10 victory. The undermanned Jets never really had a chance. Woodall threw two interceptions and was sacked six times, while the team also lost two fumbles. There was no joy in Jetville after that shellacking.

The second regular-season meeting between the two New York teams, four years later, was the first one that was truly competitive. And it was historic, as well. The NFL instituted the sudden-death rule for non-playoff games that season. The first game to go into overtime came in Week 2 when the Steelers and Broncos stood at a 35–35 standstill after four quarters at Mile High Stadium. Neither team could muster up so much as a point in the extra 15 minutes, though, so the game ended in a tie.

On November 10, 1974, the Jets and Giants also went into overtime, but this time there would be a victor, the first non-postseason overtime winner in NFL history. The two teams would clash once again at the Yale Bowl, the temporary home of the Giants. After eight games in a 14-game schedule, neither squad was going anywhere. The Jets were a less-than-sparkling 1–7, while the Giants were only slightly better at 2–6. So this game was more for bragging rights than anything tangible that could be gained by a win. Playoff implications would not be found anywhere near the state of Connecticut on this sunny, 50-degree afternoon. But it was a chance for the Jets to exact revenge for their 1970 loss and to humble the holier-than-thou Giants once again.

Namath was healthy in 1974, only one of four seasons in the 1970s where he would appear in 10 or more games. But Snell, Maynard, and Sauer were all gone, and John Riggins was out with an injury. They still had the first-rate Boozer to run the ball, along with rookie Robert Burns. Rich Caster, Jerome Barkum, David Knight, and Eddie Bell were Namath's new aerial targets. There was a fresh face roaming the sidelines, too, as Ewbank's son-in-law, Charley Winner, replaced the legendary coach.

Just like the previous pair of games, the Jets scored first. Namath whipped a 19-yard pass to Knight to give his team the

New York Giants Carl "Spider" Lockhart (43), Doug Van Horn (63), and Jack Gregory (81) greet Jets running back Emerson Boozer (32) before the teams' November 10, 1974, matchup at the Yale Bowl. Boozer caught the game-winning touchdown in overtime as the Jets won the game 26–20. (Ross Lewis/Getty Images)

early lead in the first quarter. Old AFLer Gogolak, who was in his final season, booted a 26-yarder to close the gap. Along with the bidding war for Namath, the Hungarian soccer-style kicker was one of the central characters in the two warring leagues' decision to hold a mutual draft. The Giants stole Gogolak away from the Buffalo Bills after the 1965 season, enraging the AFL. The outcome was one draft for two leagues.

The Giants took the lead in the second quarter when tight end Bob Tucker caught a 2-yard touchdown pass from old Dallas Cowboy

Craig Morton. But rookie placekicker Pat Leahy nailed a 34-yard field goal to knot the game at 10. While Gogolak was on the way out after a nine-year stint in New York, Leahy was in the first of his 18 seasons as a Jet. He finished his career as the franchise's all-time games-played leader with 250, and he was a First-Team All-Pro in 1978. After Leahy's boot, the Giants' kicker returned the favor with a 22-yarder, giving his team the lead once again going into halftime.

Every time the Giants went ahead, the Jets answered right back. In the third quarter, Leahy put another one through the uprights, tying the game at 13. But every time the Jets caught up, the Giants went back ahead. They did it again when Morton threw a 12-yard touchdown pass to Bob Grim. But that was the final time the old New Yorkers would overtake their younger upstarts.

Down by a touchdown with the clock ticking away in the fourth quarter, the Jets drove all the way to the Giants' 3-yard line. They then tied the game on a play that no one could have expected. Even the Jets didn't know what was happening. Namath hadn't scored a rushing touchdown in five years. Even in his prime, he never came close to being described as a scrambler, and at this stage of his career it took all his willpower just to walk to the line of scrimmage, let alone dash and scurry around the field the way Fran Tarkenton could. But on this day, he had one more sprint in him. Well, limp is probably more like it.

In the huddle, Namath called for a handoff to Boozer up the middle. He took the ball from center, turned, jammed it into the running back's gut, but pulled the ball back and kept it himself. With his 10 teammates expecting the handoff, and 11 Giants converging in the middle to tackle Boozer, Namath hobbled around the left end untouched on a naked bootleg—and a secret naked bootleg at that. Boozer had looked back, thinking the ball was fumbled. Shock and awe filled the Yale Bowl. It was Namath's last-ever rushing touchdown. Just jogging those three yards was an arduous task for the 31-year-old, who was so fragile at that point that he put a hand out, desperately signaling the defenders not to touch him the way a cantankerous old man might wave people away who were offering to help him cross the street.

That touchdown sent the game into overtime. The Giants had the first crack at scoring and having the honor of being the first NFL regular-season overtime winner, but Gogolak missed a field goal. When the Jets got the ball on their first possession of the extra period, they took advantage of the opportunity needing two plays to gain 62 yards. Namath completed a 42-yard pass to Caster to open the drive, which was followed by a 20-yard reception by Barkum. Three straight running plays brought the ball all the way to the Giants' 5-yard line.

Namath was done running for the day—and pretty much for the rest of his career, as he would gain a total of 16 yards on the ground in his last three seasons—so he called a play-action pass. After taking the snap, he faked a handoff and gunned a pass to Boozer just out of the reach of linebacker Brad Van Pelt. The game was over, and history was made with the Jets' 26–20 win.

Namath and Morton produced eerily similar games. Broadway Joe, who would be named the Comeback Player of the Year that season, went 20-for-31, throwing two touchdowns and totaling 236 yards, while Morton completed 21 passes on 32 attempts, threw for one more yard than his Jets counterpart, and also tossed two touchdown passes. Neither had a pass intercepted, and there were only three penalties the whole day. The little-known Burns, a ninth-round draft pick by the Jets that year, enjoyed a career day. He rushed for 101 yards on 21 carries. His time in the NFL lasted just that one season, and in the other four games in which he notched at least one rushing attempt, he gained 20, 11, 26, and 0 yards. So yes, this was his best day in the NFL, and he helped his team to a groundbreaking victory.

The Giants would lose every game the rest of the way that year, ending with a pathetic 2–12 record, while the Jets would win their last five, finishing at 7–7 but two games behind the wild card Bills. The two teams would play another overtime game 29 years later, but this time it was the Giants who would come out on top. After Chad Pennington tossed two fourth-quarter touchdowns to tie the game, Brett Conway kicked a 29-yard field goal in overtime to win it for the Giants.

By the time the 1980s rolled around, the bitter feelings between the two teams had fizzled out. They shared a stadium and were now partners in the conglomerate known as the NFL. Just as people grudgingly had to accept newfangled fads like the horseless motorized carriage, the spellbinding moving-picture show, the magical talking box of television, and that wondrous, perplexing invention called the computer, the Giants caved in and accepted the Jets' right to exist.

In 1986, Giant linebacker Harry Carson said, "The Jets-Giants rivalry doesn't exist as far as the players are concerned. It is strictly a fan thing." Wesley Walker stated, "I always took it as it's a rivalry because we're both in New York. It's just like any division game. You know, they're a New York team, we're a New York team, who's really the best. It's just competition. And when you play this game, it doesn't matter who you're playing against." Raul Allegre, who kicked for both teams, claimed, "There's no Jets-Giants rivalry. Trust me, we didn't see the Jets as we saw the Eagles or the Redskins or the Cowboys. We went to a lot of functions together. We still do. Back then I didn't feel that it was a rivalry."

And the teams would even root for each other, though they of course had their own interests at heart, as happened at the end of the 1981 season when the Giants needed the Jets' help to gain a playoff berth. Lawrence Taylor noted, "We all went back to the stadium the next day to watch the Jets and Green Bay on TV. When the Jets won, these older guys just went crazy again. There was champagne everywhere, and they were crying—it was a sight to see—and all the while I was standing there thinking, 'It's not that big a deal.' We still had some unfinished business out there." It was a big deal for both teams, though, as it was the first time either would qualify for the postseason since the '60s, and it was the first time ever that the pair would make the playoffs in the same year.

That's not to say that if one had the chance to play spoiler for the other, there wouldn't be some satisfaction gained. On December 18, 1988, just such an opportunity arose. The Giants came into the last game of the season with a 10–5 mark and needed a win to gain entry into the postseason. The Jets, at 7–7–1 and with their playoff prospects expired, were playing for pride and for one more chance to bury their local rival.

Old standby Leahy opened up the scoring by nailing a 41-yarder. Two-time Pro Bowler Mickey Shuler caught a 5-yard touchdown pass from Ken O'Brien, and Leahy added another field goal, giving the Jets a 13–0 second-quarter lead. But the Giants woke up and began their comeback when Phil Simms connected with Stephen Baker, bringing them within six at the half. A Freeman McNeil rushing score preceded another Baker touchdown. And a fourth-quarter Lionel Manuel 9-yard touchdown reception gave the Giants a narrow 21–20 advantage.

It looked for all the world as if the Giants, who had won the Super Bowl just two years prior to this season, would get another crack at the Lombardi Trophy. But with only 37 seconds left in the game, Jets great Al Toon would snag his league-leading 93rd catch of the season, a 5-yard touchdown pass from O'Brien that would give Gang Green their eighth win of the season and break the hearts of the Giants, knocking them out of the playoffs. They may have been friendly rivals by 1988, but they were still rivals. And maybe what Carson and Allegre said was true about the players' feelings toward each other, but Jets fans certainly rejoiced over the victory and what it meant to the fans of the other team in town.

The Jets had their chance to take over the city in the 1970s, but that fate remained just out of their grasp. They had Joe Willie Namath, a Super Bowl win following the 1968 season, a first-place finish and playoff appearance in 1969, and the Giants spiraling into

Raul Allegre

Raul Allegre is living proof that not all New York Giants are bad. Near the end of the 1991 season, Leahy injured his back, and the Jets, wanting someone with experience, picked up Allegre, who had recently been released by the Giants. The Jets needed to win their final game against the Dolphins to qualify for the playoffs, and Allegre was the hero, kicking a game-tying field goal as time expired in regulation and the winner in overtime. He recalled his brief yet successful tenure with Gang Green:

"They called me on a Monday, and I was there the next day on a Tuesday. I remember it was very cold that week. We couldn't practice outside. We had to go to a gym at Hofstra. We couldn't go out because back then the Jets didn't have an indoor practice facility. I didn't get to practice with the center and the holder once. The first time I got to work with them was during pregame. So I was just trying to figure out the timing—Louie Aguiar was the holder and Trevor Matich was the snapper—just trying to get some rhythm.

"The game started and I still struggled with the first kick. I missed my first kick, which I believe was a 41-, 42-yard field goal. I pushed it right. Then I had another field goal and a few extra points. But every kick was different. Game conditions are quite a bit different than pregame. The field goal prior to tying the game—I believe it was a 26-, 28-yard field goal—I banked it off the upright. So when I went in at the end, we were winning 17–13, and then Marino had a drive at the end and they scored, I believe, with about 48 seconds left. We had two timeouts. We got a good kickoff return and eventually got in position for a 44-yard field goal. But by then I was just trying to get comfortable with mediocrity and playing an unimaginative brand of football. While the Giants were trading away Pro Bowlers such as Tarkenton and Fred Dryer, the Jets had all the charisma and star power. They had everything going their way. They were ready to take over New York. But Namath's knees, along with injuries to Snell and Boozer, the retirements of Maynard and Sauer, and the departure of Riggins, along with bad decisions and other forces, sent them into a decade that went from mediocre to atrocious.

the center and the holder. And that 44-yarder I hit pretty good, and we went to overtime. We won the toss and took the ball and scored on a 30-yard field goal and eventually got to play Houston the next week.

"We lost a game that we should have won against Houston, but Bruce Coslet, in his infinite wisdom, decided that we needed to score touchdowns, so we passed up four field goal attempts inside the 20-yard line and we ended up losing 17–10. He felt that with Warren Moon and the run and shoot we had to score touchdowns, so he went for it on fourth down and we passed on those field goals.

"The guys were really nice. Everybody treated me great, and I didn't have any problems. But during the game I was more focused on trying to figure out what I needed to do and trying to mentally get up to speed with what I needed to do with my timing, which eventually I did. To me, that game, I was probably the most proud of any game that I've ever played because I didn't panic. I figured it out. It was a high-pressure game, and I hadn't had much chance to practice and I just figured it out. When we needed to have the field goals I was ready. And the last two kicks were just as perfect as they could be. So I was pretty proud of adjusting on the fly.

"I really enjoyed my time in New York. Obviously with the Jets, it was very short, only two games. I wish it could have been longer, but they had other plans. But the two games that I got to play there were significant. One made a difference. And a lot of people remember that game. The fans still remember that Miami game, and to me it's unbelievable how vividly they remember all the details. I don't get to go to New York much, but when I do run across Jets fans, they remember."

While the Jets rebounded from that black hole in the '80s and onward, their local rivals did, as well. But the Giants' rebound was just a little bouncier as they captured three Super Bowls. The gang in green and white has just never been able to catch up. Over the last five decades, the Jets have been wailing the lament of the little brother. But with the new Rex Ryan Jets blowing like a hurricane throughout New York and New Jersey, Gang Green has another chance to conquer the city. They have the stars, the headlines, and the swagger once again. The Giants may be ahead in the all-time series, seven games to four, but it was the first game the two teams played, the one that didn't count, that counted most of all. And the Jets are standing on the doorstep with one more chance to pick up where they left off on that August afternoon in New Haven in 1969.

CHAPTER 6

IT'S GOOD TO BE JOE NAMATH

JOE NAMATH ONCE OWNED THE WORLD. He could make guarantees that would come true. Women would flock to him with the slightest twitch of a dimple. He could drink scotch all night and throw touchdown passes the next afternoon. He could swing like Sinatra, play it cool like Elvis, and film motorcycle movies like Brando. He wrote an autobiography titled, *I Can't Wait Until Tomorrow...'Cause I Get Better Looking Every Day*. He was the Joe Namath of being Joe Namath.

What was it like to be Broadway Joe when he was the biggest superstar in America? The opening scene of his 1970 movie *C.C. and Company* perfectly epitomizes The World According to Joe Willie Namath. Namath's character, C.C. Ryder, strolls into a grocery store, grabs a shopping cart, and casually makes his way to an aisle. As lighthearted muzak plays in the background, he loads up his cart with a random selection of cans to feign shopping. A packet of knives is hanging at the end of a shelf, and he slips one out of the cardboard packaging, then opens a loaf of bread, takes two slices, and carefully wraps the loaf back up. Nonchalantly continuing on his way, he unseals a pack of cheese with the knife and places a slice on the bread that he's laid out in his cart. He next loads up his bread with ham and lettuce. He glances around with an air of indifference and squeezes a blob of mustard onto his handiwork. He puts his sandwich together, takes a bite, and nods in approval. Strolling once again, while chewing, he stops at the beverage section to grab himself a small carton of milk, downs the drink, and throws the carton in a nearby trash can.

The store manager walks by, and Ryder has the following exchange:

"Excuse me."

"Yes, sir?"

"Where are the cupcakes?"

"11-B, sir. Right over there."

"Thank you."

"Not at all."

He unwraps what appears to be a Twinkie, happily devours the snack until he reaches the paper goods aisle, and opens a box of napkins. He neatly dabs his face and then restocks the shelf with the cans from his cart. Now cartless, he saunters to the checkout area, snags a pack of Fruit Stripe gum costing 10 cents, and, while waiting for his change, a couple of chicks stop and giggle at him. He smiles back at the girls, retrieves his money from the checkout girl, walks out of the store, climbs on his chopper, and roars away.

The world was at Joe Namath's fingertips. He took what he wanted, when he wanted, and he did it all in a good-natured, winking-at-everything way. He didn't have to steal while threatening anybody or drawing a gun. He disarmed with a smile, not a snarl. He took his time, and while he was pilfering his treasure, he drew you in with his charm and charisma. Sure, he just made himself a sandwich in the middle of a grocery store without paying for a cent of it, but he was so polite and casual about the whole thing that no one was the wiser. And besides, he bought a pack of gum out of the goodness of his heart.

Joe Namath and actress Raquel Welch arrive together at the 1972 Academy Awards in Los Angeles. (Fotos International/Getty Images)

In 1966, when Namath was 23 years old and just entering the height of his groovy swingerdom, he stated his philosophy of life: "I believe in letting a guy live the way he wants to if he doesn't hurt anyone. I feel that everything I do is okay for me and doesn't affect anybody else, including the girls I go out with. Look man, I live and let live. I like everybody. I don't care what a man is as long as he treats me right. He can be a gambler, a hustler, someone everybody else thinks is obnoxious, I don't care so long as he's straight with me and our dealings are fair. I like Cassius Clay, Bill Hartack, Doug Sanders, and Hornung, all the controversial guys. They're too much. They're colorful, man. If I couldn't play football, I'd like to be a pro golfer. But I like everybody. Why, I even like Howard Cosell."

And Namath could swing with the best of them. "I used to drink with Sinatra, Dean Martin, and Sammy Davis at Jilly's in New York," Broadway Joe said. "Those guys were crazy. They stayed up all night. Every night. They didn't have anything to do in the morning. Didn't have to get up. Me, I had to go to practice. The good thing, though, was the Jets practiced late. I didn't have to be there until noon. I could stay up pretty late and still get some sleep before practice started."

"No, I never met the Beatles. But I met Elvis. I knew him a little bit. I will love Elvis forever for one thing—the way he treated my father. I took my father to see him in Vegas. My father loved Elvis. We went backstage afterward. My father and Elvis got along. They sat on a couch for a half hour, maybe 40 minutes, just talking about everything. It was something to see, my father and Elvis, just sitting there, bull—— about football and music."

The 1960s Joe Namath was an outlaw. He was an anti-establishment hero with scandalous long hair and an anything-goes style of living. He was lumped in with all the anarchists, kooks, and hippies of the counterculture who were trying to destroy all-American America. He scared the squares. He was the Elvis Presley of sports—the 1950s Elvis Presley, that is. The don't-show-him-below-the-waist Elvis. A different girl every night? That's not how Bart Starr or Johnny Unitas conducted themselves. Namath was threatening, and he was dangerous. He consorted with the wrong kind of people, and he didn't apologize for anything. He did what he wanted, when he wanted to do it, and with whom he wanted to do it with. The FBI had a dossier on him. The CIA kept a file on him. He was on Richard Nixon's enemies list. He transcended sports and was more than a football player. Joe Namath was a desperado.

The morning that Namath arrived in Miami for the Super Bowl, he had a pair of guests knock on his door. They weren't autograph-seekers but law enforcement agents. Namath recalled, "On our last trip to Miami, to play the Dolphins, some distinguished citizen had threatened to kill me. Later, when all those stories were going around that I was the new headman of the Cosa Nostra—hell, I'm not even eligible; I just *look* Italian—this gentleman was rumored to be one of my closest friends. I don't think that's a very nice way to show friendship.

"I lived through that previous trip, and the two visitors said they hoped I'd do just as well on this one. 'A routine checkup,' one of the guys told me. He was very happy about the particular room I'd picked. He said that because of the position of my balcony, anybody who wanted to shoot me would have to fire from a wide-open spot on the beach behind the hotel. 'There's nothing to worry about,' said the investigator. 'If he shoots you, he can't possibly get away.' That really made me feel a lot better."

The law wasn't just around to protect Namath; they had been tailing him for most of that season. "I'm pretty sure they started keeping me company right after we lost a couple of games to Buffalo and Denver," he said. "It was nothing personal, but, as I mentioned earlier, I had five passes intercepted in each of those games, and the D.A. or the CIA or somebody like that got a little curious. Nothing serious. They just checked all my bank deposits. I don't blame them, I guess."

"Not too long after the Denver game, Ray Abruzzese, my roommate, and I began to get the feeling that we were being tailed and that our phone in our apartment was being tapped. Ray, who used to play for the Jets, thought maybe the phone was being tapped by an irate husband, but I told him it probably wasn't that serious, probably just the CIA We were both pretty amused, but we stopped cracking funny jokes on the phone about point spreads."

As for his after-hours activities in the '60s, Namath wasn't just a participant in the Manhattan nightlife scene, frequenting hot spots like Toots Shor's and Dudes 'N Dolls—he owned part of it. After the Super Bowl victory, Namath—along with friends Abruzzese, Bobby Van, and Joe Dellapina—opened the nightclub Bachelors III, on Lexington Avenue and 62nd Street. Namath, Abruzzese, and Van were the three bachelors. (Dellapina was married.) And again, it was his supposed association with objectionable Tony Soprano–types that got him into hot water.

What started out as a comfortable and safe place for a celebrity to relax, have a drink or two, and meet a girl or three became a hangout for unsavory sorts. Rumors were swirling that known gamblers were using the phones for bookmaking. And Commissioner Pete Rozelle did not care to have one of his players mingling with gambling types or shady figures. While the league didn't come right out and accuse Namath of fixing games or of having any involvement in a football gambling ring, Rozelle insisted that Namath sell his share of the nightclub. The Jets quarterback refused. He was a free thinker and a rebel, and he wasn't about to say, "Yes, sir," and comply like a weak-kneed conformist. He was Broadway Joe, and Broadway Joe can do anything he wants, baby.

"In March of 1969, when I was first shown the list of names of so-called undesirables with whom I was supposed to be associating, I took one look at the list and said, 'Hell, just give me the antipasto and the scampi and a bottle of Bardolino.' I mean, I thought it was a menu. I didn't recognize a single name on the list. Later on, when I saw some pictures and heard some first names and some nicknames, then I knew I had at least met most of the people. Sure, they'd been in Bachelors III, and they'd said hello to me, and I'd said hello right back to them."

The district attorney's office was snooping around Bachelors III, as was the NFL's office. And there were unsubstantiated rumors flying around that illegal craps games were being held in Namath's apartment by the same types of "undesirables." Namath professed his innocence to any wrongdoing and held his ground. Rozelle's request became an order, and in June, rather than divest himself of his investment, Joe Willie Namath held a press conference and retired from football. He stuck to his principles and even shed a tear or two while the likes of Frank Gifford, Kyle Rote, and Howard Cosell looked on in amazement at what they were hearing.

The commissioner's office shed a tear or two, too, as Namath was the biggest star in the league and the top TV attraction on Sunday afternoons. The standoff lasted until July. A compromise was reached—football needed Namath and Namath needed football, after all—when Namath agreed to sell his share of Bachelors III in New York, but he would retain his interest in the Ft. Lauderdale and Boston branches of the club. Did he really want to quit football? Of course not.

He reported to Jets training camp. Since he wasn't just your run-of-the-mill football player getting ready for the season—he was Joe Namath, for crying out loud—he began work on his very own TV talk show, *The Joe Namath Show*. His co-host was Dick Schaap, and the program aired for one season, spanning 13 episodes from October 1969 until December of that year. In New York, it aired on WOR channel 9 on Friday nights, while also being syndicated across the country.

Guests ranged from Tom Seaver, Willie Mays, and Dave DeBusschere to Jimmy Breslin, Woody Allen, and Peggy Fleming. Disparate pairs of guests would also be featured, doubling the fun. Truman Capote appeared with Rocky Graziano, while actor Maximilian Schell (yes, the co-star of *Heidi*) was on with O.J. Simpson. Actress Louisa Moritz jiggled, giggled, and read the mail. Booze flowed before, during, and after the broadcast, making for one big party. It was the low-budget, hipster's version of *The Tonight Show*.

Unrelated to his TV show, there was even a Broadway Joe theme song around in the late-'60s. It was a funky, groovy number sung by the Super Chicks with far-out lyrics:

He's kind of mod and very hip
With lots of heart and lots of lip
A swinging ladies' man who has a ball
But put a football in his hand
And right away you'll understand
Why Broadway Joe's the greatest of them all
He's a hero, he's a pro
He's a mister something else our Broadway Joe
He's a groovy super guy
He can pass a football through a needle's eye
What a feeling, what a sight
When we see that number 12 in green and white
One, two, three, hut, go, go, go
No one else can throw like Broadway Joe

In the late-'60s, Namath couldn't even grow a beard, or shave it off, without it becoming headline news. During the 1968 season,

Broadway Joe grew a Fu Manchu, which became the most famous Fu Manchu in America. Teammate Verlon Biggs suggested the team forego shaving until they had their division clinched. But Namath being Namath, any old facial hair wouldn't do—it had to be mod, groundbreaking, and cool. And when he decided to shave it off, he turned it into a $10,000 profit. "I woke up one morning and I just felt like shaving. So I called up Jimmy Walsh, my lawyer in New York, and said, 'Jimmy, I'm ready to shave. See if you can get a commercial.' And he did."

As the decade was coming to a close, Joe Namath had his own television show, began filming movies, appeared in commercials, made guest appearances on other TV shows, owned a nightclub, had his own string of hamburger joints (Broadway Joe's), and had a song written about him—not to mention winning a Super Bowl and a few MVP awards. He was a multimedia superstar.

His autobiography, written in 1969 at the zenith of his popularity, was chock-full of numerous memorable quotations that summed up the Zen of Being Joe Namath, and what it was like to be young, gifted, charismatic, and one of the most famous figures in America. "Women are the best thing going in the world," he wrote. "I've got nothing against guys. They're great to drink with and play cards with and to laugh with, and I like to have them blocking for me on the football field. But if I have to, I can go a week or two or even three without seeing a guy. I don't want to go a day without seeing a woman." Yes, he loved the ladies: "I love football. I really love football. As far as I'm concerned, it's the second best thing in the world."

His thoughts about having the world on a string: "The thing I like best about my life is that I can do almost whatever I want to do. I don't have to conform to anyone else's standards." And he felt no need to conceal his actions, no matter what endeavor he partook in. "I gamble out in the open. I do everything out in the open. I've got a lot of faults, just like almost everyone I've met, but I'm not a hypocrite. I don't hide things. I hate hypocrisy more than anything else in the world." And, of course, he penned a personal credo: "I like my women blond and my Johnnie Walker Red."

Unlike 1960s Joe Namath, though, 1970s Joe Namath lost his edge. But he became a full-fledged pop-culture icon. Elvis lost his danger when he joined the Army and began churning out goofy, harmless movies. And a similar thing happened to Namath as he went from a gambling, drinking, free-thinking, long-haired threat to the establishment to becoming the mainstream. Namath played his last postseason football game in 1969, and in the following decade, he would be famous for being famous. The 1970s Joe Namath was a brand. But when you're Broadway Joe, that's really not such a bad thing.

The first movie that Namath filmed was *Norwood* in the summer of 1969, but the first one to be released was *C.C. and Company* in 1970. The film co-starred Ann-Margret and William Smith. Rhythm and blues singer Wayne Cochran, who was known for his giant white pompadour, outlandish costumes, and legendary live shows with his band, the C.C. Riders, also made an appearance. The genesis for the movie came about in the course of one conversation, according to Cochran's website:

"Ann-Margret and her husband, Roger Smith, Monica, and myself were sitting in our hotel suite at the Newport Hotel on Miami Beach one afternoon. They had also become good friends of ours. Ann would come to see me in Las Vegas. She loved the show, and I would go see hers. They were in television and of course movies. Roger said, 'Why don't we write a movie about a motorcycle gang and call it the C.C. Riders?' Of course, the Riders and I were going to play parts in it. He immediately went and wrote it. They got Joe Namath to star as C.C. Rider [sic]. That was the name of the main character. We did a guest shot in the movie performing in a dance scene with Ann and Joe."

Ann-Margret's manager, Allan Carr, produced the film, and while trying to decide who to cast in the lead, Carr thought of the biggest star in the country at the time: Joe Namath. The movie was standard motorcycle fare with Namath, a mechanic, joining a gang called the Heads. Ann-Margret plays fashion journalist Ann McCalley whose car breaks down and is subsequently terrorized by the menacing gang. But Namath's character is a motorcycle gang member with a heart of gold and comes to her rescue. There's fighting, motocross action, cool-looking choppers (Namath's has a zebra-skin seat), petty thievery, kidnapping, nudity, love scenes, Namath and Ann-Margret shaking and shimmying to Cochran belting out an electrifying version of Otis Redding's "I Can't Turn You Loose," and an ending with Namath and his co-star riding off into the sunset.

McCalley: "Where are we going?"

Ryder: "I've got to get Charlie back his money, then drop you off."

McCalley: "And then what?"

Ryder: "And then I gotta split for a while."

McCalley: "Where?"

Ryder: [Shrugs]

McCalley: "Remember we talked about looking for something?"

Ryder: "Yeah."

McCalley: "Well, I'd like to look with you. For a while, anyway."

And Namath charms his way through the whole thing. The film didn't win an Oscar, but Broadway Joe was officially an actor. In *The New Yorker*, Pauline Kael wrote, "Namath has a light, high voice, and he's generally mild and camera-shy—and he's rather sweet, in the manner of sub-teen favorites." But *Variety* called him "clumsy."

His next movie, *Norwood*, was released soon after *C.C. and Company*, also in 1970. Glen Campbell was the star, while Namath had a smaller supporting role. The two play cousins recently back from the Vietnam War. Campbell's character heads out on a road trip, and along the way he collects an odd assortment of traveling companions, including a chicken. They stop to visit Namath, and the highlight of the picture is Broadway Joe tossing around a football with a midget, portrayed by actor Billy Curtis, who appeared in *High Plains Drifter* and *The Wizard of Oz*. Namath was nominated for a Golden Globe in the Most Promising Newcomer category. He filmed one more movie while he was still playing in the NFL, 1971's spaghetti Western *The Last Rebel*.

Namath said of his acting career, "Going from an area where you are considered best to one in which you know yourself that you're not good, well, it's tough. Dealing with all the great artists I dealt with, dealing with the harsh criticism—sometimes that criticism just made you cringe. I've never known anyone who didn't cringe under it. All I can say is I worked as hard at the profession as I could. Not many people knew that I was taking acting lessons while I was still playing. I secretly enrolled in an acting course at Hofstra."

Not only was 1970 the beginning of Namath's career on the silver screen, but that year he also made a debut of another kind—as an action figure. The Mego Corporation unveiled "Broadway Joe Namath," a 12" action figure somewhat resembling G.I. Joe. Little Joe came wearing a Jets uniform and also featured a tiny football, helmet, stickers, booklet, and a spring-action arm. The packaging boasted its attributes: "Throws a toy football," "Fully jointed arms and legs," and "Turn-about-body." Did the FBI now have to add "spring-action arm" to its dossier?

Since this was a Joe Namath toy and not Daryle Lamonica or Fran Tarkenton, sold separately were 12 "Mod-About-Town Outfits." They consisted of assorted vests, fur coats, leisure suits, bell bottoms—any groovy, cutting-edge clothing ensemble

Joe Namath and Mike Lookinland, who played Bobby Brady, appear together on the set of The Brady Bunch *in 1973. In the episode "Mail Order Hero," Namath visits the Brady home after receiving a letter from Cindy Brady indicating that Bobby Brady was "very, very sick."* (AP Images)

that shouted, "It's 1970, man. Can you dig it?" Each outfit came with a name. There was "Backfield in Motion," "Maximum Effort," "Different Drummer," and "Red Dog," among others. Boys all over America were getting a crash course in A Swinger's Life 101.

With action-figure status reached, Namath became a full-blown mainstream pop-culture idol. He was up on the pedestal with the likes of Evel Knievel and others of that ilk who had lunch boxes, toys, TV shows, and every other marketing gimmick one could imagine. Namath appealed to men, women, boys, and girls. Would a toy company make an action figure of a derelict? A hippie? Or an unsavory figure? Namath was still cool, of course, but he was "safe cool" now. And what was safer than the popular TV show *The Brady Bunch*?

Namath made guest appearances on a variety of shows, including *The Sonny & Cher Comedy Hour, The Flip Wilson Show, Here's Lucy, Dean Martin's Celebrity Roast, Fantasy Island, The Love Boat, The A-Team,* and *The Simpsons,* just to name a few. But his starring turn on *The Brady Bunch* became the stuff of legend. The episode aired on September 21, 1973, during the program's final season.

The show opens with youngest son Bobby having a dream that he's on the Jets with Namath. The field is the Bradys' perfectly manicured, Astroturf-like backyard with yardage lines painted on. The opponent is seven kids dressed as the San Diego Chargers. Namath throws a bomb to Bobby to win the big game. The next afternoon, Bobby's friends brag about their celebrity acquaintances—"My Dad's cousin was on the same plane with Hank Aaron," "I know somebody who knows Lee Trevino's caddie," "My Dad rode on an elevator with Wilt Chamberlain." Bobby boasts that Joe Namath comes to his house for dinner whenever he's in the area for a game. His friends believe him, and as coincidence would have it, the Jets will be in town that week for an exhibition game.

The rumor that Namath will be at the Brady household spreads like wildfire. Bobby makes a phone call to "the stadium" and leaves a message for Namath in a desperate attempt to reach the Jets quarterback. Meanwhile, Bobby's sister Marcia reads in a magazine that actor Mike Connors traveled far and wide to visit a sickly child whose biggest wish was to meet the star of *Mannix*. That story gives Cindy Brady the idea to pen a letter to Namath claiming Bobby is "very, very sick" and would like nothing better than to meet his hero. Broadway Joe, of course, shows up at the Brady house to visit Bobby, who feigns being bedridden with Cindy at his side. Antics and misunderstandings ensue. Because the two children were raised to do the right thing, they come clean at the end, but their father warns, "You two are going to be penalized for illegal procedure." With the sticky situation resolved, Joe throws passes to Bobby in their backyard in front of all his friends, making the boy a hero in the eyes of his pals. All's well that ends well thanks to the kindness of Joe Namath.

On the set of the show, Namath was no prima donna nor did he big-league the cast and crew. According to the website TheGregBradyProject.com, actor Barry Williams noted:

"Joe Namath is one guest star who is particularly memorable and, one could say, even inspirational. Already a legendary football player by the time our fifth season of the *Bunch* got underway, I was able to spend a couple of days on the set with him. Unfortunately for me the episode called "Mail Order Hero" focused on little Brady brother Bobby. I didn't let that get in the way of playing receiver of his passes in patterns of down and outs and going long in between takes. Joe was, simply put, a gracious guy. He didn't avoid everyone by staying in his dressing room until he was called, he didn't sit in the corner waiting to get it over with. He was social, friendly, and oh yeah...pretty good with a football. I ate it up. I probably could have run more plays with him if Florence Henderson didn't keep jumping into his arms."

Namath said of his appearance, "The show was just a fun thing to do. Bobby Brady had a problem in the episode. I was there to help." There's no record that the producers of the show had to lure him to the program by pretending that actor Mike Lookinland was sick and his dying wish was to meet Joe Namath, though.

It was TV appearances like this that cemented his place in 1970s pop culture history. But another aspect of Namath's appeal was his emergence as a full-blown sex symbol, which was captured in his string of now-legendary commercials.

He donned a pair of pantyhose in one ad, and as the camera slowly pans from a couple of feet to a pair of legs, the female narrator says, "This commercial will prove to the women of America that Beautymist pantyhose can make any legs look like a million dollars." As the camera gets to the upper torso, we find that the model is Broadway Joe, clad in pantyhose, a pair of shiny short-shorts, and his Jets jersey. "Now I don't wear pantyhose, but if Beautymist can make *my* legs look good, imagine what

John Riggins

While Namath was in and out of the lineup with injuries during the first half of the 1970s, John Riggins was the best player on the Jets. Unfortunately, he was the one who got away. Another New York team let a Hall of Famer slip right through their fingers a few years earlier, when the Mets jettisoned Nolan Ryan out of town, and the Jets did the same with Riggins.

The Jets selected the rugged fullback with the sixth overall pick in the 1971 draft. The Kansas native paid immediate dividends, leading the team in rushing and receiving in his rookie season. On October 15, 1972, Riggins rushed for 168 yards against New England, while his backfield mate Emerson Boozer ran for 150. It was the only time in franchise history that two runners gained 150 yards in the same game, and the total of 333 rushing yards that afternoon is still a team record. Though he missed the final two games of the season that year due to a knee injury, Riggins rambled for 944 yards, which was a mere four yards short of Matt Snell's team record. Weeb Ewbank was not overly impressed, though. "When it came time to sign the contract, he had the audacity to tell me, 'Well, you didn't get your 1,000 yards,'" Riggins said. "That really destroyed my attitude. I grew up then and realized that professional football is a business."

Riggins held out at the start of the 1973 season, and that was really the beginning of the end of his tenure with the Jets. When he eventually returned to the team, he did so as a rebel with a cause. He roared up to the team's they'll do for yours," he says. At the end, a girl nuzzles him on the cheek, and Namath gives us that "It's-great-to-be-Joe-Namath" look.

He also paired up with a then-unknown Farrah Fawcett for a Noxzema commercial. Joe looks at the camera and laughingly says, "I'm so excited. I'm going to get creamed!" The young actress then spreads shaving cream on his face, as a bouncy Noxzema jingle plays. Again, the ad ends with a kiss and Namath giving the television audience that old girls-just-can't-keep-their-hands-off-me wink and a smile. He also starred in commercials for Ovaltine,

practice facility on his motorcycle, sporting a leather jacket and what could have been the NFL's first-ever Mohawk. Like his pal Namath, Riggins was a free spirit and an outlaw. In 1975, Riggins made the Pro Bowl and became the first Jet to rush for more than 1,000 yards in a season when he gained 62 yards against Dallas on the last day of the year.

After having previously taken a 10 percent pay cut in order to play out his option, Riggins became a free agent. And just like that, he was gone, off to the Washington Redskins in 1976. He went on to win a Super Bowl MVP and was enshrined in the Pro Football Hall of Fame. And the Jets let him walk away without receiving anything in return. In his five seasons with the Jets, Riggins did it all—he could run, catch, and block. He finished his career in green and white with 3,880 rushing yards and 129 receptions.

John Riggins was a tough, beer-drinking, wiseacre of a nonconformist. Besides his Mohawk, he also sported one mean Afro, giving him the best hair in franchise history, while also being labeled with one of the best nicknames: The Diesel. Like Namath, he also carved out an acting career, snagging a role in two of the most sought-after gigs of the last few centuries: a Shakespeare play and Law & Order. And he famously advised Supreme Court Justice Sandra Day O'Connor to "loosen up, Sandy baby" at a banquet before he himself fell asleep on the floor under a table. Would Riggins have made a difference on the early-1980s Jets? What affect would he have had on the Mud Bowl? Unfortunately, we'll never know.

Norelco, Brut, and the Hamilton Beach Butter-Up Popcorn Popper. Joe Namath could sell anything.

Meanwhile, on the football field, despite his upper-echelon salary, fame, and popularity, Namath was just one of the guys. Sure, there were occasionally bouts of awe by his teammates, as Jets defensive back John Dockery noted, "The aura and the frenzy that accompany him still make me marvel." And in 1977, when Namath joined the Rams, receiver Billy Waddy was beside himself. "This is like a dream to me. Here I met Joe Namath the other day. Joe Namath! Man, I've been watching that guy on television since I've been in elementary school. And now he's throwing passes to me, Billy Waddy from Boling, Texas."

But deep down, Namath was just a football player who loved his teammates. During Jets training camp, he had Maryland crabs shipped in for the team for their Wednesday night happy hours. "Crabs and beer; we had our own crab fest," said center John Schmitt. Joe Willie's nightlife and extracurricular activities didn't bother his teammates or coaches in the least, and his dedication to the sport and football intelligence were never questioned. Don Maynard said, "Always, whenever you read about Joe's football ability, you have to multiply it to get a true picture. And what you read about his nightlife you have to divide."

Weeb Ewbank once stated about his star quarterback, "I never had any trouble with Joe. I don't care anything about his social life, but he has always been a dedicated football player, willing to do anything to help the club. He'll take a movie projector home and study game movies for two, three hours a night, I guess. He plays with pain and never moans about it. And he hasn't changed."

Even Jets players who never got the chance to be his teammate think the world of the superstar. Wesley Walker said, "He's one of the best people I've ever been associated with. I wish I had the opportunity to actually play with him. Jerome Barkum and

Richard Caster used to talk very highly of him, and after you meet him you understand why. He was very modest, just a nice, down-to-earth guy. And ever since I've met him, anytime I'm ever with him, he goes out of his way to say hello. He's just a pleasure to be around."

Of course, though he blended right in with the other Jets, he was still Joe Namath. While in training camp, he was wary about giving out his phone number, so he gave out John Schmitt's instead, with the result being the Jets center sleeping with his head under his pillow while Broadway Joe chatted through the night with his girlfriend in his teammate's room.

In 1975, the World Football League attempted to lure Namath to the new league, which was about to enter its second season. They offered him $400,000 to play for their Chicago franchise. The league didn't crave him because he was still a great quarterback; instead they wanted him because he was a top attraction and an icon. Namath ended up re-signing with the Jets for $900,000 over two seasons. He finally did leave New York when that contract expired, though. The Jets wanted to part ways with him, but a trade couldn't be worked out, so he was put on waivers.

Broadway Joe hooked up with the Rams for one last shot at glory. If not New York, what better place for him than Los Angeles? An unnamed NFL executive said of the move before it became official, "He wants to get into acting, and he knows a lot more doors will open for him if he's still playing. It gives him an identity, a base. Imagine if he's playing for the Rams next season, and on the Friday night before a big game he shows up at the Polo Lounge with some starlet. There'll be 18,000 reporters after him for a story. Pictures everywhere of him and the broad. A young actor can't buy that sort of publicity. But if Namath's not playing football, who would care? There wouldn't be any news there. Everybody already knows Namath likes broads and booze."

Namath only played four games for the Rams and called it a career. He then took a stab at the ultimate American pop culture art form—the sitcom. In the fall of 1978, he starred in *The Waverly Wonders*. It was a low-rent *White Shadow* played for laughs. Namath's character, Joe Casey, was a retired professional basketball player turned high school history teacher/basketball coach. Instead of Carver High's Salami, Coolidge, and Thorpe, Waverly High School featured Tony Faguzzi, Hasty Parks, and the team's best player, Connie Rafkin. A running gag on the program involved a fellow faculty member who couldn't keep her hands off of Casey. He *was* Joe Namath, after all. NBC aired the sitcom on Friday nights at 8:00 PM. Nine episodes were filmed but only three made it over the airwaves before it was given the ax, ending Joe Namath's time in the 1970s limelight.

In the following decades, Namath went on to act in plays, along with doing more film and television. He became a football broadcaster with a brief stint on *Monday Night Football.* He got married, quit drinking, became a father, played the role of team ambassador for the Jets, got divorced, began drinking again, embarrassed himself on national TV when he confessed that he wanted to kiss Suzy Kolber, and gave up drinking once again thanks to that shameful display of inebriation. He became a grandfather. And he came out of it all alive and healthy. He has endured.

Joe Namath straddled the line between booze, broads, and gambling on one side and toys, sitcoms, and kids on the other. He was escorting Raquel Welch to the Academy Awards one night and appearing on *The Brady Bunch* the next. He went from outlaw to icon to legend. And whether it was in the 1960s, 1970s, or beyond, he proved one thing—it's good to be Joe Namath.

CHAPTER 7

THE NEW YORK
SACK EXCHANGE

ONE BY ONE THEY CAME. The first to arrive in New York was Abdul Salaam in 1976. Joe Klecko was next in 1977. Two years later, Marty Lyons and Mark Gastineau joined the Jets. As a group, they would terrorize the NFL landscape. And as a foursome, they would go down in franchise history as the greatest defensive line the team has ever known. They were famous, infamous, notorious, barbaric—and very, very talented.

Though the quartet would switch positions as the years went on, their beginning configuration had the wild, mercurial Gastineau at left end, the quiet steady Salaam setting up at left tackle, the tough blue-collar Lyons at right tackle, and the strong best-of-the-bunch Klecko at right end. The first season that all four were full-time starters was 1980, but it wasn't until 1981 that they received their nickname. A handful of colorfully named lines and defenses preceded them, including the Fearsome Foursome, the Purple People Eaters, the Steel Curtain, and Orange Crush. This gang of Jets ruffians joined their defensive ancestors when a fan held up a bed sheet at a game at Shea Stadium in 1981 that read, "The New York Sack Exchange."

The New York Sack Exchange—from left Joe Klecko, Marty Lyons, Abdul Salaam, and Mark Gastineau—poses on the floor of the New York Stock Exchange in June 1982.
(Ronald C. Modra/Sports Imagery/Getty Images)

The team at first wanted to market Klecko and Gastineau alone with that moniker, but Klecko refused to participate unless all four were involved. Lyons said, "Joe told them, 'It's not just Mark and me, it's the four of us.' Joe told them, 'If you're going to market the four of us, okay, but if you're only going to market two of us, no.'" They were the four horsemen, in it together, for better or worse, in sickness and in health, through jealousy and discord.

By the late 1970s and early '80s, the sack was just beginning its era of romance. Klecko once said, a sack isn't "exactly like a touchdown, but it's a big play, both materially and emotionally." The term "sack" is thought to have been born in the 1960s with the Los Angeles Rams' vaunted defensive line of Deacon Jones, Merlin Olsen, Rosey Grier, and Lamar Lundy.

Sacks did not become an official statistic until 1982, partly due to the popularity of the Sack Exchange. At one time, sacks were registered as Opponents Tackled Attempting Passes. "OTAP" just doesn't have the same ring and zing as "sack." Preceding that humdrum recognition, they weren't acknowledged at all—bringing down the quarterback was considered just a routine tackle, the same as wrapping up a running back after a 2-yard gain. The unofficial sack record is thought to be held by Coy Bacon of the Cincinnati Bengals, when he buried 26 quarterbacks in 1976, but no one can say for sure who really has the pre-1982 mark.

One thing that is known, though, is that the Sack Exchange transformed the New York Jets. The team went from 16 team sacks in 1976 to a league-high 66 five years later. And they improved from a 4–12 record in 1980 to an 11–5–1 mark the next year. The 1981 season was the first time since 1969 that the team qualified for the postseason, and the four defensive monsters were a paramount reason for the club's success. The gang of linemen rose to prominence and peaked in that same 1981 season. In November, they rang the bell at the New York Stock Exchange, cementing their place in nickname history. They had four unique personalities and came from diverse backgrounds, and they often squabbled amongst themselves. But together on the field, they were fast, strong, menacing, and crazed. Together, they formed a frightening alliance—frightening for quarterbacks, that is.

Abdul Salaam was the George Harrison of the contingent. He was the quiet, spiritual Beatle of the Sack Exchange. If Harrison had ever been a defensive tackle, he would have been Abdul Salaam. Salaam's given name was Larry Faulk, but in 1977, to underscore his personal philosophy of tranquility, he changed it to Abdul Salaam, which means "Soldier of Peace." On the field he was anything but peaceful, of course, but off the field, he was an introspective, serene man of few words.

Born in New Brockton, Alabama, he went on to become an athletic legend in Ohio. Salaam was a three-sport high school star in Cincinnati. And for a man of peace, he didn't have a problem throwing other people around or throwing punches, as he wrestled and was also a Golden Gloves boxer. He went to nearby Kent State and played on their "Carat Gold" defense. Taken in the seventh round of the 1976 draft by the Jets, he made his way into every game in his rookie season and started four times. The following year, he moved into a permanent starting role, and over the next six seasons he only missed five games.

Aside from a personal philosophy, he also had a defensive philosophy: "I look at it this way. The offensive linemen are trying to make a cup, we're trying to empty it. We force the quarterback out of the pocket so the guys on the end can catch him." With Klecko and Gastineau racking up the sacks, it was up to Lyons and Salaam to stuff the run, and one of Salaam's greatest examples of his playmaking ability came in a crucial showdown with the Miami Dolphins in Week 12 of the 1981 season.

With Miami leading 12–9 and on the doorstep of the Jets' end zone, Salaam made a huge tackle, forcing the Dolphins to settle for a field goal. Richard Todd drove the Jets offense downfield and hit Jerome Barkum with an 11-yard touchdown pass with 16 seconds left to win the game 16–15, which was the key victory of the season that led to a playoff berth. The Jets' defense was the team's bread and butter, and Salaam was literally right in the middle of it all.

The team was continually shifting players around and maneuvering their positioning. "The big difference for me was when the coaches took me out of the guard-center gap and put me head-up on the guard. I'd been in a read-and-react situation before, but now I could work on beating my man and putting pressure on the passer. Instead of survival, my game was now domination."

Injuries limited Salaam to just one game in 1983, his eighth and final season with the Jets. He was traded to San Diego but never played a down for the Chargers, choosing to retire instead. Salaam was not the wildest or most talented of the Sack Exchange, nor did he pile up the accolades the way his teammates did, but he was a solid rock of granite. He was the stable, consistent, level-headed member of the gang of four. Every group needs a quiet contributor to be the poised voice of reason. Wesley Walker said of his teammate, "Abdul Salaam was the quietest guy, and then he would say something that you would be surprised at."

Coach Joe Walton summed up his giant tackle in the 1983 Jets Yearbook: "Abdul fills the role on our defensive line as the steadying influence. He makes few mistakes, plays the defense called, and also seems to make the key tackle."

In the sixth round of the 1977 draft, the Jets made one of the best decisions in franchise history when they selected Joe Klecko. The Chester, Pennsylvania, native was born into a football family, as his father was a gridiron veteran. But the younger Klecko didn't take to the sport immediately. In fact, the baby-faced kid was often pushed around. "Man, I was a terrible sissy, always, always getting beat up."

The future Jets great didn't begin his football odyssey until his senior year in high school. Instead of pursuing football glory, his interests ran more toward cars and trucks. He had a job pumping gas and spent his leisure time converting a '55 Chevy into a dragster. His days of taking a beating were over, though, as he grew into a jumbo-sized teenager to go along with that baby face, and he added construction and truck driving to his professional résumé before graduating from high school.

Klecko eschewed college life and the quest of a football career when his high school days were over and continued as a truck driver. "Listen, I couldn't go through another year of *Jane Eyre*." Instead of quietly sitting in a nice, warm classroom studying the classics, he hauled the big rigs around the U.S. "I once fought my way across the country carrying a propeller for a supertanker. The thing weighed 130,000 pounds and was 22 feet across, wide as most highways." Let's see Charlotte Brontë try that.

But Klecko didn't give up on football altogether. He hooked up with a local semipro team called the Aston Knights. In order to keep his eligibility, as he hadn't ruled out college completely, he played under the pseudonym of Jim Jones from Poland University. "You know, good old Krakow A&M," he said. The Kleckos were pure-bread Polish, after all.

It wasn't the NFL, but the league was tough, and many of the players might as well have walked right off the roster of the Oakland Raiders. "If a guy missed a block, he'd roll over and snap at a passing leg, trying to rip out a calf muscle. Listen, we were playing the Hagerstown Bears, and I had been beating my man on the pass rush every time. Finally he hauled off and kicked me in the groin. It almost killed me. I crawled back to my team, all doubled over, and you think I got sympathy? 'Get him, you dummy,' they said. So on the next play, I steamrolled him over backward and then drop-kicked him in the ribs. That settled that."

The league fostered a players-have-to-do-what-players-have-to-do atmosphere, which involved a pregame training regimen of drinking blackberry brandy. Nine-fingered quarterbacks were also not uncommon. "We'd go on a trip, the bus would be loaded with [the brandy]. We'd get to a town where we were going to play, and first thing, five guys would be dispatched to buy a case. Those guys couldn't suit up without it. The brandy made them fierce and kept their guts warm on cold days. The one-thumbed quarterback sometimes played so drunk he'd lean against the center to keep from falling down. He'd bark out, 'Hut, hut, *hut!*' and everybody's eyes would water and guys would almost faint. The fumes hung over us like a mushroom cloud."

Klecko's time with the Knights led directly to his college career. Aston's equipment manager took the same job with Temple University, and he informed the school's football coach about the talented defensive lineman. Klecko was recruited and subsequently enrolled at the university, where he was back to cracking open books along with cracking open heads. He led the Owls in tackles three consecutive seasons, and he twice made the All-East Team. And like his future teammate, Klecko boxed, reportedly winning 34 out of 35 matches. No one was calling him a sissy at this point in his life.

When Klecko joined the Jets, he soon earned the nickname Killer by his teammates. And he could eat like a pro, too. On his first day of training camp, he sat down and consumed 12 pork chops. Joe Klecko was ready for the NFL. And he had the right attitude, as well. "Hate quarterbacks. Well, no. I mean, I don't hate them as people. They're probably nice guys who brush their teeth and call Mom once a week. I hate what quarterbacks *stand* for. They stand between me and success."

The Jets finished with a lowly 3-11 record, but the rookie got on the field in 13 games and started six of them, mainly playing on the inside at left defensive tackle. The following season, the team improved to 8–8, Klecko became a full-time starter at right end, and the pieces to their early-1980s playoff teams started adding up, with Richard Todd, Bruce Harper, Mickey Shuler, Wesley Walker, Marvin Powell, and Greg Buttle all on the team to go along with Klecko and Salaam. Klecko didn't see himself as a traditional defensive end, though. "You take 10 guys and put 'em in a room, and I'd be the last one you'd put outside on the end. Big offensive tackles used to see me line up and they'd laugh. 'What's that short, squatty guy doing out there?'"

Lyons and Gastineau became Jets in Klecko's third season, and Klecko was starting to make a name for himself as his talent and intensity were being noticed around the league. Packers coach Bart Starr said of the defensive star that there was "something within him that flames very hot." And Vikings defensive tackle Doug Martin stated, "He does some things you just can't copy, like grabbing his opponent by the shoulders and just walking him back to the quarterback. He's an exception."

The 1981 season was when Klecko and his linemates put it all together. The Sack Exchange was instrumental in the Jets qualifying for the playoffs, and Klecko unofficially led the NFL in sacks with 20.5. But the team was beaten in the first round of the playoffs by Buffalo. The Bills stormed out to a 24–0 lead, the Jets fought and clawed their way to come within four points, but they eventually fell by a 31–27 score. Klecko made his first Pro Bowl and was a First-Team All-Pro. That was the second and ultimately last season that the Sack Exchange would be together for a full schedule, though.

The next season, the Jets fell one step short of a Super Bowl appearance. The team featured a high-flying offense to go with their bruising, sack-happy defense, but injuries put a damper on their aspirations. Klecko ruptured the patella tendon in his right knee in the second game of the season, and he wasn't able to return until the second round of the playoffs. The Jets easily handled Cincinnati 44–17, and with Klecko back but not at full speed, they narrowly defeated the Los Angeles Raiders 17–14. But the Jets were doomed in the Mud Bowl, when they were beaten by the Dolphins 14–0.

Klecko was back to playing a full season in 1983, but now he was a left defensive tackle, taking over for the injured Salaam. He made his second Pro Bowl, at his second position, and was viewed as one of the top defensive players in the NFL. He repeated his performance the next season, again earning Pro Bowl honors as a defensive tackle. His first coach, Walt Michaels, said of his star player, "You can sense the success in him. I look at Klecko and the words 'pass rusher' jump into my mind. It's his incredible quickness and the strength of his hands. If he gets a quarterback in his grasp, he's down."

The Jets returned to the playoffs in 1985, this time losing to the Patriots in the first round. And Klecko was on the move again as he became a nose tackle in the team's three-four defense. All he did was become the first player in NFL history to make the Pro Bowl at three different positions, and he threw in a First-Team All-Pro selection, as well. His teammates couldn't help but notice Klecko's work ethic and the high bar that he set for himself. Lyons commented, "Joe had a certain standard he played by and lived by—to be the best, the strongest, the best prepared." There were no shortcuts for Joe Klecko.

The former truck driver played two more seasons with the Jets with the team losing in heartbreaking fashion to the Browns in Klecko's last career playoff game in January 1987. He finished out his time in the NFL playing one season with the Indianapolis

Colts in 1988. In 2004, Klecko was the third Jet to have his number retired when his No. 73 joined Joe Namath's No. 12 and Don Maynard's No. 13, never to be worn again. He made four Pro Bowls, two First-Team All-Pro squads, was inducted into the Jets' Ring of Honor in 2010, and was enshrined in the National Polish Hall of Fame. He also dabbled in acting, as he had bit parts in four Burt Reynolds movies—*Smokey and the Bandit, Smokey and the Bandit II, The Cannonball Run,* and *Heat.*

But his next stop should be the Pro Football Hall of Fame. Klecko's credentials speak for themselves, but the fact that sacks were not made official until well into Klecko's career may have hurt his chances, as he only had 24 official sacks. But two offensive linemen he battled with for years, Hall of Famers both, are of the opinion that Klecko deserves enshrinement in Canton.

Longtime Bengal Anthony Muñoz once said, "In my 13 seasons, Joe is right there at the top of the defensive ends I had to block, up there with Fred Dean, Lee Roy Selmon, and Bruce Smith. Joe was the strongest guy I ever faced. He had perfect technique—hands in tight, great leverage. My second year, 1981, we went to Shea and beat the Jets 31–30 but he was such an intense, smart player, I knew I was in a battle. He was the leader, the guy who kept that unit together."

And Joe DeLamielleure, who played for Buffalo and Cleveland, has no doubts about Klecko's Hall of Fame merits. "You can't think of his 10-year period without him. I had to block Joe Greene and Merlin Olsen when I was playing and, believe me, Joe Klecko was equal to those two guys. If Joe Klecko had played one position for 10 years, he'd have been considered one of the top two or three players at that position, whichever one it was. There's not another player who went to the Pro Bowl at three different positions. You take a defensive end and put him at nose tackle and he's just as good there, that's a great player. We need to get Joe Klecko in the Hall of Fame."

But maybe the greatest compliment given to Klecko came from Jets teammate John Roman. "You want talent? Not long after I met Joe, he opened 12 bottles of beer with his teeth. Now *that's* All-Pro."

When Marty Lyons arrived on the New York Jets scene, he had already made a name for himself in the previous winter's Sugar Bowl. While playing for the University of Alabama, his defense made one of the most famous goal-line stands in collegiate history. Penn State had a first down at the 8-yard line. After gaining 7-plus yards on the first three downs, they were 1 foot away from a fourth-quarter, game-tying touchdown. When quarterback Chuck Fusina inquired how far the ball was from the goal line, Lyons shouted out a warning: "You better pass." Penn State ran, couldn't gain an inch on the play, and Alabama won the game 14–7, and with it, the national championship.

Lyons was born in Takoma Park, Maryland, but grew up in Pinellas Park, Florida, where, like Salaam, he was a three-sport star at St. Petersburg Catholic High School. He chose a future in football at Alabama, and he made the correct decision, of course, as he went on to be an All-American playing for Bear Bryant. Lyons said of the famous stop in the Sugar Bowl, "Football is a team game. Penn State would have scored if every guy on our defense didn't do his job."

Taken in the first round by the Jets with the 14th overall pick in the 1979 draft, Lyons earned a starting job right from the first game of his rookie season. Like Klecko, Lyons would play tackle and defensive end in his career, but it was his second season when the Sack Exchange settled into their familiar positions with Lyons anchoring the inside at right tackle.

Teaming up with Salaam, Lyons and his fellow tackle did the dirty work, holding the opposition's running backs in check and keeping the offensive line occupied while the two defensive ends received the glory and glamour of sacking the quarterback. That was fine with Lyons, though, as he was a blue-collar and team-first guy.

Off the field, Lyons was just as unselfish. In March of 1982, his father died, and only two days later, a boy who Lyons had been a Big Brother to passed away from leukemia. The tragedies inspired the Jet to form the Marty Lyons Foundation, which fulfills wishes for terminally ill children.

"When you go from the ultimate high to the ultimate low, you ask yourself why. You are 25 and playing for the New York Jets. What are you doing wrong in life that all this happened? Two months later I knew there was nothing I could do to bring back my dad or Keith. But what I could do was help other people. It was a wake-up call from the man upstairs who told me there was more to life. He told me he gave me the God-given tools and now there were more important things to do."

For his selfless altruism, Lyons won the Walter Payton Man of the Year Award in 1984. Marilyn Green, president of his foundation, said, "If you took the heart out of Marty's chest, it would expand enough to fill the universe." And the acorn didn't fall far from the tree, as Lyons' son also performed an unbelievable heroic act when he was a mere five years old in 1987.

The Jet's wife and son were driving home from a friend's house late one night when their pickup truck hit a pothole. The vehicle swerved off the road, flipped over, rolled down an embankment, and landed upside down. Lyons' wife covered her son, nicknamed Rocky, who was sleeping in the front passenger seat. The boy was safe, but his mother smashed her head against the crumpled driver seat door and was bleeding profusely, unable to see with blood caking her eyes.

Rocky crawled out of the truck and attempted to pull his mother out of the window. While that maneuver was not successful, the boy climbed back in the truck and was able to push his mother out of the vehicle. He then pleaded with her to let him walk up the embankment and go for help, but she felt it was too dangerous for the child to go up to the road alone in the dark. So she crawled up the hill, with Rocky pushing her from behind, and all the while the boy reminded her about The Little Engine That Could for inspiration. Once up to the side of the road, the pair flagged down a car, and the driver took them to the hospital, where Lyons' wife had immediate but successful surgery. Just like his father, little Rocky was a hero. And just like his father, Rocky devoted his life to helping others. Impacted by his mother's accident, the younger Lyons became a doctor in 2009. "That's what started me on this long road so many years ago," he said. "Dr. Holifield saved my mother's life. He wasn't on call that night, but he spent 10–12 hours in the operating room with my mom."

Meanwhile, just a few weeks after the accident, the Miami Dolphins didn't think so highly of Rocky's dad on the field. In a December game at Joe Robbie Stadium, Miami fumbled the ball, then Jets cornerback Bobby Humphrey scooped it up and ran it back 46 yards for a touchdown. On the play, Lyons blocked Dwight Stephenson, who had to be carted off the field. The Dolphins' center tore ligaments in his left knee, which ended the four-time First-Team All-Pro's career. Stephenson's teammates felt Lyons' block was not a clean one. Lyons disagreed with their analysis of the play.

"Their players and coaches were yelling 'cheap shot' at me right there on the field. But if I had wanted to cheap-shot him, I wouldn't have been down on one knee trying to call for their trainer and their doctor. I wouldn't have stayed out there with him for several minutes. And I wouldn't have walked into their locker room to see him afterwards."

Stephenson also didn't see eye to eye with his Miami teammates. "Marty was all shook up," the center remembered. "He's a good guy. I hold no grudge. We played together three years at Alabama. He was a year ahead of me. He told me he didn't even see me on the play. He just reacted. I'm one of the last people he would want to cause any harm. We're pretty close. We get together. I know his wife and little boy. I knew about the automobile accident they were in a few weeks ago, how their little boy helped his mother get out of the car and up an embankment."

Of course, it wasn't all grave and solemn moments when it came to Marty Lyons, as he was in the middle of one of the great comic penalties in football history. In a 1986 game against the Buffalo Bills, Lyons was flagged for a personal foul committed against quarterback Jim Kelly. Though he mistakenly got the uniform number wrong, saying it was No. 99, referee Ben Dreith announced that Lyons was giving him the business down there.

Lyons also wasn't immune to pulling training-camp pranks. He once assembled a stink bomb and placed it under the car of assistant coach Mike Faulkiner. "He got halfway across campus, and his car was filled with smoke. It was funny, but I don't think the two fire trucks liked it too much."

Marty Lyons was the blood-and-guts member of the Sack Exchange. He played 11 seasons in the NFL, all with the Jets, and he recorded 29 official sacks, along with two safeties. While he never made a Pro Bowl, he has been inducted into numerous halls of fame: The State of Alabama Hall of Fame, the Nassau County Sports Hall of Fame, the Suffolk County Sports Hall of Fame, the Maryland Sports Hall of Fame, and the Tampa Bay Sports Club Hall of Fame. He also belongs in the Good Guy Hall of Fame, as Marty Lyons was the ultimate unselfish teammate and is the ultimate unselfish human being.

The fourth member of the New York Sack Exchange was the most controversial. Unlike his three linemates, Mark Gastineau was not a spiritual Zen master. He did not set an example for his teammates to follow, nor was he a selfless humanitarian. He was a volatile, flashy, and often misunderstood showoff who was unpopular around the league as well as in his own locker room. Conflict and headlines followed him wherever he went.

Born in Ardmore, Oklahoma, Gastineau moved to Arizona when he was seven. His father built him a rodeo ring, and by the age of 12, young Mark was competing in rodeo events. He didn't perform a rodeo version of his sack dance, though. "A quarterback and a steer are two completely different animals. I've never danced on a steer." His surroundings were also an impetus for another hobby— he's been a lifelong collector of Indian artifacts.

Gastineau weaved his way through three different colleges— Eastern Arizona Junior College, Arizona State University, and East Central Oklahoma State University—before being selected by the Jets in the second round of the 1979 draft. His speed set him apart from other defensive linemen, as he ran a 4.8 40-yard dash in college, which he whittled down to 4.56 once he became a pro.

Many of his teammates took an instant dislike to the flamboyant defensive end. "I went through a lot of major problems when I was coming into the league, with people not liking me and me not knowing why they didn't like me," he said. "They didn't treat the other rookies that way." The unofficial no-dancing policy the veterans had may have had something to do with their disapproval of the unbridled greenhorn.

"After the first couple of times I did it, about six guys came over with their arms folded and said, 'We don't do that stuff on this team. We're not going to let you dance.' Well, that was a wild situation. I'd never had anybody except a coach tell me I couldn't do something."

Lyons tempered his opinion of Gastineau by 1984. "We all had to learn who Mark Gastineau was and accept him for what he was. That was harder to do at first than it is now." But there was at least one teammate who was on his side, as Wesley Walker said of him, "Loved him! Loved Gastineau!"

In Gastineau's debut season, he played in all 16 games but came off the bench. The following year, he was named the starting left defensive end, completing the Sack Exchange, as the three other members were now entrenched in the starting lineup. It was in his third season where Gastineau flourished, earning a spot on the Pro Bowl roster for the first of five consecutive seasons. His 20 sacks were second in the league, only half a sack behind Klecko.

After sacking six quarterbacks in the shortened 1982 season and helping his team make it all the way to the AFC Championship Game, Gastineau led the NFL with 19 sacks in 1983. Despite being a First-Team All-Pro for the first of three straight seasons, he wasn't voted in as a Pro Bowl starter due to the animosity of his fellow players. "A lot of people don't like me, so they won't vote for me. They're allowed to vote for a third-stringer if they want to, and that is *not right.*"

One of Gastineau's many critics was Raider Howie Long, who said of the Jet in 1985, "To me, there are two ways to play defensive end. You can be flashy like he is—which is the kindest way I can put it—or you can take a blue-collar approach, as I do. You make your play then go back to the huddle. He's three parts show and one part sincerity. He drives his Rolls-Royce and he wears his fur coats when he goes to visit children in the hospital. Does that sound like he cares? Can you imagine me owning a fur coat?"

Besides being looked down upon by Jets players and non-Jets players alike, Gastineau was also looked down upon by the police due to a few brushes with the law in 1983. He got into a little trouble for drug possession, and on September 30, 1983, he and Ken O'Brien were arrested and charged with third-degree assault after getting into a brouhaha at Studio 54. Their trial took place the following summer, and the two couldn't practice with the team as they spent their days in court. Gastineau moved into a hotel near Central Park and ran sprints in the park after dark. "If anyone tries to mug me, I'll sack him," he said at the time. "I told a couple of the doormen at the hotel that next week I'm bringing my pads in and I'll practice some rushes against them. They looked kind of nervous." Gastineau was convicted of misdemeanor assault and sentenced to 90 days of community service, while O'Brien was acquitted of all charges.

Mark Gastineau celebrates after sacking Green Bay Packers quarterback Lynn Dickey in 1982. (Gene Kappock/NY Daily News Archive via Getty Images)

In 1984, Gastineau set the official sack record when he took down 22 quarterbacks. The record stood until 2001 when Michael Strahan broke the mark with a dubious sack of Brett Favre. The Green Bay quarterback was seemingly in cahoots with his friend from the Giants when he all but fell down for Strahan. Technically, it may not even have been a sack as Favre took off on a naked bootleg without making an attempt to throw the ball downfield. To his credit, Gastineau accepted the record-breaker with class and dignity.

After his fifth straight Pro Bowl selection in '85, Gastineau battled injuries for much of the '86 season. He missed the final five games as the team stumbled into the playoffs. But they breezed through Kansas City 35–15, which set up a match with the Cleveland Browns. With just more than 4 minutes left to play and the Jets holding a 20–10 lead, the Browns found themselves in a second-and-24 hole. Bernie Kosar threw an incomplete pass, but Gastineau was flagged with a questionable roughing the passer penalty, which gave Cleveland new life. The Browns ultimately tied the game and won it in overtime. His teammates defended Gastineau and disagreed with the penalty. The referee was the same Ben Dreith of Marty Lyons and Jim Kelly fame. This time it was the ref who gave the Jets "the business."

Gastineau became embroiled in more controversy the next season when he crossed the picket line during the players' strike. He claimed he had no choice because he needed alimony money. Teammate Dave Jennings said, "We expected it from Mark. He's always put himself in front of the team. He's a very selfish individual." But things got out of hand when Gastineau drove into the team's parking lot and some of his fellow players spit at him. He got into a tussle with backup center Guy Bingham and a few other players. Reggie McElroy, the team's assistant player representative, ultimately issued a statement of apology. Gastineau said of the incident, "When someone spits in your face, I don't care how many of them there are, there's no way in the world I'll ever take that." Lyons and Klecko both crossed the picket line a little later.

In 1988, actress Brigitte Nielsen waltzed into the world of the New York Jets. She and Gastineau were dating, and she made a spectacular entrance when she drove up in a limo onto the sidelines of a Jets-Redskins scrimmage at Lafayette College in Pennsylvania and was trailed by a stream of paparazzi. She was also in the middle of the storm a few months later when Gastineau shocked everybody with the announcement that he was retiring seven games into the season, ostensibly to care for Nielsen, who he claimed was suffering from cancer.

Years later Gastineau admitted he quit for another reason. "When I was in the NFL, I was doing steroids. I had been checked okay two times, and the third time was going to be in the papers and, you know, be out. So I didn't want to be embarrassed." After nine-and-a-half seasons, for whatever reason, that was the end.

What was Mark Gastineau most famous for, though? Aside from his mullet and his obsession with his own physique? (His first wife Lisa once said, "We go through razors like most people go through toothpaste.") He was known for his sack dance. It wasn't really so much of a dance as wild, uncoordinated, frantic gyrations of a man who has just poked a hornet's nest. Though he never did it near an offensive lineman or standing over a quarterback, his celebration rubbed most opponents and even some teammates the wrong way. Lyons once said, "Against Green Bay he did it after one of mine. I told him, 'If you're going to dance, do it on your own sacks.'"

In his sophomore season, Gastineau refrained from doing his thing. "That was in 1980, my second year. I'd let other people influence my thinking. I'd seen my teammates fold their arms and walk away from me. I'd been told, 'We don't do that hot-dog stuff on the Jets.' In God's truth, what I'd been doing had been a natural reaction. So for one season I didn't do the dance. It was the most unhappy year of my life. I'd get a sack and I'd say, 'Don't jump, Mark, don't jump.' I'd want to rip my mouthpiece out and start chewing on it. In the offseason I talked to my wife and parents about it. They told me to do what I wanted to do. I talked to our coach, Walt Michaels, and our president, Jim Kensil, and even to the owner, Leon Hess. They all said, 'Go on and do it if it makes you happy.' So last year I danced again."

And again, Walker was on his side. "Didn't bother me at all. I mean I look at these guys who make a regular little tackle and they're dancing around and it's disgusting. But he could back up his play. It wasn't just about the dance. He was physical; he could play. Sometimes you would think he was one dimensional because he was so focused on getting to the quarterback they could run underneath him sometimes. But people didn't even give our defensive backs a little credit, because if you're getting a sack, those guys are covering back there, too. So it's a team game. It's not just one guy. It takes a team. It takes a lot more effort. How did they get there? The Sack Exchange was certainly a force to be reckoned with, and anybody would tell you they would be intimidating. The dance never did bother me. If he was doing something in a derogatory way, maybe. If he's celebrating because he's happy and to do whatever...it got him a lot of exposure, a lot of people were jealous of him, but it didn't bother me one bit. What bothered me is the things that they did to him because I just thought it was like a jealousy."

Not only did Gastineau's dance cause resentment, it was the source of fisticuffs. On September 25, 1983, at Shea Stadium, Los Angeles Rams tackle Jackie Slater took extreme umbrage at Gastineau's antics after a sack of Vince Ferragamo. Slater chased Gastineau around the field, and a full-on fracas ensued. "One lousy tackle and he puts on a big act. Why don't I dance every time I block him out?" Slater exclaimed. A total of 37 players were fined a combined $15,750, with Gastineau losing $1,000.

"There were guys on our bench who might not have liked me much, but they all came out on the field," Gastineau said. "It was a good feeling to see them come out for *me* during the fight." There was some disagreement about which players were on which side, though. A Jet confided to Ram Bill Bain that Gastineau was an "ass," and they were hoping to see Gastineau get his clock cleaned by Slater. Bain said, "I loved it. I almost fell down on the field laughing."

Walker put it all in perspective, though, "Some people get intimidated or they get frustrated because they're really getting beat. You know, nobody wants anybody celebrating, but the bottom line, Slater was getting beat. That's the only thing I could think of. Gastineau was just celebrating on his own, that was the thing. He didn't do anything derogatory—that's my opinion anyway. But people were just jealous of him. But Jackie Slater wants to go off on him, sometimes you get mad, it can be competitive. I watched Lyle Alzado rip Chris Ward's helmet off because he's frustrated, he's getting beat. That's what guys do. They get frustrated."

The next season the NFL put a stop to all the post-sack festivities. The party was over. The league instituted a No Dance rule, which resulted in a 5-yard unsportsmanlike conduct penalty for "any prolonged, excessive, or premeditated celebration." The rule was directly aimed at the Redskins' Fun Bunch and a certain member of the New York Jets, and it unofficially became known as the Gastineau Rule. It was only loosely enforced, though, and as the years have gone on there's dancing of some sort or another on almost every play. The Jets defensive end may have just been ahead of his time.

Gastineau ended his career with 74 official sacks and an unofficial total of 107.5, the most in franchise history. He was a three-time First-Team All-Pro as well as a five-time Pro Bowler, and *Sports Illustrated's* legendary football guru Paul Zimmerman ranked Gastineau the No. 7 greatest pass rusher of all time. But when Gastineau's NFL career ended, that didn't mean the controversy and trouble ended, too.

He made a football comeback in 1990 with the BC Lions of the Canadian Football League, but it lasted all of four games. A boxing career came next. He had starting training for that sport during the 1982 strike, and later trained with Gerry Cooney. "A lot of people in football think because they have big bodies they can get in a ring and go rounds with these guys," he said. "But when you think about it, you don't see a lot of boxers going out and trying to be football players." His record of 15–2 from 1991–96 may have been tainted; there is some sentiment that a few of his opponents had taken a dive.

More difficulties ensued when Gastineau was hit with domestic violence charges, and in 2000, he spent 11 months in Rikers for parole violations. Since getting out of prison, though, he has turned his life around, becoming a Born Again Christian. The past decade, there's been a new humble Mark Gastineau. In fact, he's kept such a low profile that a younger generation may be familiar with the name "Gastineau" more for E!'s reality show *Gastineau Girls*, starring the former Jet's ex-wife Lisa and daughter Brittny, which aired for two seasons beginning in 2005 and was a precursor to *Keeping Up With the Kardashians*, than for Mark Gastineau's colorful football career. "Peace. That's what I want out of life," he said. "I want to be happy with all these new things happening in my life— it's nothing but peace and happiness. It's a great beginning for me; and I'm really excited about getting started."

The New York Sack Exchange was only fully together for two seasons, 1980 and '81. But they made their mark not only in franchise history but NFL history, as well. The group was comprised of four wholly different individuals: Abdul Salaam was the spirit, Joe Klecko was the example, Marty Lyons was the conscience, and Mark Gastineau was the id. Wesley Walker, who had a front-row seat for the whole wild ride—the good, the bad, and the ugly—encapsulated the essence of that roller-coaster era:

"If I had my MVP of all the Jets, Joe Klecko would be my No. 1 guy. I've never seen anybody that has that ability. What's disheartening, they never gave Abdul Salaam the credit because he tied everything up. He made Joe Klecko and Mark Gastineau. Those were two phenomenal ends. Joe Klecko made All-Pro at every position. There's no one—no one!—that could handle him one on one. And people just didn't know how good some of our players were, and injuries may have hurt that.

"They weren't together as a unit personality-wise, though. Joe Klecko and Marty Lyons *hated* Mark Gastineau, and I don't know why. There were a lot of things that went into that whole thing, and I used to sit there and talk to him and it would be disgusting. We were supposed to be teammates, and here they have one of the best defensive lines in the National Football League and they hate each other. There's no reason for that. That's not what makes the success of a team, and I never could understand that.

"But guys would be jealous—guys would even be jealous over women you weren't dating. They're arguing before a game, which was ridiculous. You're going to play a football game. And I don't know how anybody could say anything about another individual, about their families, and say anything derogatory. Because we're all different, we all bring something to the table, but we're not going to be like *you*. But certain guys had these little cliquish things, and I would sit there and just watch this stuff, and it was just disheartening. And I really believe that's why we weren't successful. But you cannot tell me the Sack Exchange wasn't one of the best things that ever happened to the Jets."

CHAPTER 8

JUST GIVE ME THE DAMN FLASHLIGHT

IN ONE CORNER, THERE WAS HUMBLENESS. In the other resided chutzpah. On one side lived Mr. Third Down. Across from him was Mr. Me. It was quietude vs. obstreperousness. It was East Coast vs. West Coast. Suburbs vs. mean streets. 5'10" vs. 6'4". Jet vs. Jet. Jet vs. ex-Jet. White vs. black. Walk-on vs. No. 1 draft pick. The battle lines were drawn. It was Wayne Chrebet vs. Keyshawn Johnson.

On the field, Chrebet and Johnson were strikingly similar—tough, not afraid to venture over the middle, battlers, warrior-like mentalities. But off the field, they had as much in common as Hollywood does with Garfield, New Jersey. Which, of course, is nothing at all. They were the Ali-Frazier of the NFL...only they were on the same team.

Wayne Chrebet had no chance to play in the NFL. He was too small, too slow, too white, too everything. The one thing he had, though, was the nerve to try. His father even had doubts about a high school career. "We eventually signed the consent waiver for football because we never thought Wayne would get in to play," he said. Of course he did get in to play. And he continued to play in college at Hofstra. He wasn't there on a scholarship nor was he highly recruited, but that didn't stop him from setting numerous school records and tying an NCAA mark held by Jerry Rice when he caught five touchdown passes in one game. Though he was almost turned away at the gate on his first day in professional football, Chrebet continued his underdog, not-a-chance-in-the-world football career as an undrafted invitee with the Jets.

Unimpressed security guard Harry Fisher, on first laying eyes on Chrebet at the opening of training camp, declared, "Players only." Chrebet argued, "But I'm on the team." "Like hell you are," was the answer. "I thought Wayne was just another kid from Hofstra," Fisher said later on.

Chrebet eventually made his way into camp, and one person he did impress was John Griffin, coordinator of college scouting for the Jets. Chrebet's first workout with the team raised eyebrows. "If I had to use one word to describe Wayne's workout, it would be *spectacular*. Richard Mann, our receivers coach, threw him about 50 balls, and Wayne didn't drop one. Obviously the object of the game is to throw balls that are either very hard or impossible to catch, but Rich couldn't get any past him."

Chrebet was 12th out of 12 on the depth chart at the receiver position, but he surprisingly made the team, when Coach Rich Kotite took a shine to the unheralded rookie. And Chrebet provided instant production, catching 66 passes, second on the team to Adrian Murrell's 71. Though nobody noticed him coming out of college, he quickly earned a name for himself around the league with his fearless style of pass-catching over the middle where the animals of the defense roam. "I live in the middle of the field where a lot of receivers won't go. Someone told me when I was in college, 'Make something about you stand out. Whether you shave your head or have some weird ritual, do something to stand out.' In the pros I figured I'd catch everything. Go across the middle, get drilled, catch the ball, and get up and act like nothing happened. Show them toughness. That's what I live by."

Jets wide receiver Wayne Chrebet (80) pulls in the game-winning 18-yard pass in the fourth quarter to give the Jets a 21–17 victory over the Tampa Bay Buccaneers on September 24, 2000. (AP Images)

The keys to Chrebet's success were hard work—he was a relentless weightlifter (which he inherited from his father, who was a bodybuilder and former Mr. New Jersey and Mr. East Coast) who often swam to exhaustion once his workout session in the weight room was finished—and a feeling like his football career was all just a mirage. As his mother once said, "Wayne plays every day as if somebody in authority is going to tap him on the back and say, 'It's time. Clean out your locker. Go home.' It all goes back to who he is and where he's from. Nobody ever wasted millions on Wayne."

Chrebet just had a way of sneaking up on everybody, including his doubters, his coaches, his opponents, and even his father. "Don't play gin with him, because he'll set you up," the elder Chrebet said. "He'll lead you to believe you have him beat, and then—wham!—he's won again." In his second season, the 1996 1–15 debacle, Chrebet snuck up on his defenders to the tune of a career-high 84 catches, leading the Jets. And he never had fewer than 48 pass receptions in his first eight seasons.

But his bread and butter was the third-down reception, whether that meant getting creamed while making a leaping catch over the middle or having his block knocked off by a head-hunting safety. His nickname of Mr. Third Down was hard-earned. "I don't care if they bring in Jerry Rice. My role is the same—to be the league's best third-down receiver," he said.

While Keyshawn Johnson may not have respected the undersized receiver, his opponents knew what he brought to the table. Colts cornerback Jason Belser had to deal with Chrebet firsthand: "He's their big-play guy. And he'll do anything for his team. If they need Wayne to block, he'll block. If they need him to run a route across the middle, he'll run it. Wayne is fast, too. He's the type of player who in the fourth quarter is still moving at the same pace as in the first quarter. Much of that is desire, but there's no denying it—the guy's got a lot of ability."

Unfortunately, it was his fearlessness that shortened his career. On November 6, 2005, in a game against the Chargers, Chrebet was knocked unconscious while making yet another third-down catch and sustained his last in a long line of concussions. While he lay on the ground motionless, he of course held onto the ball for the first down. But that was the last catch he would ever make. He finished his unsung career with 580 receptions, second only to Don Maynard on the all-time franchise list. He gained 7,365 yards, third most in team history behind Maynard and Wesley Walker. His 41 touchdown receptions also placed him third on the all-time team list behind Maynard and Walker. And he has the third-most career receptions in NFL history by a nondrafted player, only trailing Rod Smith and Gary Clark.

Chrebet was a fan's player, a coach's player, and a player's player. His heart and desire were everything one could want in a football player. And no matter how successful he became, he never once put on airs or even hinted at a show of pomposity, which bled into his personal life, as well. His future wife got a taste of the Wayne Chrebet directness, unaffected by pretension, when he got down on one knee and proposed marriage with the untraditional, "So, do you have my back?" She did. And she became Mrs. Third Down.

Keyshawn Johnson, on the other hand, was born to play in the NFL. That doesn't mean he was born with a silver spoon in his mouth with all the advantages one needs to become a top-flight athlete. On the contrary. Growing up, he barely had any spoons at all, and he probably stole and then sold the ones he did have.

The feud between Johnson and Chrebet was often framed in a Good vs. Evil light. But Keyshawn Johnson was not evil. He was just loud. Unlike Chrebet, who came from a stable two-parent household, Johnson never knew his father. He was the youngest of six kids, but his older siblings often lived with relatives, leaving Keyshawn alone with his mother in South-Central L.A. The two spent time in a shelter, and for a nine-day stretch they once lived out of a car.

Johnson's rocky childhood found him getting into all sorts of trouble, mischief, scams, and schemes, often involving illegal activities. He scalped tickets, sold drugs, mapped out burglaries, fenced merchandise, and in his late teens a bullet found its way into his leg. A couple of juvenile camps also served as residences for the young Keyshawn. Maybe he wasn't born to play in the NFL, after all. Maybe he was just born to survive.

But amongst all that hardship and affliction, Keyshawn wandered onto the nearby USC campus and finagled his way into being the football team's ballboy. He may have only been a youngster, but he possessed the magnetism of...Keyshawn Johnson. Marcus Allen was starring for the Trojans at the time and said of the precocious go-getter, "You could see he had the magic then. He had charisma. The kid had a presence at an early age, and I think he knew exactly what he wanted to do.... He's been around ballplayers his whole life, and he certainly had that exposure at 'SC. He was sort of like a little brother. Everybody knew him. He was never a nuisance, but he was a character."

Despite his troublemaking background, Johnson became a high school football star, though he attended a number of different schools. He continued his academic odyssey in a few junior colleges before finally latching on with USC, where he went from ballboy to legend. A two-time All-American, Johnson was named the MVP of the Cotton Bowl in 1995 and earned Player of the Game honors in the 1996 Rose Bowl. At a press conference after his final college game, he brazenly announced, "Okay, I'm ready to go play for the New York Jets."

The Jets, of course, did select him with the first overall pick in the 1996 draft, and the following day Keyshawn threw, in his own words, "the biggest party in the history of drafts." Tupac attended, along with assorted actors, athletes, and the requisite contingent of beautiful women, while Coolio and the Westside Connection performed. Like Reggie Jackson before him, Keyshawn Johnson didn't become a star in New York—he brought his star with him.

After holding out and with negotiations dragging into August, Johnson finally signed a six-year, $15 million contract. But he found himself coming off the bench to begin his rookie season and playing behind a certain diminutive, hard-working receiver. Johnson ultimately started 11 games that year, catching 63 passes for 844 yards. Of course, he announced to the world that he was not at all satisfied with that output. But each season with the Jets, Johnson's statistics gradually increased, inching up to 70 catches in '97 and 83 and 89 the following two seasons, which earned him a place in the Pro Bowl both years. He was named co-MVP of the '98 game.

Johnson was the complete package. He had size, strength, speed, and ability. He wasn't afraid to cross the middle of the field, and he was an adept blocker. He may have been flashy off the field, but on it he was an old-fashioned hard worker. And Chrebet wasn't the only receiver to take care of his body. Johnson relentlessly ran through the hills of California to stay in tip-top shape. He worked as much as he talked.

The crowning moment of Johnson's Jets career came on January 10, 1999, in a 34–24 playoff victory over the Jacksonville Jaguars. Nine catches for 121 yards and a touchdown reception is a memorable day for any receiver. But how many pass catchers can add 28 rushing yards with a touchdown, a fumble recovery, and an interception to their stat sheet? All in the same game? The only things he didn't do were play quarterback and reenact his time as a ballboy. But he probably could have. He wasn't just blowing smoke when he stated, "I don't think there's anybody in the league like me, period. I just don't. On the field, off the field, at home. I'm just different."

Sure, Keyshawn Johnson was brash, a braggart, boastful, a self-promoter, and he had an ego as big as his mouth. But he also had a humanitarian side to him. He was a misanthrope at times when it came to his teammates, but he was the Good Samaritan when thinking of his community. He founded Key's Kids for underprivileged children and the Keyshawn Johnson Education Fund, handing out much-needed scholarships to youths who otherwise wouldn't have been able to attend college. Johnson also appeared with President Clinton on panels discussing race in athletics. "I'm really proud of that," he said in Keyshawn-speak. "How many people get to chop it up with the top dog?"

After four seasons, his days with the Jets were over. Bill Parcells, who was always a Keyshawn Johnson fan, traded the receiver to the Tampa Bay Buccaneers for two draft picks, which turned into John Abraham and Anthony Becht. The deal ostensibly was made with the thought of rebuilding, but Johnson felt that new owner Woody Johnson and Coach Al Groh didn't want him around. "The only thing I can think is that they're trying to buy time. If I look like the bad guy, then they can say, 'Well, we had to trade him, and since we did, now we have to rebuild.' But if that's so, just come out and say it—don't lie to the fans."

Johnson spent four seasons with the Bucs, making one Pro Bowl and winning a Super Bowl. But he ran afoul of Coach Jon Gruden and was deactivated for the final six games of the 2003 season. He moved on to Dallas for two years and a final season in Carolina, finishing his career with 814 receptions, 10,571 yards, and a total of 66 touchdowns. He was also the first player to score a touchdown with four different teams on *Monday Night Football*.

Of course Keyshawn Johnson also had one prominent, glaring characteristic that informed much of his career—he was completely obsessed with Wayne Chrebet. "We lead the league in guys from

Hofstra. We've got more guys from Hofstra than we do from USC or Notre Dame," Johnson said in his rookie year. After Chrebet led the team in receptions in 1996, Keyshawn was exasperated. "Why draft me if you're not going to give me the rock? I mean, c'mon. Give me the goddamn ball and let me do my thing."

After his rookie season, Johnson penned a book detailing his experiences with the Jets. Most athletes wait until their career is over or until after they've won a championship or maybe broken a record to write about their exploits. Keyshawn waited one year. And it was a 1–15 year at that. The book came with the never-to-be-forgotten title of *Just Give Me the Damn Ball!: The Fast Times and Hard Knocks of an NFL Rookie*, though it might as well have been called *Just Get Wayne Chrebet the Hell Away From Me*. Staying in character, he dedicated the book to the Lord Savior Jesus Christ, his mother, his daughter, and to himself "for not giving a damn about what people think."

Sure, he skewered quarterback Neil O'Donnell and Coach Rich Kotite, but most of Johnson's venom was saved for Chrebet. Keyshawn labeled his rival a "mascot," a "pet," and somebody who "wouldn't even make anybody else's team." After the book's release, Chrebet responded to what had been written about him. "To be honest, it makes me kind of nervous that a grown man thinks about me so much. Between you and me, I think Keyshawn has a crush on me. Why is he worrying about Wayne Chrebet so much? I thought he was Mr. Hollywood, the guy who got more than $6 million just to sign. Big contract, a big house, big everything. What's he bothering with me for? I'm Wayne Chrebet. Who's Wayne Chrebet?"

Johnson felt that Chrebet was getting special treatment, which led to fewer balls being thrown his way. Keyshawn was a nationally known college football star. Why was this little guy from a Podunk college getting all the passes and all the accolades? Besides, Chrebet's a complementary player, not a focal point of a defense's attention. As Johnson pointed out, "He can play. But here's the question I ask: Does he line up on every play knowing other teams are geared toward stopping him and still beat them?"

Race came into play, too, according to Keyshawn. The guy from South-Central works just as hard, if not harder, than the pipsqueak from Garfield. Why isn't Keyshawn the people's choice—or, more importantly, the coach's and quarterback's choice? "Keyshawn's problem is that he hyped himself up so big that he'll never be able to live up to it," Chrebet said. "So what does he do? He makes an excuse. He takes the attention off himself by blaming something else—in this instance, race."

Johnson wasn't too worried about the effect the book would have on his teammates. "We're all professionals," he said. "Everyone on the team should have a positive attitude about it all." Of course, they didn't. During most of their time together on the Jets, Johnson and Chrebet had adjoining lockers. For good or bad, they were linked together, literally and figuratively.

The rivalry came to a head on September 24, 2000, at Raymond James Stadium, home of the Buccaneers. Keyshawn was in his first season with Tampa Bay, and his new and old teams came into the game with matching 3–0 records. In the week leading up to the game, Johnson entered a new zone in the trash-talking arena. He reached a zenith when it came to insulting Chrebet. He also flipped off a CNN camera along the way.

With the football version of the Fight of the Century or Thrilla in Manila only days away, Keyshawn called Chrebet everything short of a gorilla, but mainly because it didn't rhyme with Tampa Bay. What he did say was this: "You're trying to compare a flashlight to a star. Flashlights only last so long. A star is in the sky forever." From that statement, came a new nickname for Chrebet—the Green Lantern.

Keyshawn Johnson, left, hugs former Jets teammate Curtis Martin after the Jets' win over Johnson's Buccaneers on September 24, 2000. Martin, a running back, threw the game-winning touchdown pass to Wayne Chrebet. (AP Images)

Neither player was much of a factor early in the contest. Tampa Bay jumped out in front with a Martin Gramatica 22-yard field goal, while the Jets' John Hall answered back with a 41-yarder of his own, ending the first quarter in a 3–3 tie. The Bucs' Dave Moore caught a 3-yard touchdown pass from Shaun King in the second quarter. Hall struck again for Gang Green with a 27-yard boot.

Ronde Barber opened up the second-half scoring when he picked off a Vinny Testaverde pass and ran it back 37 yards to give Tampa Bay a 17–6 bulge. With 1:54 left in the game, Curtis Martin made his way into the end zone, catching a 6-yard pass from Testaverde to cut the lead to three.

All the while, Johnson and Chrebet had just caught one pass each. Keyshawn's was essentially a handoff, as his catch of a shovel pass gained all of 1 yard. Chrebet's reception was good for 14 yards. But the Jet would end the day with bragging rights and be the hero, as well...much to the delight of his teammates.

After the Martin touchdown, Groh passed on an onside-kick attempt, which proved to be a fortuitously wise decision. On Tampa Bay's second play after the kickoff, Marvin Jones caused a Mike Alstott fumble, and the ball was recovered by Victor Green. When the Jets took over on Tampa Bay's 24-yard line, Richie Anderson went into motion, and Martin took a handoff and gained 6 yards following a Chrebet block.

Offensive coordinator Dan Henning then pulled a rabbit out of his hat for the key blow of the afternoon. And it was a gutsy, startling rabbit at that. With 52 seconds remaining in the game, the Jets lined up exactly as they had on the previous play, and as Testaverde took the ball from center, Anderson, Martin, and Chrebet moved as if they were repeating the first-down play. Except this time, Chrebet pretended to miss his block and got lost in the end zone. And Martin rolled out instead of barreling up the field. The running back spotted an open No. 80 and uncorked a wounded duck of a throw, which wobbled over the outstretched hands of a desperate Damien Robinson. Chrebet, with the most effective way of exacting revenge on his former teammate at his fingertips, leaped and made a phenomenal, acrobatic catch for the final points of the game. The Buccaneers would fumble the ensuing kickoff to clinch the 21–17 win for the Jets.

Martin's lob was the first game-winning touchdown pass thrown by a running back since 1969 when Preston Ridlehuber of the Bills turned the trick. That's the same Preston Ridlehuber who recovered the fumble and scored at the end of the *Heidi* game. The Jets running back said of the trick play, "They actually laughed at me. That play was the joke of the week. I told them, 'Just wait 'til the game. I'll get it done in the game.'"

Martin's performance that day was prodigious as well as versatile. He gained 90 yards on the ground, caught eight passes for 30 yards, hauled in a touchdown pass, and tossed one, too. But Chrebet was the man of the hour, coming down with the game-winning catch while his arch nemesis could only muster up that one measly reception. Johnson was thrown to five times but was well-covered by Marcus Coleman. A vexed Johnson said, "I can't explain it. How can I explain it? That's the plays we called and we ran them efficiently and we ran the ball well. I think the rain took us out of our passing game a little bit there. That was pretty much it."

Chrebet's catch came with two opposing points of view, of course. One was from the man who made the catch: "I jumped too soon. It was hanging up there so long, I said, 'Man, I've got to go up and get it.' Fortunately, I came up with it." And the other, from the man who stood helplessly on the sidelines watching his enemy gather in not only the game-winning touchdown pass but all the glory, as well: "I pretty much just said, 'Damn, wow, they let somebody get open.' At the beginning, I didn't know he caught it. Then, touchdown. They ran the toss fake and threw the ball. He was open and scored the touchdown. There's really nothing you can say about it other than they scored a touchdown and won the game."

No one was happier for Chrebet than his teammates. They wanted to win the game for Wayne as much as for themselves. As far as they were concerned, it was a storybook ending with the good guy coming out on top. And all the talk centered on the infamous flashlight quote. "Looks like a flashlight was good enough today," said a happy Groh. "The power of 46 flashlights can be pretty bright sometimes." Victor Green chimed in, "Keyshawn who? The flashlight outshined the star."

The verbal bouquets thrown Chrebet's way circled the Jets' locker room. Testaverde stated, "After all the stuff he went through, he certainly deserved to have the winning catch. He never answered any of the remarks. He handled himself in a classy way. Good guys do finish on top." And Kevin Mawae was ecstatic for his

Lam Jones

Over the decades, track stars have been turned into football and baseball players with varying results. On the positive side, there was the Dallas Cowboys' Bob Hayes, a three-time Pro Bowler. At the negative end stands Herb Washington, the Oakland A's failed experiment as a designated runner in 1974 and '75 who had zero lifetime at-bats, stole 31 bases, but was caught 17 times. And somewhere in between is Johnny "Lam" Jones. He was a Texas high school track legend, won an Olympic gold medal at the age of 18 in the 1976 games, starred on the University of Texas football team (along with "Ham" Jones and "Jam" Jones), and was the second overall pick in the 1980 NFL draft by the Jets.

Jones signed a then-record six-year $2.1 million contract, but his NFL career lasted only five seasons (1980–84) all with the Jets. Unlike the success that Chrebet and Johnson achieved, Jones is considered one of the franchise's biggest busts. He caught 138 career passes, but he was more known for his drops than the ones he hung on to. Over the years, he's battled social anxiety and drug and alcohol addiction (but has been sober since 1990), and the last few years he's been fighting myeloma cancer. Through all his troubles on and off the field, his heart has always been in the right place, which is best exemplified by his unselfish donation of his cherished Olympic gold medal to the Special Olympics. Where did his football career go wrong? Teammate Wesley Walker has a theory:

teammate. "That's poetic justice, man. It goes to show you we've got a flashlight who, at the biggest point of the game, can shine brighter than anyone on the field. Wayne's humble, and he kept quiet all week long, but the rest of us were ready to pop off for him."

Did Johnson learn any lessons after getting a big taste of humble pie? Um, no. "So you want to get me? You want to shut up the loudmouth kid from the ghetto? So what? That's not going to do it. You're not going to humble me. That's not going to make me regret doing anything," he said. Even Bucs guard Frank Middleton

"I wish he would have had a coach that took the time with him," Walker said. "I tell him this all the time: I wish I would have been his coach. We were young, and I did my bit of partying and doing my thing, but when it came to work, you worked. You're there in the offseason. You're working with the quarterback. Lam would be there for a week or two, and then you wouldn't see him for six weeks or eight weeks or something. He didn't help himself.

"I remember when he dropped a couple of balls, Joe Walton and Rich Kotite would yank him. His confidence got really low. But I saw a talent there. And I'll never forget [what] Dan Henning told me, because I had my share of drops my rookie year—you're going to catch more than you're going to drop. If [Lam] would have had a coach that took him aside like Dan Henning, this guy would have been all-world.

"I've never seen anything like him. I love this guy. Because when you can catch the ball, and have speed and run routes, there's nobody that can catch you. And he could do it. He just never worked at his craft. Or he never developed the confidence where he could become good at it because they would yank him. There's no athlete on this earth that could go in there for one play and then you yank him out. You have to get into the flow of things, and he never got that. But I've never seen anybody that had this ability of speed, hands, could catch, run routes, and he learned from us. Nobody nurtured him. And that's all he needed."

couldn't help taking a pot shot at his teammate. "He went at it by trash-talking, and they didn't. Usually when that happens, the team that shuts up and plays football usually wins."

Chrebet summed it up best with his simple take on the whole matter. "It's just easier to go about your job when all you have to worry about is catching the football."

No matter their differences, Johnson and Chrebet were two of the greatest receivers in franchise history. One of their forefathers, Wesley Walker, added his two cents on the sparring duo. "I love Wayne Chrebet. I watched him when he was at Hofstra. Here's a guy that's not very big. You don't need to be—you just need the opportunity, and he made the most out of his opportunity. Keyshawn Johnson, he had all the ability in the world, but here's a guy that could be flamboyant and do it in a negative way, which I never liked, where it could become demeaning. But he's a guy that I would go in a foxhole with because he comes to play. I didn't like some of his antics, what he did to some of his teammates like Chrebet, because he was so focused on just me, me, me, me. That's the only thing I didn't like about him."

Chrebet and Johnson were teammates for four up-and-down contentious years. They went through a laughingstock 1–15 season together, but also rose all the way to the AFC Championship Game in 1998, only one half away from a Super Bowl. They could have been perfect complements to each other, and in some ways they were, despite their mutual animosity. But in five decades of Jets football, there's never been a feud to match the one fought by these two unique, distinct players. The star vs. the flashlight. The little guy came out on top that day down in Florida, but Keyshawn Johnson and Wayne Chrebet both made their singular marks in the history books of the New York Jets.

CHAPTER 9

MONDAY NIGHT MADNESS

ONE DAY WHILE JOE NAMATH was the toast of the town, living it up in Manhattan, Howard Cosell came around for a visit. That was one of the benefits (or pitfalls) of being a celebrity in the 1960s and '70s—Howard Cosell might come around for a visit. The two larger-than-life personalities sat in the living room chatting. Well, Cosell did the majority of the talking. And his booming, nasal, unmistakable voice echoed throughout the apartment. As the tête-à-tête went on, a bedroom door opened, and Namath's roommate, Jets safety Ray Abruzzese, who had been sleeping, groggily walked into the living room. He headed straight for the TV and then froze when he spotted Cosell sitting on the coach. "Oh, you're *here*," he said. "I was just coming in to turn you off." And such was America's relationship with Howard Cosell.

Through the decades, professional football games have occasionally been played on Mondays, going all the way back to October 10, 1921, when the Rock Island Independents defeated the Chicago Staleys 14–10. A few dozen games were played in the ensuing years, with even the New York Jets toppling Houston 26–17 as late as October 20, 1969. None of those contests featured Cosell, though, or even "Dandy" Don Meredith for that matter. So even though they were played on a Monday, those games weren't

"Monday Night Football." They were just warm-ups—or appetizers to the buffet that was to come, if you will.

But on September 21, 1970, football on Monday nights was truly born with the arrival of ABC's *Monday Night Football*. Commissioner Pete Rozelle wanted a prime-time game and originally tabbed Friday night as his designated evening. He was talked out of that decision, though, as it would interfere with high school football games played all over America on that night. He settled on Monday, and the plan began to take shape.

CBS and NBC, who were already broadcasting the NFC and AFC, respectively, wanted no part in this risky venture. Football at night? And on a Monday? Who in their right mind would watch something like that? It would be the downfall of the whole network. You might as well have a show about a celebrity dance-off or just film a bunch of rich, crazy housewives and put it on the air. Besides, isn't *Laugh-In* already airing on Mondays? We'll stick with Rowan and Martin, Goldie Hawn, and "Sock it to me," thank you very much.

Rozelle went to the last network left, ABC, which was bringing up the rear in the network sweepstakes. And even they had doubts, as well as second, third, and fourth thoughts. Already wallowing in last place, they didn't want to become a laughingstock, as well. But they reluctantly agreed and tabbed Roone Arledge to oversee the mad, crazy experiment. He envisioned the broadcast to be more than just a football game, though. He wanted it to be a spectacle, a happening, an extravaganza. Arledge would add more cameras, more graphics, more everything. And that included more announcers.

His first choice to fill the three-man booth was Frank Gifford, but the former Giant was under contract with CBS for 1970. With Gifford unavailable, Arledge hired Keith Jackson as his play-by-play man. Gifford recommended his pal Meredith, who signed on.

Announcers Howard Cosell and Don Meredith pose in the days leading up to the first Monday Night Football *broadcast on ABC. The Jets lost to the Cleveland Browns 31–21.* (New York Daily News Archive via Getty Images)

And Arledge's secret weapon was Cosell, the man America loved to hate but the man they just couldn't seem to turn off.

In Woody Allen's 1973 movie *Sleeper,* his character, Miles Monroe, wakes up after being cryogenically frozen and finds himself 200 years in the future. A historian, while viewing a video of Cosell, tells Monroe, "We weren't sure at first what to make of this, but we developed a theory: We feel that when people committed great crimes against the state, they were forced to watch this." Without missing a beat, Monroe answers, "Yes. That's exactly what it was."

Cosell was annoying, he was fascinating, he was intelligent, he was overbearing, he was articulate, he was loved, and he was hated. Say the words "Howard Cosell" to any football fan in the 1970s, and he could sound off for hours with his opinion of the announcing legend, sometimes punctuating his thoughts with irrational violence.

If this demented laboratory experiment was going to work, the NFL and ABC would need a top draw to bring in viewers. The Kansas City Chiefs had just defeated the Minnesota Vikings in Super Bowl IV the previous winter. Roman Gabriel of the Los Angeles Rams was the reigning NFL MVP. Bart Starr was still throwing bombs in Green Bay. Johnny Unitas was a legend and enduring in Baltimore. Gale Sayers and Dick Butkus were roaming the field in Chicago. O.J. Simpson was electrifying the city of Buffalo. Daryle Lamonica and the Oakland Raiders were consistent winners and consistently entertaining. The Dallas Cowboys were the Dallas Cowboys. The Giants were the grand old team of New York. But the No. 1 sensation at the time was Namath and the New York Jets.

The choice for the first *Monday Night Football* game was easy— it had to be the Jets. They were the biggest attraction around. Even though they were a year and a half removed from their legendary Super Bowl win that came with a guarantee, the Jets were still a shooting star—the cool, hip team that was all the rage with the kids. They were the bad boy that your parents didn't want you to date. But that just meant they were made for television. And prime-time television at that. They were coming off a 10–4 season in 1969, good for first place in the AFL East. But they lost to Kansas City 13–6 in the divisional playoff round. However, that defeat didn't dampen the glow of their reputation or marketability.

One reason for the success of *Monday Night Football* was its immaculate timing. The arrival of the Monday night game coincided with the NFL/AFL merger. The Jets' opponent was the Cleveland Browns, who would be making their debut in the new American Football Conference. They moved over from the old NFL, along with the Baltimore Colts and Pittsburgh Steelers. These were the post–Jim Brown Cleveland Browns, but in 1969, they finished atop the Century Division with a 10–3–1 record and whipped Dallas in the Divisional playoff round 38–14 before falling to Minnesota 27–7 in the NFL Championship Game.

So with the matchup set of two high-profile teams that came close to meeting in the Super Bowl a few months prior to this contest, the mellifluous Southern twang of Keith Jackson opened the broadcast (but over the original theme song, which preceded the longtime iconic jingle): "From Municipal Stadium in Cleveland, Ohio, two powers in professional football meet for the first time ever as members of the new American Football Conference of the National Football League—the New York Jets, led by the passing wizardry of Joe Namath, and the Cleveland Browns, led by the power running of Leroy Kelly."

Cosell interviewed Namath and Jets linebacker Al Atkinson on the field, which was followed by the modern-technology magic of a split-screen banter session with Cosell, "Dandy" Don, and Jackson. The kickoff was next, and television and football were never the same again.

The hometown Browns got on the board on the first possession of the game, marching 55 yards downfield and culminating the drive with an 8-yard Gary Collins touchdown catch of a Bill Nelsen pass. Monday nights were not quite ready for the end-zone antics of Billy "White Shoes" Johnson or Chad Ochocinco, though, as Collins casually and politely flipped the ball to the referee before jogging back to the Cleveland sideline as the Browns' marching band played the team's fight song. When the Browns got the ball back after the Jets punted, they did it again, this time scoring after a long, sustained 84-yard drive, which was helped along by two pass interference penalties. Fullback Bo Scott dashed around the left end and dove into the end zone for a 2-yard touchdown run, giving Cleveland a 14–0 lead and striking up the band yet again.

In the second quarter, Emerson Boozer scored the first of his two touchdowns to cut the Cleveland lead in half, and the teams went into their locker rooms while Cosell narrated the halftime highlights. When Howard was finished, former Giant Homer Jones, the originator of the end-zone spike and playing in his first game with his new team, ran back Jim Turner's kickoff 94 yards to extend the Brown lead. Boozer soon followed with his second score.

And at some point in the game, Don Meredith began his long history of making risqué, somewhat inappropriate remarks when he commented on the quirky name of one of the Browns receivers. "Isn't Fair Hooker a great name?" he asked. Cosell wouldn't take the bait, "I pass." "Dandy" Don continued, showing America what it could look forward to with this whole new zany Monday night concept: "Fair Hooker...well, I haven't met one yet."

Every time the Jets climbed within sniffing distance, Cleveland would turn around and counter with a score themselves. A Don Cockroft 27-yard field goal gave the Browns a 10-point cushion to end the third-quarter scoring. The Jets would come back again, though, this time with a 33-yard Namath touchdown pass to George

Sauer. The score capped off Sauer's incredible evening. He caught 10 passes for 172 yards. When the Cleveland offense was done for the night, the Jets had one more chance, down by three, with less than a minute left in the game.

With Namath behind center, Sauer and Don Maynard running downfield, and Boozer and Matt Snell in the backfield, the Jets had a full arsenal at the ready. But when Namath took the snap at New York's 18-yard line and dropped back to pass, he threw a sinking liner that was picked off by Browns linebacker Billy Andrews at the 25-yard line, who ran it back for a touchdown to break the back and the heart of the Jets. It was Namath's third interception of the game, and it was the exclamation point to Cleveland's 31–21 victory.

One of ABC's many cameras panned to Namath, who stood frozen on the field for what seemed an eternity with his hands on his hips staring at the ground, defeated. It was a portrait of a beaten man. When the broadcast signed off, director Chet Forte used that image to bid adieu to the viewers. The television camera was now an artist's paint brush, and games became more than games—they were stories of triumph and heartbreak.

The Jets racked up 454 total yards compared to Cleveland's 221, but the interceptions, a fumble, and 13 penalties doomed New York. In fact, they would finish the year with a 4–10 record, Namath would embark on his long line of missed games due to injuries, and their descent into 1970s oblivion would begin.

However, the fans who tuned in to this curiosity weren't disappointed by the exciting game and groundbreaking broadcast. They may have turned their TV dials to ABC to witness this exotic novelty, but the strong ratings continued, of course, and *Monday Night Football* became a cultural icon. In hindsight, how could it have failed? America had (and still has) an insatiable appetite for football, and fans would surely watch a game whichever day it was broadcast, whether morning, noon, or night.

Jackson was replaced by Gifford the following year, but Cosell continued for more than a decade, and his sparring with Meredith became legendary, while the old Cowboys quarterback's warbling of Willie Nelson's "The Party's Over" whenever he felt the outcome of a game had been decided became a staple of the broadcast. Cosell's drinking prowess took a hit, though, when he reportedly lost his lunch on Meredith's boots later in that first season and "Dandy" Don and Jackson had to continue the game as a duo. But the first broadcast was a landmark, and the New York Jets were there.

Gang Green didn't just play in the first *Monday Night Football* game, they also played in the best. Exactly three decades after history was made in Cleveland, the Jets hosted the rival Miami Dolphins in a game that was so thrilling, unbelievable, and far-fetched that you may not have believed it even if you saw it with your own eyes. If Cosell were still around for the broadcast, he probably would have described it as such: "The preposterous, almost apocryphal nature of this engagement between two fractious adversaries will go down in the annals of sport as one of the most implausible, abstruse, and capricious contests ever chronicled." But, alas, Howard had passed away five years previous to this Monday night classic, so it was up to Al Michaels to wax poetic about the Miracle at the Meadowlands.

Miami and New York were both 5–1, they were fighting for first place, and they both had reason to believe they were Super Bowl contenders. The Jets had reached the AFC Championship game two years prior but lost a heartbreaker to Denver after holding a 10–0 lead. In the first game of the 1999 season, Vinny Testaverde suffered an Achilles tendon injury, which sabotaged the Jets' season. But the gang was back to together in 2000, and they got off to a flying start.

The Dolphins were coming off of three consecutive playoff appearances, but 2000 was their first season since 1982 that Dan

Marino wouldn't be behind center. Long Island native, boyhood Jets fan, and future Jet Jay Fiedler had the distinct honor of being the Richard Todd of Miami, taking over for the legendary Marino. Both teams featured new coaches: Dave Wannstedt replaced Jimmy Johnson in Miami, while Al Groh roamed the sidelines in his only season in New York, supplanting Bill Parcells who kicked himself upstairs to concentrate on his football operations duties.

The date was October 23, 2000, and most of New York's sports-world focus was centered on the Yankees-Mets World Series. The Bronx Bombers were holding a 2–0 lead, and the bizarre Roger Clemens bat-throwing incident with Mike Piazza had taken place only 24 hours before the Jets and Dolphins would kick off at the Meadowlands. Clemens was, in fact, on the field before the game, making an appearance for the Home Shopping Network. ABC announcer Dennis Miller dug up a baseball bat and asked the pitcher if he would break it and autograph it for him. Clemens signed it but neglected to snap it in half.

This AFC East regular-season game would be a leisurely, mild distraction on an off day of the Subway Series, right? But what took place on this evening in East Rutherford rivaled anything in that memorable Series.

It would take a while, though. For the first 45 minutes of the game, the only unforgettable aspect of the contest for the Jets was the utter embarrassment they must have been feeling. Dolphins kicker Olindo Mare opened the floodgates with a 28-yard field goal. Fiedler chucked a 42-yard touchdown pass to Leslie Shepherd. And the Jets' Swiss-cheese defense continued when Lamar Smith dashed 68 yards for another score. The scoreboard read Dolphins 17, Jets 0 before most of the fans had settled into their seats and stopped asking each other, "Did you see the game last night?"

New York finally got on the scoreboard when Wayne Chrebet caught a 10-yard pass from Testaverde, but Mare booted a

44-yarder to up the score to 23–7 at halftime. A miracle comeback seemed like the last thing on anybody's mind. Rick Reed's chances against the Yankees the following night was most likely a bigger topic of conversation in the stands than the unlikely probability of the Jets storming back in the second half. "Oh, man, it was humiliating. That wasn't our team. Defensively, we played like… there aren't even words," summed up safety Victor Green.

The mild-mannered, understated, and serious Groh was a contrast to the bellicose Parcells. Once asked about the dissimilarities between the 1999 Jets and the 2000 version, Groh quipped, "The head coach isn't as funny as the last one." But in the locker room at halftime, Groh broke out of character and threw a tantrum. He hurled a metal stool. He kicked a laundry bag as if he were angrily booting a field goal. If Mike Piazza were anywhere nearby, Groh, too, would have heaved a broken bat at the Mets' catcher.

But when the Jets took the field for the second half, not much changed as they continued their offensive feebleness, unable to put any points on the scoreboard. After another Lamar Smith touchdown gave Miami a seemingly insurmountable 23-point lead, Fiedler declared the game over to teammate Jason Taylor, who was miked up for the telecast. But all that did was jinx his team, and he would find out the hard way that the opponent wasn't a group that easily gave up. As Jets defensive tackle Ernie Logan stated, "Even if we're down by 30, we're never lying down. If you get comfortable and you're playing us with a lead, you better watch out."

Things changed for the Jets at the start of the fourth quarter when they switched to a no-huddle, hurry-up offense. With no time to waste waiting for plays to be sent in from the sideline, Testaverde barked out orders at the line of scrimmage. And with the deficit so large, improvisation was also needed, and the Jets quarterback began calling plays the team hadn't practiced since training camp. But everything he did turned to gold, and the Jets' offense absolutely exploded. The Dolphins were suddenly facing a different team. The comeback began with a 30-yard touchdown pass to Laveranues Coles. Tight end Jermaine Wiggins caught a 1-yard touchdown pass from Testaverde. And John Hall booted a 34-yard field goal. Bing, bang, boom—just like that, the Jets closed the gap to 30–23.

But Testaverde and the Jets were just warming up. When they got the ball back after those three unanswered scoring drives, Chrebet, as he would throughout his career, came through again in a tight spot, catching his second touchdown pass of the night on a 24-yard pass from Testaverde, tying the game. But the euphoria was short-lived. On the first play after the kickoff, Fiedler gunned a 46-yard touchdown pass to Shepherd to retake the lead. But as we've already seen, the Jets weren't going to lie down and die. Not on this night.

There was one more drive to go in the fourth quarter. And it could only end one possible way—memorably. Starting on their own 43-yard line, the Jets went to work. They made it all the way down to the Miami 5-yard line but were facing a fourth-and-1 situation. But this was a night when the Jets would overcome every obstacle thrown in their path. Richie Anderson, who would finish the game with 12 catches good for 109 yards, caught a 2-yard pass, enough for the first down and setting up the play of the game.

With three yards to go, the Jets had many weapons at their disposal. There was Anderson, who was having a fine game. There was Curtis Martin, who was in the midst of the sixth of his 10 consecutive 1,000-yard seasons. There was one of the great clutch players in Jets history in Chrebet, who hauled in six passes for 104 yards that night. There was talented rookie Coles. So who did the Jets choose to go to as their make-or-break playmaker? Left tackle Jumbo Elliott. That's right, Jumbo Elliott.

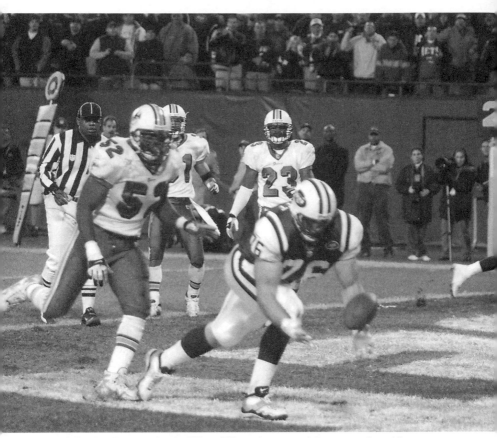

Offensive lineman Jumbo Elliott (76) catches a touchdown pass from Vinny Testaverde with 42 seconds remaining to give the Jets a 40–37 overtime win over the Miami Dolphins in 2000. (Corey Sipkin/NY Daily News Archive via Getty Images)

The play only took a few seconds to develop, and the Dolphins never knew what hit 'em. Testaverde took the ball from center, and faked a handoff to Martin. He took another step or two back, and then, doing his impression of a basketball player taking a fade-away jump shot, leaped and tossed the ball into the waiting hands of a wide-open Elliott in the end zone. Easy, right? Well, this is a 300-pound offensive lineman we're talking about, not a soft-handed veteran receiver. As the ball fell into Elliott's hands, he fell down himself, juggling the ball along the way. But by the time he hit the ground, the ball was nestled safely in his arms. Touchdown Jets, and the game was tied once again.

Elliott never doubted that it was a legal catch, even though the play had to go through a replay-review confirmation. "I know I caught it," he said. "My hands were below the ball. They were giving me air time so Dennis Miller could crack jokes about it." And Elliott was impressed with his own pass-receiving prowess. "It was very Lynn Swann–like. I still can't get the smile off my face. It was fun. I'm glad it came at a crucial time; it wasn't like we were up by three touchdowns."

It was on to overtime, and no matter what mistakes the Jets would make, after all they had been through and with all the momentum on their side, a Gang Green victory was in the cards on that Monday evening. The Dolphins got the ball first, but Marcus Coleman intercepted Fiedler's second pass of the game. Here was the Jets' chance. That was the final break they were looking for, and the outcome would be a happy one, no doubt. But the Jets weren't going to make it easy for themselves. Before Coleman could be brought down safely with possession of the ball, he fumbled it right back to Miami. Would he be the goat of the game? Would the Jets come this close only to lose in heartbreaking, mind-numbing fashion? On a fumble off an interception, of all things?

No, they wouldn't. For it was a case of déjà vu all over again, as Coleman intercepted yet another pass on the same drive, but this time there would be no butterfingered ending to the play. It only took the Jets six plays to get into field-goal range. And the inconceivable and unthinkable was finally complete when Hall hit a 40-yard field goal four hours and 10 minutes after the opening kickoff.

It was the Jets' fourth fourth-quarter comeback of the year, and Groh invoked the all-time legendary quote master to express his feelings of the marathon come-from-behind upset, "I don't think anybody could say it any better than the fella who lives about seven or eight miles from here, who wore No. 8 in pinstripes for a long time. Yogi said, 'It ain't over 'til it's over.'"

It was 20 years earlier when Al Michaels asked, "Do you believe in miracles?" This surely was an appropriate night to dust off that line once again. Coles, Wiggins, and Elliott all caught their first career touchdown passes (and for Elliott, it was his only

Arnold Schwarzenegger: Psychic

Monday Night Football is no stranger to celebrity guests visiting the announcers' booth. Spiro Agnew, Kermit the Frog, John Lennon, and Ronald Reagan have all made appearances during broadcasts. Lennon and Reagan were interviewed during the same game on December 9, 1974, when the Redskins took on the Rams at the Los Angeles Coliseum. Off-camera, the future president put his arm around the former Beatle and explained the rules of American football to the Liverpudlian, and while being interviewed by Cosell, Lennon opined that football "makes rock concerts look like tea parties."

Monday Night Football has also been a staple of popular culture from its inception. The announcing booth was used as a scene for two different episodes of *The Odd Couple*. In "Big Mouth," aired on September 22, 1972, Oscar Madison and Felix Unger find their way into Cosell's booth during a Giants-Cowboys game, and when Cosell instructs Madison to take over the play-by-play, the sloppy sportswriter freezes in fear, so Unger, speaking as Madison, commandeers the microphone for one of the most refined yet strange play descriptions in football television history:

"As Staubach takes the snap from center, he fakes a handoff to Duane Thomas elegantly and fades back to pass. He's looking for a receiver...he can't find one...he's scrambling...he's scrambling with the dexterity of a lizard. And now he looks to run with it himself, and he's stopped cold at the line of scrimmage for no gain on the play. No gain, but a lesson for us all. And what is that lesson? It is the lesson that is the message of all sports—try, try again, for career reception). Testaverde went 18-for-26 with 235 yards and four touchdowns in the fourth quarter alone. It was the biggest comeback in Jets history. During *Monday Night Football*'s 500th telecast, this game was voted the greatest of all Monday nighters. But Curtis Martin said it all after the game: "We've had a few comebacks, and every time I find myself saying, 'That was one of our sweetest victories.' But this...this was by far our sweetest victory. How can you top this?"

all men, no matter what their race, creed, or color, no matter who they are, the common ground for all their trying is the love of fair play. And speaking of fair play, this is Oscar Madison signing off and reminding you that a quitter never wins and a winner never quits. And now back to Howard Cosell."

A second *Monday Night Football*–themed episode, "Your Mother Wears Army Boots," aired on January 16, 1975. During a Jets-Bengals preseason game, one in which a highlight of a Joe Namath-to-Rich Caster completion is shown, Unger tells his roommate, who has just unleashed a bevy of inappropriate insults at Cosell, "For the first time in broadcast history, you've got an audience rooting for Howard Cosell."

So when a celebrity guest visited ABC's broadcast booth during the Monday Night Miracle and turned into an all-knowing soothsayer to boot, it was no surprise and it just symbolized how strange, bizarre, and memorable that game would truly become.

Arnold Schwarzenegger, chatting with Al Michaels, Dan Fouts, and Dennis Miller to promote his latest movie, had complete faith in the Jets even though they were being destroyed every which way down on the field. Down by 20-plus points? With the Jets showing no inkling of a comeback in the making? That didn't deter the Terminator from not counting out Gang Green. "Wayne Chrebet is going to pull it off. I think as usual the Jets are going to come from behind, you will see...I think the Dolphins have to be terminated." When Chrebet scored the tying touchdown to even the score at 30–30, Schwarzenegger looked liked a genius. Maybe Arnold really does come from the future.

CHAPTER 10

RICHARD TODD AND THE BATTLE OF THE MUD PEOPLE

IT ALL ENDED IN THE MUDDY SLOP of the Orange Bowl on January 23, 1983. The Jets' first chance for a Super Bowl appearance since their stirring, historic victory over the Colts in 1969 came to a grinding halt in the swampy Florida muck. But the road to the 1982 AFC Championship Game began in 1976.

With rabid Jets fans in attendance on draft day, holding up signs reading, "Don't blow it, take Todd #1," NFL Commissioner Pete Rozelle pointed to the animated members of Jets Nation and announced, "You got it. The Jets on the first round select Richard Todd, quarterback from Alabama." The fans wanted another University of Alabama product as the heir apparent to the legend whom they had embraced the previous 11 seasons, and they got their man.

Todd hired Joe Namath's agent, who secured him a Namath-like five-year, $605,000 contract, and the comparisons to Broadway Joe began. Unfortunately for Todd, they never ended. Todd stated that coming to the Jets and replacing Namath was a dream come true, but there was no way he could have known what he was getting himself into. His teammates dangled him upside down from a sixth-floor Hempstead window during a training-camp rookie hazing ritual, and most of his tenure with the Jets must have felt just as dizzying and frightening.

The two quarterbacks split time during that 1976 season, with Namath starting eight games and Todd six. When the aging star went out to Los Angeles to play for the Rams, he handed the car keys to Todd. The Jets were all his. "When I came to New York, I was in awe and scared to death of the city," he said. "First of all, Namath was here. There were things I never had, like Chinese food and French food and all that. But hanging around Joe was fun."

The fun didn't last long, though, as the Alabama native struggled to find any kind of success, and the sentence "Richard Todd is no Joe Namath" became a local catchphrase. Even though his predecessor was in California and then subsequently retired after the 1977 season, Todd was constantly haunted by the Ghost of Joe Willie Namath. Every time Richard Todd's name was mentioned, the name of Joe Namath soon followed. Everywhere Todd turned, there was Namath. Fans reminded him. Newspapers reminded him. When he turned on the TV, instead of seeing Walter Cronkite, there was Namath's visage staring back at him. Instead of Fonzie, it was Broadway Joe cruising through Milwaukee on a motorcycle. Instead of Captain Stubing doling out sage advice on an antic-filled cruise ship, it was Joe Willie. When Namath joined the Jets, he had no one to live up to, but Todd lived in the shadow of a hero who guaranteed a Super Bowl victory. And there was no escape.

For his first five seasons, Todd threw more interceptions than touchdowns every single year, with the lowlight of leading the league with 30 picks in 1980. One of the big mistakes he made was in trying to emulate his hero. His teammates noticed. Years later, Bruce Harper told 1240 WGBB's Sports Radio New York, "Richard

Todd was a really good quarterback. I think it was just difficult for him coming from Alabama after Joe Namath, going to the same team that Joe Namath went to. You know, the expectations were very high. I think had he played his own game, if he was trying to be himself, it would have helped a lot more."

Wesley Walker concurred. "I think his biggest problem was that he followed in Joe Namath's footsteps and tried to be kind of like him instead of just being Richard Todd," Walker said. "For him to come from a wishbone quarterback and become a drop-back passer, he certainly improved at that and became a player, but— and I'm sure he'll be the first one to tell you—if you don't have the coaching around you, you're never going to flourish, and that can hurt you."

When Namath's descendent failed to live up to his promise, the wrath of angry Jets fans rained down upon Todd like a hail storm out of the Apocalypse. The euphoric Jets fans of draft day turned into an angry mob, carrying pitchforks and torches. Things got so bad that Todd stopped leaving Shea with his wife at his side after games so she, too, wouldn't be pelted with trash. A frustrated Todd was caught on camera flipping off a group of Jets fans. "Sure the boos hurt me. I'm human, too. They would even boo me during the introductions," he stated. "I've caught a lot of abuse. Fans are unreasonable everywhere. Fans are fans. They expect you not to make any mistakes. But this is a humbling game we play. There are no supermen. There are great players, but no supermen."

The pressure slowly built up for Todd, and things erupted on November 4, 1981, when he attacked sportswriter Steve Serby of the *New York Post*. "About a month or six weeks earlier, I had written a column," Serby remembered. "The headline was, 'With Todd at Helm Jets Will Never Win Super Bowl,' or something like that. Obviously, I don't write the headlines, but that was the gist of it. He was very upset about it. We didn't talk for a month or six weeks, whatever it was. He also didn't like the fact that I was a supporter of Matt Robinson, who was the backup quarterback at the time. He was the guy that I felt was a better fit for that team.

"So Todd and I hadn't talked for a while, then one day, November 4, in the locker room, myself and Ed Ingles, who worked for CBS Radio at the time—apparently Todd was upset with him, as well—we went up to Todd and tried to patch things up. This was right before practice, and Todd wanted nothing to do with it. He and I engaged in an expletive-laced exchange. I was standing around 12, 15 feet away from him. I had my notebook at my side, and I had this feeling that he was going to charge me. And sure enough he did. He lunged at me, grabbed my neck with his right hand, pushed me backwards, and smashed my head into the locker of a wide receiver named Bobby Jones, who was already out on the practice field I believe. I slumped to the bottom of the locker. I must have been out for a few seconds because the next thing I remember was Mark Gastineau standing over me and saying, 'You better get to the hospital. It looks like you broke your nose.'

"It turned out I didn't break my nose, but I was pretty shaken up. I was driven to the Nassau County Medical Center, I believe it was, which is right near Hofstra where the Jets used to train. They examined me, and they sent me home. The *Post* kept me off the beat for the next two weeks because they filed a civil suit against the Jets, but the Nassau County D.A., Denis Dillon, ruled against the *Post*. I went back to work two weeks later. The Jets played a game in Cleveland about a month later, and I remember Todd and I shook hands after that game. Now he never apologized. He never apologized to me, but we shook hands and we didn't have a problem after that."

The sensitive Todd felt that local sportswriters should be supportive instead of constantly in attack mode. "They should be for you," he said. "I'm sorry I lost my temper like that, but there comes a time when you can only take so much. I'm a moody person. I could understand bad things being written about me last year. Hell, I threw 30 interceptions. But when everything is negative, negative—well, there's only so much you can take."

Ironically, 1981 was the season that things started turning around for Todd and the Jets. At the time of the locker room throw down, the Jets' record was 4-4-1, but they won six of their last seven to finish 10-5-1, which was the first winning record for the Jets, and the first time the team qualified for the playoffs, since 1969. The Sack Exchange spearheaded the defense, while Walker, Harper, and Freeman McNeil teamed up with Todd to form a dangerous, electrifying offense. The malicious Todd-hating Jets fans were now waving "Todd Is God" banners in the Shea Stadium stands. Todd's interceptions dwindled all the way down to 13 as he tossed 25 touchdown passes and completed 56.1 percent of his passes.

The highlight of the season came in Week 12 in a first-place showdown with Miami. Todd had cracked a rib in the previous week's game, a win over New England, and he had sprained his ankle in the second quarter of the Miami game, which made it difficult for him to plant his leg while unleashing a pass. Before the game, he took an injection to deaden the pain in his side, and he wore a Casco Rib Protector and Byron Donzis Flak Jacket.

With 3:10 left in the game, the Dolphins held a 15-9 lead, but the Jets had one more chance to score seven points. As Todd hobbled onto the field for the final drive of the game, starting at the Jets' 23-yard line, the old comparisons to Namath popped up again. But this time they were positive. Jerome Barkum, who played with both quarterbacks, said, "Oh yes, I was thinking of Joe. I was thinking about how many times I saw him come out on that field hurting. The way Richard's head was down, the way he hunched over, that reminded me of Joe. It took me back. Joe playing on those busted-up knees of his, Richard playing today with the broken rib and the bad ankle—those things take courage."

While Namath called his own plays, Todd took his orders from the sidelines. But he was Namath-esque in leading his team downfield with not a second to spare. He completed six passes to six different players, getting his team to the Dolphin 11-yard line with 16 seconds left on the clock. For the finale, tight-end Barkum was split left with two receivers on the right. The play was called 45-Option. Barkum tore across the middle, caught Todd's bullet, and the game was tied. Pat Leahy added the extra point, giving the Jets a 16–15 victory.

Coach Walt Michaels said of his persecuted quarterback, "He played in pain, and he pulled it out for us. I looked at his face every time he came off the field, and there wasn't one time I saw an unusual expression on it—except for a win look. What's a win look? It's something Namath had, something all the good ones seem to have. I think this game will be a milestone in his career."

The Jets beat Green Bay on the last day of the season to finish in second place and earn a wild card berth in the playoffs. After the victory over the Packers, Joe Klecko declared, "We're a big, grown-up football team now." Their season ended a week later when, after falling behind the Bills 24–0, the Jets stormed back but ultimately came up short 31–27. In a bit of foreshadowing, a Richard Todd pass intended for Derrick Gaffney was intercepted at the Buffalo 2-yard line with just a few seconds left to seal the win for the Bills. But that season proved that the New York Jets were finally more than just Joe Namath.

Richard Todd and the Jets continued their resurgence in 1982. They seemingly had it all—in the shortened nine-game season, Todd again threw more touchdowns (14) than interceptions (eight) and sported a 58.6 completion percentage, while Freeman McNeil (a league-leading 786 rushing yards), Wesley Walker (39 receptions,

620 yards, six touchdowns), and Mark Gastineau (six sacks) all went to the Pro Bowl. The offense finished third in points and fourth in yards gained, while the defense was 10th in points allowed but sixth in yards given up. They had a quarterback coming into his own, a top ground game, an aerial attack that rivaled any in the NFL, the Sack Exchange (though Klecko missed the final seven games due to an injury), Lance Mehl and Greg Buttle at linebacker—it may have been the most talented Jets team yet.

Their 6–3 mark qualified them for the postseason. The Jets faced the 7–2 Cincinnati Bengals in the opening round, and just like the previous year against Buffalo, they quickly fell behind 14–3. But they stuck to their game plan of daring Pro Bowl quarterback Ken Anderson, whose league-leading 70.6 completion percentage was mainly due to a short passing game, to beat them with the long ball. The plan worked to perfection. The Bengals could only manage a field goal the rest of the way, as Anderson was sacked four times, picked off three times, and knocked out of the game twice.

Meanwhile, the dangerous Jets offense exploded for four touchdowns and two field goals in the final three quarters, and safety Darrol Ray scored on a 98-yard interception return, giving the Jets a resounding 44–17 victory. Walker caught eight passes for 145 yards and reached the end zone once, while the well-balanced offense was on display as McNeil ran for 202 yards and not only rushed for a touchdown but threw one as well on an option play. Todd completed 20 passes on 28 attempts for 269 yards with a touchdown. He wasn't intercepted, nor was he sacked. McNeil called his quarterback "a great man and a great general."

The following week, the Jets won a slugfest against the Raiders 17–14. Walker (seven catches, 169 yards, and a touchdown), McNeil (101 yards), and the defense (two sacks, three interceptions—two by Mehl) starred again, while Todd acted as the consummate leader, hanging in against a brutally tough Los Angeles defense.

The Jets were rewarded with a trip to Miami for the AFC Championship Game. Of the four remaining quarterbacks, Todd was the leader in playoff passing yardage while Walker was the most productive receiver. The Jets had speed coming out of the backfield, speed at the receiver position, and even speed on defense. Although they had lost both of their games to the Dolphins in 1982, the Jets were 7–0–1 against their rivals in the previous four seasons, so they were in no way intimidated by Miami. There wasn't anything that could stop the 1982 Jets. Well, there was one three-letter word that proved to be their kryptonite—*mud*.

On January 22, 1983, it rained in Miami, Florida. And the following day, it continued to rain. And all the while the Orange Bowl field remained uncovered. There wasn't a tarp in sight. Walker had a premonition that this wouldn't be the Jets' day. "I do remember waking up and it was like a monsoon. And I always look out of my window to see how the day's going to be, and when I woke up and it was like a monsoon, I said, 'Oh my God.' This changes the whole complexion of the game. I'm a receiver. You know we're going to change; we're going to run the ball. Then it becomes a game of field position and turnovers."

After 24 hours of rain, the field was a mess, with mud, puddles, and ooze as far as the eye could see. The game might as well have been played in the Okefenokee Swamp. The Dolphins insisted the field didn't need a tarp. Stadium manager Walt Golby said, "It's not necessary on this type of field." And he reassuringly added, "Look, I just inherited this job."

Jets president Jim Kensil was furious. "The Orange Bowl doesn't even own a tarp, and the league bylaws say that every facility has to have one," he said. "A tarp costs about $4,000. The Orange Bowl people said that their Prescription Athletic Turf has pumps that

Jets quarterback Richard Todd is taken down by Dolphins Kim Bokamper during the second half of the AFC Championship Game on January 24, 1983. Todd was intercepted five times as the Dolphins won 14–0. (AP Images)

suck out the water, but they didn't get the job done today. We could have brought our own tarps down from New York if we'd known. They said that a tarp would kill the grass underneath, but I'd rather play on dirt than this stuff."

The league handed out a release in the press box stating, "Based on the amount of rain already fallen, if the rain was to stop at 12:00 noon most of the surface water would be gone in two hours." Even though Commissioner Rozelle demanded that the rain end by noon, it turned out he wasn't quite that powerful, as Mother Nature had a mind of her own and it kept right on raining throughout the game.

Groundskeepers swept off the field using squeegees before kickoff, but all that accomplished was to turn the sidelines into a lake. A good old-fashioned game of mud football is usually a thrilling prospect, but not when a conference championship is on the line.

The game kicked off as scheduled, and the Mud Bowl got underway. If Jets fans looked up to the heavens and pleaded with God to send them a sign that this would finally be their lucky day, the sign they received was not one to their liking. On the Jets' initial possession, Lam Jones ran a down-and-in pattern, and Todd's very first pass was picked off by Glenn Blackwood.

With the Dolphins keying on Walker, Todd targeted Jones for most of the day. He threw Walker's way once in the first half, while he attempted six passes to Jones, only completing three. Miami's defensive guru, Bill Arnsparger, who was the mastermind of the Dolphins' No-Name Defense Super Bowl teams of the previous decade, mapped out a strategy that took advantage of the poor playing conditions.

"The bump. Jones wasn't used to getting that bump on the line of scrimmage," said Dolphin cornerback Don McNeal. "It bothered him. That's one thing Coach Arnsparger stresses every day. Get that good jam when a guy starts his pattern. It's especially effective on a muddy field. It makes a receiver slip and it throws his timing off, getting into his pattern. When a cornerback plays 7 yards off, then the receiver has an advantage on a muddy day because the defensive guy's the one who's gonna slip."

In the first half, the Jets offense couldn't get anything going. In fact, they could only make it past the 50-yard line once all game without help from the defense. But Miami's offense was just as feeble, since Gang Green's defense was playing at a championship-quality level. The game was predictably scoreless at halftime. Though neither team was making any headway on the scoreboard, the two teams weren't fumbling the ball away, either. Sure, Todd and Dolphins quarterback David Woodley kept throwing the ball to the wrong team, but neither offense was capitalizing.

The key play in the second half, and possibly the game, was a fumble that wasn't fumbled. Miami was in the midst of a drive that started at the Jets' 48-yard line when Pro Bowl fullback Andra Franklin lost the ball. The Jets recovered, and it looked like this would be the turning point they were waiting for. It *was* a turning point, but things turned the wrong way as the refs ruled that Franklin didn't fumble after all. Miami kept possession of the ball and completed a seven-play drive that was helped by a penalty called on cornerback Bobby Jackson, who protested a Miami completion. Former Jet Woody Bennett sloshed into the end zone from the 7-yard line to give Miami a 7–0 lead.

As the fourth quarter got underway, Miami's defense kept thwarting Todd, forcing him to throw over the middle by disguising their coverages and then swooping in for another interception. The Jets defense, though, was stymieing Woodley with just as much success. But Todd's arch nemesis that day, linebacker A.J. Duhe, provided the backbreaker when he picked off his third pass of the game and ran it back 35 yards for a touchdown.

"I was in a down-lineman position, rushing from left defensive end," Duhe said. "I wasn't getting anywhere on my rush, and then I saw Bruce Harper take that little hitch that he does when he's going to drift out wide. I saw Todd look downfield and then look back to Harper, so I drifted out with him. I jumped for the ball, and it hit me in the hands or the forearm or something. I saw it falling, I bobbled it, then I had it and I was gone. [Bob] Baumhower was yelling, 'Lateral it! Lateral it!' but I wouldn't."

The final score was 14–0. The Jets wouldn't get this close to a Super Bowl for another 16 years. After a scintillating playoff run,

Walker caught one measly pass with 1:25 remaining in the game for zero yards. Jones had three receptions and Barkum only two. McNeil got stuck in the mud, gaining 46 yards on 17 carries. The offense only produced two plays that went for more than 10 yards and gained a less-than-impressive 139 total net yards on the day. And Todd? He completed 15 passes in 37 attempts, threw for 103 yards, rushed for 10, and was sacked four times. And he tossed five interceptions.

Not everybody blamed the quarterback, though. "I remember our defense picked up a fumble, we recovered, but they gave it back to Miami," Walker said. "I remember if we got that fumble we probably would have scored. It was just things like that, despite Richard Todd's turnovers. But we still had a chance to really win this game. I think I caught one pass toward the end of the game, and I was just so disappointed. But I just remember waking up to it being rain soaked. It wasn't Richard Todd's fault. I just know we were going to change the whole complexion of the game because we're just going to be a different type of team. And it couldn't have been more positive for Miami because we could run and we could throw. But under those field conditions it was going to detract from what we do best. It just worked in Miami's favor. And we just played one of our worst games ever, despite those conditions. But two teams [were] playing in the same conditions and there [are] no excuses. But it's one of those memories where you only get so many opportunities. I played 13 years, and we'd been to the playoffs multiple times, but we had two times where we had a chance to go to the Super Bowl and we blew it. It was very disheartening."

The Jets fielded two different teams that day. While the offense was woeful, the defense played courageously. Gastineau sacked Woodley twice, Marty Lyons and Kenny Neil each recorded a sack, Buttle intercepted a pass, and safety Ken Schroy picked off two

Jets running back Freeman McNeil carries the ball against the Miami Dolphins during the 1982 AFC Championship game, often referred to as the Mud Bowl due to the condition of the field at Miami's Orange Bowl. McNeil ran for just 46 yards in the loss after totaling 303 rushing yards in the Jets' first two playoff games.
(Focus on Sport/Getty Images)

passes. Schroy said of the discrepancy, "You stop 'em and stop 'em and force turnovers, and it doesn't get you anywhere. Maybe our offense didn't play up to its capacity, maybe they didn't make the right adjustments. Something was wrong out there."

Is it any consolation for Todd that his Dolphin counterpart was almost as ineffective as he was? Woodley tossed three picks of his own, without any touchdown passes, and went a poor 9-for-21 for 87 yards in the air. And does it make any difference that in their previous playoff game a week earlier, this same Miami defense intercepted Hall of Fame quarterback Dan Fouts five times, as well? The Charger's line reads eerily similar to Todd's: 15-for-34, 191 yards, one touchdown, five interceptions. Todd was understandably terse after the game. "They beat us, period. They deserve to go to the Super Bowl, and that's all I'm going to say."

The big mystery of the game was this: Did the Dolphins purposely let the rain turn the field into a bog to slow down the Jets' high-powered offensive attack? While Jets president Kensil was enraged after the fact, no Jets official made provisions for the field to be covered beforehand. They took the Dolphins' word that the field would be in acceptable condition. No Jets player used the marshy conditions as an excuse for the loss, though. Buttle simply stated, "It was muddy for both teams."

When asked if Miami was up to any subterfuge and slopped up the field to slow down the speedy Jets, Harper answered, "That's what people say. I don't know if it's true or not, but it sure did seem like it." Walker gave the Dolphins a little credit. "It doesn't really matter if they did. If it was purposely done, they would have been smart to do that. I know I would have done it to slow us down or whatever. There were always these rumors. But that was smart on their part if they did flood that field." After the game, Michaels didn't want to talk. "Look, I'm not a wealthy s.o.b. I can't afford the fines."

The 1982 Jets almost made it to the Promised Land. They were one rainy day away from a Super Bowl, but soon after, they had the rug pulled out from under them—Walt Michaels was fired. He led the Jets to their best season since the glory days of Super Bowl III, and in place of a raise, he got canned. The move was mysterious and controversial, though some of the reasoning was due to Michaels' willingness to name names (Don Shula) and ask the Dolphins what they knew and when they knew it regarding the lack of a tarp on the Orange Bowl field.

The firing certainly took the players by surprise. Walker said of his first coach, "Loved him. The problem with Walt, and I tell him to this day, I love him, and when you sit down with him, he's very knowledgeable, and he knows the game. But he didn't come across sometimes as being real knowledgeable and as a player's type of guy. We have this conversation, 'You're very pleasurable to be around.' You have a different feeling for him. Because there were guys who were glad to see him go. Sometimes Walt could be very standoffish and quiet, and he didn't come off being very knowledgeable. He had this demeanor about him; it wouldn't be very pleasurable and so you didn't know how to really judge him."

The early 1980s Jets had talent up and down the roster but just couldn't quite reach the top of the mountain. Despite Harper's take that it "was a real close team," Walker felt otherwise. "We weren't together as teammates, as a family. There were prejudices, there were cliques, guys didn't hang out with each other. And when I got drafted—I'm from Berkeley, I'm like a black hippie, I love everybody—the guys were separate. Prejudice, jealousy, and I can't believe this is happening. And I think that's what really kept us from being together as a team and being more successful."

The next year, the Jets fell to 7–9, which was also Todd's final season in New York. He may have finally learned to be comfortable in his own skin, but it was probably too late. "I don't worry about my image anymore," he said. "I found out when I was trying to please everybody that I was making myself unhappy. And I learned I can't be concerned with people who come to games to scream and boo and cheer and drink." He again was back to throwing more interceptions (26) than touchdowns (18), and he was traded to the Saints after the season. He spent two years in New Orleans before retiring.

When Richard Todd came to New York, he embraced the role of being Joe Namath's successor. But he ultimately spent eight seasons with the Jets trying to wiggle his way out of Broadway Joe's shadow. Namath threw 215 interceptions in his 12 seasons with the Jets while tossing 170 touchdown passes. Like his hero, Todd also had more passes picked off (138) than he threw for touchdowns (110). While Todd had a higher completion percentage in his Jets career than Namath did, 54.6 to 50.2, and won the same amount of postseason games (two), Namath's defining moment was the unbelievable Super Bowl III victory. Todd's was the disappointing loss in the Mud Bowl.

As for his contentious relationship with the press, he said, "I wish I was more patient with the media. But being a quarterback in New York isn't easy." And though Jets fans were relentless in their negative feelings toward Todd, he wanted to win them over, as he said in the summer of 1983. "The fact is, I'm lucky. If I leave this earth tomorrow, it has been a blast. But I've always wanted to stick it out and show the New York fans they were wrong about me. Being a survivor is what's important."

Richard Todd was in the wrong place at the wrong time. He should have been anywhere else but New York and followed any quarterback but Joe Namath. He joined a losing team and was thrown into a no-win situation from day one. But despite those long odds, along with never-ending criticism and nonstop booing, Todd led the Jets to a conference championship game. Unfortunately, the worst game of his career came in the biggest game of his career. When his football days were over, he turned philosophical. "If I could do it all over again, maybe I'd be a backup quarterback. Everybody likes them."

CHAPTER 11

I AIN'T GOT NO HOME

I ain't got no home, No place to roam
I ain't got a home, No place to roam
I'm a lonely boy, I ain't got a home

I ain't got no sister, I ain't got a brother
I ain't got a father, Not even a mother
I'm a lonely boy, I ain't got a home
                    — Clarence "Frogman" Henry

THE NEW YORK JETS (NEE TITANS) were like stray dogs from the very beginning. Or maybe orphans is more like it. They've been wandering through New York and New Jersey for five decades in search of a home to call their own.

When they first emerged, they were plopped down in the orphanage that was the Polo Grounds. It was a home for the abandoned as it was abandoned itself. After four years surviving on mush and gruel, they were taken in by a nice family named the Mets in the modern split level of Shea Stadium. A period of peace and bliss ensued, but cracks were found in the foundation, family troubles ensued, and the house began to fall apart. Resentment crept in, as they weren't a blood relative and were made to wait outside after school because they weren't trusted with a key of

173

their own, nor could they enter the abode without permission. They moved on to a foster home in East Rutherford, New Jersey. The place was nice, warm, and safe (though a little windy), and they were given three meals a day, but it was never really theirs. They never truly felt at home. Finally, they got an apartment of their own, but they had to suffer the indignity of having to share it with their foster brother.

Thus has been the fate of the Jets. They've been living their own version of *The Odyssey* in constant pursuit of a residence where they can feel comfortable and at home. When the New York Titans joined the AFL in 1960, they were relegated to playing their home games in the decaying Polo Grounds. It was vacated by the New York Football Giants, who moved across the river to Yankee Stadium in 1956, while the New York Baseball Giants fled to San Francisco following the 1957 season. The stadium was old and crumbling, it was in a neighborhood that wouldn't be featured in *Better Homes and Gardens,* and it couldn't draw flies. Actually flies were all it could draw. But the one feature it did have was the absence of another tenant. The years 1960 and 1961 were the only two seasons that the Jets/Titans have ever had a stadium to themselves. It may have been a dilapidated, ramshackle dump, but it was their dilapidated, ramshackle dump.

The version of the stadium up in Harlem that the Titans called home was actually the fourth edition of the Polo Grounds. The original was built in 1876 for the sport of polo and was located at 110th Street between Fifth and Sixth avenues. It was referred to in the lowercase "the polo grounds," but eventually uppercased its way into its proper name. Baseball's New York Giants began playing there in 1883. Football was also a minor presence, as Yale hosted a few of their games at the uptown site.

In 1889, the powers that be in New York City decided to extend 111th Street, which would cut right into the grounds. That meant that a second Polo Grounds was needed. Version two of the park, and all future ones as well, was located at 155th Street and Eighth Avenue. The Polo Grounds II was temporary until the Polo Grounds III was ready, with the second version being renamed Manhattan Field and the new version Brotherhood Park, which opened for business in 1890.

A fire raged through the grandstands in 1911, which meant yet another version of the park had to be built. The Polo Grounds: The Final Version ("This Time We Mean It") reopened later that year and also regained its Polo Grounds moniker once again. The Giants attempted to call it Brush Stadium, after owner John Brush, but the people of New York wouldn't fall for it and the somewhat awkward yet unique Polo Grounds name stuck.

Football's New York Giants were born in 1925 and settled in the Polo Grounds for 31 seasons. The Yankees were temporary tenants from 1913 to 1922. And the Mets also played there in 1962 and '63. But in 1960, the Titans had it to themselves—and with a lack of fans attending their games, they were almost truly alone.

They debuted on September 11, 1960, and defeated the Buffalo Bills 27–3. The Titans/Jets' home-field advantage was slight with a record at the Polo Grounds of 14–13–1 in four seasons. Their final game was played on December 14, 1963, also against Buffalo. The Bills defeated the newly named Jets 19–10. Don Maynard scored the last home-team touchdown on a 73-yard pass from Galen Hall. Dick Guesman put the final Jets' points on the board with a 17-yard field goal. And the last points in a football game at the Polo Grounds fittingly came on a safety when Hall was tackled in the end zone for Buffalo's last two points of the game. The Titans/Jets did not reach the playoffs in their years at 155th Street.

With the 1964 season came the arrival of the new, state-of-the-art Shea Stadium. And the Jets would enter a whole new world, a new dimension they had never experienced when they

175

unloaded their moving van in Queens. Changes began percolating the previous season when Sonny Werblin bought the Titans and renamed them the Jets in anticipation of the move into their new digs just a Curley Johnson punt away from LaGuardia Airport. He also hired Weeb Ewbank as coach. Ewbank had led the Baltimore Colts to two NFL titles in 1958 and '59 and brought instant credibility to the struggling AFL franchise.

Shea Stadium was built to bring National League baseball back to New York City, but it did have football in mind. In an example of the modern world gone innovation-crazy, field-level seats for the expressed purpose of being used for a football game were stored underneath the permanent stands and were located on underground tracks that could be rolled out on football Sundays. Plans were made to fill in the upper decks so that Shea could hold 90,000 fans, and a dome was also proposed. Both ideas were scrapped, though, and Shea remained as it was.

The team had a new home, a new name, a new coach, a new identity, and a new popularity. After four years playing under a black cloud and keeping their fingers crossed that their home stadium wouldn't collapse around them, the Jets began a new era. And Shea was hugely instrumental in transforming the team and its image. It was not just a place to hang their helmets, though—it was a paradise. From the beginning fans came in droves. After drawing fewer than 5,000 fans to many of their games in the ancient Polo Grounds, they were now bringing in upwards of 60,000 supporters. Of course it was noisy, with jets flying overhead throughout each game, but that just added to the unique ambiance, and it was thematically copasetic with the team's new name and image.

The Jets christened the stadium on September 12, 1964. While the fans were going crazy for Wahoo McDaniel, the team pounded the Broncos 30–6 with Jets tight end Gene Heeter scoring the first touchdown in the stadium's history, a 16-yard pass from Dick

The Shea Stadium crowd looks on as Jets receiver Don Maynard advances the ball upfield during a September 1965 game against the Kansas City Chiefs. (Olen Collection/ Diamond Images/Getty Images)

Wood. Denver's Gene Mingo kicked the first field goal, a 32-yarder through the uprights. Jim Turner chimed in with three field goals of his own. Don Maynard scored on a 39-yard pass from Wood. And the final points were put on the board with a 5-yard touchdown run by a promising rookie making his professional debut.

Helping to kick-start the Shea Stadium era was the Jets' first-round draft pick, Matt Snell, who gained 82 yards on 22 carries in his and the stadium's initial game. In only his fifth professional game, he gained a team-record 180 yards vs. the Oilers at Shea and went on to win the Rookie of the Year award and earn All-Star honors, racking up 948 yards, which was good for second in the league. His crowning achievement, of course, came in Super Bowl III. Joe Namath won the MVP, but it was Snell's 121 rushing yards that were the key to the game. Snell made three AFL All-Star teams and was a first-team All-AFLer in 1969. Unfortunately, he was plagued by injuries for much of his career, battling constant knee problems and a ruptured Achilles tendon. He finished his career with 4,285 yards and 24 rushing touchdowns. And in a footnote to entertainment history, he appeared in the first Miller Lite commercial, setting a trend for retired athletes everywhere.

Snell was the Jets' first Shea Stadium star, along with fan favorite McDaniel. Namath would arrive in Year 2, and a Super Bowl would be won in the fifth season, with the AFL Championship Game being the first playoff game to be played in Queens. (They beat the Mets to the postseason by nine and a half months.) The Jets would host only two more playoff games in their time at Shea—a 1969 playoff loss to the Chiefs and a 1981 wild card defeat to Buffalo. Both games ended with a Jets quarterback throwing an interception. Down 13–6 to Kansas City, Namath (14-for-40 in the game) doomed the defending champions when he tossed his third pick of the game, dashing his team's hopes of a Super Bowl repeat. It was Namath's last playoff appearance. Twelve years later, a Richard Todd interception sealed a 31–27 win for the Bills.

Shea Stadium and the Jets reached a pinnacle on October 5, 1968, when a then-AFL record 63,786 fans witnessed Emerson Boozer score a last-minute touchdown to beat San Diego 23–20. Unfortunately, the Jets' home in Queens saw just as many highlights for the opposition as it did for the home team. In Weeb Ewbank's final game at the helm of Gang Green, on December 16, 1973, Buffalo Bill O.J. Simpson ran wild in a snowstorm for 200 yards on 34 carries, which gave him a then-record 2,003 yards for the season, helping his team to a 34–14 victory. If that wasn't bad enough for the Jets, Simpson's backup, Jim Braxton, gained 98 yards on the ground himself. Ewbank finished his Jets career with a 71–77–6 record—but he never attempted to elude the police while riding in a white Ford Bronco as the record-setter who spoiled the coach's finale did.

After the initial utopian period with record crowds, unparalleled popularity, and a championship season, the Jets' last decade at Shea would not go as smoothly. Their downward spiral on the field of play coupled with their heavy-handed landlord, the New York Mets, who did not care to have them as their tenant, made the 1970s an unhappy time for the franchise. To make matters worse, they had to shove over and make room for two more occupants in 1975, as the stadium became awfully crowded when four New York teams used it as their home—the Mets, Jets, Yankees, and Giants. The Yankees were in their second year in Queens as they awaited the renovation of Yankee Stadium to be completed. And after playing their home games at the Yale Bowl in 1974, the Giants temporarily moved to Flushing the following year.

One Jet who had mixed feelings about playing at Shea was Wesley Walker. "It wasn't really our own stadium, but I felt we had more identity there because it was right in Queens and it was still New York and it was closer to home, and we did have a home," he said. "But I felt like it wasn't our stadium because we shared it with the Mets. I had met a bunch of the guys that were really good friends of mine. I still remember meeting Tommie Agee and the coach Frank Howard. There were friends of mine that were there, but we shared that stadium. And then during the preseason, we're playing, and half the field would be covered in baseball dirt, and I never liked that. But we still didn't have our own stadium, and that did bother me."

Bruce Harper was more adamantly positive in his outlook toward Shea. "Shea Stadium was home," he said. "That was home, you know. We really had a home-field advantage with the planes going overhead and the wind coming off the water and the stands. Boy, those stands used to rock. And the fact that it was a baseball field—the Mets played on it—the grass, the turf was gorgeous. It was beautiful. It was just wonderful to run on it, of course after they took up the baseball diamond. That was really, really home. We had our own and complete identity."

The most oppressive aspect of the Jets' lease was the Mets' right to have complete control over Shea during the summer and

Introducing Broadway Joe: Namath Makes Debut at Shea Stadium

Joe Namath came to the Jets as the $427,000 man. That may seem like a paltry sum in today's sports world, but in 1965 that amount was a pro football record. The NFL's St. Louis Cardinals drafted him with the 12th pick, while the AFL's Jets made him the league's first overall selection. (The Jets acquired the rights to negotiate with Namath in a trade with Houston.) After a bidding war, Namath chose the higher offer, which included a $225,000 bonus, a $7,000 Lincoln Continental, a $25,000 salary for three years, and no-cut and no-trade clauses. The battle for the star quarterback from the University of Alabama was an impetus for the two leagues' shared draft and ultimately led to the merger between the NFL and AFL.

New York, of course, was made for Broadway Joe, but his decision to go there wasn't based on his visions of the high life in the Big City. "I didn't know enough about New York at the time to like it or dislike it, and I didn't know anything about St. Louis. If I'd known then what I know now, I would have taken the Jets' offer even if it had been smaller, but back in 1964, when the two clubs started bidding, I just made up my mind that I was going to accept the better offer."

When he arrived in training camp, his teammates were wary of their young, rich quarterback. After getting the cold shoulder from many of the veterans, Namath stood up in a players-only meeting and asked them to judge him by his play on the field and not by the size of his bank account. Once they saw that he worked as hard as they did, he was accepted. Two of his fellow Jets that season were rookie receiver George Sauer and veteran Don Maynard.

early fall. The Jets were forbidden to use the stadium until the Mets played their final game, which meant starting every year on the road and sometimes not playing their first home game until well into the season.

While the 1969 Miracle Mets were captivating a nation with their World Series run, they were also keeping the Jets out of New York. After five games on the road, the Jets finally made their debut at home that season on October 20. Things were even worse in 1973

All through training camp, Namath worked with both. Maynard practiced with the rookie quarterback, relentlessly going over pass routes hour after hour—5 yards, 15 yards, 20 yards—building a chemistry and foundation that would last for eight seasons.

The Jets lost their season opener to the Oilers 27–21 with Mike Taliaferro taking all the snaps. In their second game—on September 18, 1965, against the Chiefs—Taliaferro again started. But in the second quarter, after only completing four passes in 12 attempts for 24 yards, Taliaferro was replaced by Namath, who jogged onto the Shea Stadium turf for the first time. The Jets were losing 7–3, and in the fourth quarter they'd fall behind by a 14–3 score.

But all the hard work Namath and Maynard put in over the summer paid dividends for the first of many times that afternoon. With New York driving and on Kansas City's 37-yard line, Maynard took control of the huddle. The strong-willed receiver told his quarterback exactly where he'd be and when and how to throw the ball. And it worked like a charm. Namath took the snap, Maynard ran a quick out pattern to the left, and the rookie quarterback fired the ball, hitting his receiver in stride. Maynard turned up the field and raced into the end zone. Broadway Joe had his first touchdown, and it was only fitting that Maynard was on the receiving end.

The Jets lost the game 14–10 with Namath completing 11 of 23 passes for 121 yards. His (and the team's) first win wouldn't come until Week 7 in a 45–10 romp over the Broncos, with Namath and Taliaferro again splitting time. The Jets finished with a 5–8–1 record, but Joe Willie Namath was named the AFL's Rookie of the Year, and his path to stardom had begun.

when the Mets were "Ya Gotta Believe-ing" their way to the seventh game of the World Series against the Oakland A's. The Jets began that season with six consecutive road games, not playing at Shea until October 28. They had already dug themselves a huge hole with a 2–4 record before being able to sleep in their own beds the night before a game. It wasn't until 1978, after a court decision ruled in the Jets' favor, that Shea's football tenant didn't have to wait until the Mets went home for the winter to unpack their bags and stay a while.

The Mets also didn't care for the revolutionary mobile stands, which tore up the playing field. And adding to the discontent of the Jets was the decline of Shea Stadium itself. With every passing year, it was becoming more and more like the Polo Grounds, with plumbing and drainage issues galore, not to mention the bitter, swirling winds that often made for Siberia-like conditions. The Mets' tyrannical rule over their tenant finally drove the Jets away.

The Jets' 20th season at Shea was also their last. The final game came on December 10, 1983, against the Pittsburgh Steelers (which was, coincidentally, the last game of Terry Bradshaw's NFL career). Pittsburgh blew out the Jets 34–7. Lam Jones scored the final points for New York on a 27-yard touchdown pass from Pat Ryan. The last points at Shea came on an 18-yard Cliff Stoudt pass to Calvin Sweeney, with Gary Anderson kicking the extra point. When the game ended, fans stormed onto the field and ripped it to shreds. They tore down the goalposts, yanked up the turf, and went home with whatever they could get their hands on. It was a looting fest worthy of a blackout. If they could have walked away with the baseball dugouts or Freeman McNeil, they would have. And in a final farewell, the scoreboard read, "N.J. Jets."

The Jets were in search of a home yet again, and this time they would leave New York altogether. And with the move, their second-class citizenship was cemented when they decided to

Fans take down the goalposts at Shea Stadium after the Jets' final game at the ballpark, a 34–7 loss to Pittsburgh in December 1983. The Jets moved to New Jersey to play in the Meadowlands in 1984. (James Hughes/NY Daily News Archive via Getty Images)

camp out in Giants Stadium, another beyond-windy venue. They would spend 26 years suffering the indignity of not only playing their road games in another football team's stadium but their home games, as well. But at least they didn't have to wait until baseball season was completed to have home-field advantage.

Sharing a venue didn't have much of an affect on either the Jets or Giants players, though. "Sometimes we knew because we were going to go on the road, and we always came to the stadium and took a bus," Raul Allegre said. "We knew that they were going to be there the next day, but they didn't get there until Sunday. So we really didn't cross paths very much. We shared a stadium, but we didn't share a locker room. They had their own locker room, so they did their thing, we did ours. The fact that we shared a stadium was not an issue."

And as for the wind, the kicker stated, "After a while you figure it out. You just have to be smart about it. I knew where the ball was going to go. The key was just keeping an eye on whether the wind got worse after pregame. In pregame I would tell Parcells we need to have the ball on this yard line going this direction and this yard line going the other direction. You just have to pay attention to make sure that the wind didn't shift, and usually it didn't. I do remember one time the wind shifted but that was it. You knew your limits. You knew that going in one direction if you went past the range that you told the coach, chances were that you weren't going to make the kick."

Not every Jets player was thrilled with the move to the Garden State. If Walker was hazy about his fondness for his former home in Queens, he was unequivocal in his opinion of the Meadowlands: "I hated going to New Jersey, period. I hated going to see Giants Stadium, and I still hate the New Meadowlands Stadium. I live in Long Island, and I always practiced at Hofstra. I was hoping they would even get a stadium in Long Island. I wish we were in

Long Island somewhere. But we never had that, our own stadium. The one thing I did learn: It's not about the fans, it's not about the players—it's a business. They could give a crap about the players, the fans. This is business. When we moved to the Meadowlands, we weren't supposed to say anything. I mean I'd be hurt or you'd come home, it would take two, three hours to get home after a game. I hated it! We couldn't say anything bad or negative toward it. We just had to keep our mouths shut, and that was just the business aspect of it. But I hated it!"

There was talk of changing the name of Giants Stadium when the Jets joined their New York (now New Jersey) football brethren in East Rutherford, but a clause in the lease gave the Giants the final say in approving such a change. And they gave their final say. They said "no." During the Jets home games, there was an attempt to "green" up the stadium, but it was really just window dressing.

One of the outcomes of having two teams share a stadium, though, was that Giants Stadium would set the record for the venue with the most NFL games played. A more unfortunate result of the Jets' move to New Jersey was that many of their fans lived in Queens and Long Island and didn't want to travel far away to a neighboring state to watch their favorite team play. It took a few years, but the Jets finally started filling "the Meadowlands," as it would be known to non-Giants lovers, the way they packed Shea back in the '60s.

On September 6, 1984, in their 25th year of existence, the Jets took the field for their first game in their new home after beating the Colts 23–14 on opening day the previous week. That was the Colts' first game in *their* new home in Indianapolis after escaping Baltimore in the middle of the night. The Jets left Queens in plain daylight, though, with many witnesses, and they would be facing the Steelers once again to begin a new chapter in their gypsy-like history. And like the outcome of the final game at Shea, Pittsburgh would come out on top on this day at 23–17. Steelers receiver Louis Lipps scored the first touchdown on a 6-yard pass from Mud Bowl adversary David Woodley, while Walker would put the first Jets points on the scoreboard on a 14-yard touchdown reception from Ryan.

The Jets played the last game at the Meadowlands on January 3, 2010. (The Giants closed out their season on the road.) And the Jets went out in style, walloping the Cincinnati Bengals, 37–0. With the classy Walker scoring the first Jets points, it was only fitting that the last points came when the just-as-classy Thomas Jones reached the end zone on a 2-yard run. In those 26 seasons, the Jets qualified for the postseason nine times and hosted four games. In 1985, they lost to New England 26–14 but came out on top the next season when they crushed the Chiefs 35–15. They won their next two home playoff games, as well, defeating the Jacksonville Jaguars 34–24 in January 1999 and destroying the Colts 41–0 in January 2003.

For many of the years that the Jets called the Meadowlands their home, the team's unruly fans (hey, they're an unruly team) took part in an uncouth tradition that wouldn't quite be acceptable in a tearoom or while lining up to meet the Queen of England. But in a football stadium, after hours of tailgating? Well, that's a different story.

A few of the more ill-mannered and discourteous patrons, looking to entertain themselves at halftime, would throw a few bucks down a spiral walkway. And while poor, unsuspecting fans, who couldn't believe their luck—what's more lucky than found money?—bent over to pick up the small windfall, the money-tossers doused the far-from-lucky schmucks with beer. As the tradition became more well-known, fans began wearing raincoats, but that just caused the troublemakers to hurl their beer even harder. Eventually, that harassing behavior was not tolerated by the Jets organization, and the custom died out. The Jets may have had a few wild experiences of their own, but even they at times have tried to maintain a certain standard of decorum. And besides, why waste all that beer?

Another staple of the old and new Meadowlands has been Fireman Ed. Through the years and spanning the country, there have been many famous fans, from Crazy Ray in Dallas and Barrel Man in Denver to Chief Zee of the Redskins and even the New York Mets' Cow-Bell Man. But for the Jets, the No. 1 fan is Fireman Ed. Since 1986, Ed Anzalone has been hoisted on the shoulders of another fan (originally his brother Frank, but now friend Bruce Gregor) to lead the famous cheer of "J-E-T-S, Jets! Jets! Jets!" While he didn't originate that battle cry—it began as a who-can-say-it-louder chant between the two upper-level end zones—he inspires the crowd, picking his spots when the Jets need a jolt.

Fireman Ed has inserted himself into the headlines on occasion, having battles with the likes of Jason Taylor, Chad Ochocinco, and even a Giants fan in the first preseason game at the New Meadowlands. His fame has spread so far that he's part of the Hall of Fans section at the Pro Football Hall of Fame. Though not every Jets fan is enamored with him—some see him as a bit of a spotlight hog—he is entrenched in Jets lore.

In 2010, the Jets moved again, but they didn't have far to go or even have to leave for another state. Giants Stadium was destroyed and the New Meadowlands was born. And much like the previous move, an issue cropped up that affected fans in a negative way—namely Personal Seat Licenses. A PSL is a onetime fee that gives a fan the right to purchase a season ticket. He can pay the license in full or finance over the course of a few years. If said fan no longer wishes to buy a season ticket, he can sell his PSL or it will be forfeited back to the Jets without compensation.

No matter the spin by the team, PSLs were a form of punishment to a loyal fan base. Many fans that had been supporting the Jets for decades refused to be hijacked by the team and gave up their season tickets. Others just couldn't afford them anymore.

But on a positive note, this time, through the wonder of modern technology, the stadium truly would turn green. And the team would induct franchise greats into a Ring of Honor to give the place a more Jets-like feel. They still share the stadium with their big brother and some still refer to the venue as "Giants Stadium," but the name of the other team in town no longer hangs on the outside. After 50 years, the Jets finally—kind of, sort of—have a home to call their own.

CHAPTER 12

THE WILD, WILD WEST

AT 3 PM ON WEDNESDAY, OCTOBER 26, 1881, Wyatt Earp, his brothers, and Doc Holliday went down to the O.K. Corral to face off with the devious Clanton gang. The fiendish, black-hatted rustlers went for their guns, shots were fired, and a shootout commenced. Wyatt stayed as cool and calm as Joe Namath in the pocket facing Baltimore's blitz in Super Bowl III, and, like Broadway Joe, he lived to tell the tale of the most legendary gun battle in the Old West.

There's something romantic about a shootout, gunfight, or duel to the death. The stakes are high. The tension is oppressive. And at the end, the winner usually gets the girl while the loser lies bloodied and dead in the street. If the participants are famous and legendary, then it's all the better. And when it's over, drinks are usually on the house. Just like an NFL game. Except the NFL doesn't play on Wednesdays.

Countless movies were filmed about the Earp-Clanton confrontation, and whether you choose Henry Fonda in *My Darling Clementine* or Burt Lancaster in *Gunfight at the O.K. Corral,* what you'll find is a classic gunfight of the Old West, a duel that is worth telling over and over again. And what can be found on a football field in 1972 and 1986 are two more shootouts, two more tales worth passing down from generation to generation.

Joe Namath, resembling the wild-haired, unruly Clint Eastwood, once rode into Baltimore searching for the old gunfighter Johnny Unitas. Like John Wayne in *The Shootist,* Johnny U. was winding down his career and not looking for any trouble. Fourteen years later, the young Ken O'Brien battled an in-his-prime Dan Marino in an unforgettable epic duel. Which was better? Which was more memorable? Choosing between Namath-Unitas and O'Brien-Marino is like choosing between Henry Fonda and Burt Lancaster. The stories are the same, but the actors are just a little bit different.

Following are two classic Jets games featuring four gunslingers, which came right out of the Wild, Wild West.

1972

The 1972 World Series was billed as the Hairs vs. the Squares, when the mod, mustachioed Oakland Athletics defeated the clean-cut, tradition-filled Cincinnati Reds. But three weeks earlier, a similar battle took place in the NFL. The Jets traveled to Baltimore in a rematch of Super Bowl III. It wasn't the teams who were opposites, though, it was the quarterbacks.

Joe Namath was 29 years old by then and no longer the brash, young upstart taking the football world by storm. But with his white cleats, a fur coat, and a chick on each arm, he was still the antithesis of the crew-cut-sporting, black-high-top-wearing Johnny Unitas, who was 39 at the time. And let's face it, when you're looking at Johnny U., you're staring straight into the steely eyes of old school.

If Namath may not have been cutting-edge cool anymore, it was only because he was ahead of his time, as teammate Dave Herman explained. "It isn't Joe who has changed. It is the world that has changed toward Joe—or caught up with him. He used to be one of the only players with long hair, for instance. By now, he's one of the few players without a mustache."

Joe Namath stands on the Jets sideline in street clothes during a home game in the early 1970s. The quarterback struggled with injuries throughout the latter part of his career. (Focus on Sport/Getty Images)

The questions surrounding Unitas at the time were all about his age and arm. Namath's uncertainties, on the other hand, were never about his rifle of an arm, football IQ, or guts in the pocket. Instead, they centered on his fragile, rickety knees. Namath had only played a combined nine games the previous two seasons, but he would be healthy enough to start 13 contests in 1972. "He has so much nerve," said tight end Rich Caster. "He stays in that pocket, and you know those knees of his are like a light bulb, ready to crack any minute."

Like the Colts with Unitas, Namath's teammates basked in their quarterback's confidence and followed his unquestioned leadership. Emerson Boozer spent 10 years lining up behind Namath, so he was a firsthand witness to what his quarterback brought to the team. "He's so cool, so much in control," Boozer said. "Sometimes it frightens me. You know, like maybe he should blow up or fall apart. But he doesn't. He does his homework, and he comes into the game sure of what we can do and he makes us do it."

A funny thing happened at Memorial Stadium on the afternoon of September 24, 1972—an aerial battle of epic proportions broke out as the two Pennsylvania natives jumped into the Wayback Machine. Unitas was transported to 1958, while Namath landed in 1968. Ten years apart, first Unitas and later Namath had authored the two most important championship victories in NFL history, The Greatest Game Ever Played and Super Bowl III.

This contrasting pair of legends may have had distinct images—and their off-the-field lives may as well have taken place on different planets—but on the field, while not quite twins, they were kindred spirits. Both were brainy, bright, courageous, gritty, daring, bold, explosive, and as unruffled as Wyatt Earp facing down the Clantons.

With the NFL/AFL merger in 1970, the Colts moved to the AFC East, ensuring two battles a year between the combatants of the most remarkable upset football has ever known. But on this fall day, the last showdown took place between Namath and Unitas. The Jets and Colts would play each other a few weeks later, but Unitas wouldn't be on the field, and in 1973, the Chargers, whom Johnny U. had signed on with for one last hurrah, wouldn't be on the Jets' schedule.

The final battle was staged for 2 PM, and it was Namath who fired the first salvo. Broadway Joe warmed up by throwing a 65-yard touchdown pass to Eddie Bell. But Unitas answered back with a 40-yard touchdown toss to Sam Havrilak. The duel had begun. The challenges were issued. The challenges were accepted.

While Namath had a hand in six of his team's seven scores, Unitas had a little more help. Longhaired Colts kicker Jim O'Brien booted two field goals in the second quarter. His hippie-like mane earned him the nickname "Lassie" when he arrived in Baltimore as a rookie two years earlier, but it didn't prevent him from becoming the hero of Super Bowl V when he kicked the championship-winning field goal with five seconds left in the game. After Namath tossed another lengthy touchdown throw, this time a 67-yarder to John Riggins, Don McCauley returned the kickoff 93 yards, giving the Colts a 20–13 lead.

One of the keys to Namath's success was his quick release. He was the fastest gun in the NFL. Oilers coach Bill Peterson said of the Jets quarterback, "[Namath] gets rid of the ball so fast you can't rush him and follows through all the way, like any quarterback who ever played for Bear Bryant." Boozer added, "Joe has a quick release, right, but Joe holds the ball a long time before he finally releases it, so you have a long time to hold your block. A lot of quarterbacks, they throw the ball too soon, but Joe never does. He always waits until the last second—or split second—until the rush is only this far away. And then he throws. And then he gets hit in the mouth. But he throws without ever thinking about possibly getting hit in the mouth."

Namath used that lightning-quick release to throw his third and fourth touchdown passes. The first went to old friend Don Maynard, playing his last season with the Jets, good for a 28-yard score. The next was caught by Caster, who was just getting his feet wet in anticipation of the big second half that awaited him. The Jets ran off the field at halftime with a 27–20 lead. Five touchdown passes had already been thrown in 30 minutes of play.

Maybe the players were exhausted in the third quarter after all that running around in the first half, because a 14-yard field goal by Jets kicker Bobby Howfield was all the offense either team could muster up. But the scoring bonanza would begin again in the final frame, with a total of 28 points being put on the board. Baltimore's McCauley began the onslaught when he ran the ball into the end zone from the 1-yard line, bringing the Colts within three points of the Jets.

But if one thought Namath's arm might have been getting fatigued after chucking four touchdown passes, including bombs of 65 and 67 yards, well, those were like easygoing sideline warm-up tosses compared to what he had hidden up his sleeve. With Namath shredding Baltimore's zone defense in the first half, the Colts tried their luck in man-to-man in the second half. But that worked about as well as their previous plan. As the speedy Bell ran deep patterns, crossing over the middle, it forced two Colts defenders to key on him, which left Caster alone in single coverage—big mistake.

With the Colts getting closer with every score, Namath and Caster would be the two to keep their team ahead and then put the finishing touches on the Jets victory. Caster, a 6'5" behemoth and three-time Pro Bowler in his time with the Jets, ran a post pattern, which resulted in a 79-yard touchdown. But Unitas threw his final touchdown pass against the Jets when he hooked up with longtime teammate Tom Matte. The score closed the gap to three points, but Broadway Joe, never one to be outdone, had one more bit of magic left in him that day. And he would outdo even himself.

Namath and Caster would team up again, and they wouldn't waste any time doing so. Backup defensive back Rex Kern came off the bench and covered Caster. "I had two receivers open, but when I saw those two clean white numbers, 44, I knew where I was going to go," Namath said. Caster began a post pattern once again but deked Kern and ran the other way. The Colts defender bit on the fake and never had a chance as the ball settled into Caster's hands for his third touchdown of the game, this one good for a whopping 80 yards. Namath and the Jets finally had enough points to withstand Unitas' onslaught and won 44–34.

The grand old man of the Colts threw for 376 yards, completed 26 passes on 45 attempts, and slung a pair of touchdown passes. But on this day, it would be second best. His younger counterpart threw an astounding six touchdowns even though he only completed 15 passes in the game. The half dozen touchdowns set a franchise record that would be tied in 2008 by Brett Favre, who had a duel of his own with Kurt Warner. Namath racked up a staggering 496 passing yards. The 872 combined total yards by the two Hall of Famers were a then-NFL record. And Namath's receivers reaped the benefits of his special day: Caster caught six passes for 204 yards, while Bell hauled in seven passes for 197 yards.

Long hair, short hair, white shoes, black shoes, new school, old school—it didn't matter on that afternoon in Baltimore. Two of the greatest arms in football history faced off and put on a show that will forever be remembered.

1986

Now let's fast forward to September 21, 1986. While this duel didn't involve a battle of longhaired hipsters vs. their disapproving father figures, it did take its roots from a wild time and place in American history—the AFL. With aerial pyrotechnics, missile projections, fireworks, and strong-armed and strong-willed warfare, the game was reminiscent of Namath himself, along with his rebel-league cohorts like George Blanda, John Hadl, and Len Dawson.

The Namath and Unitas legends were already cemented and they had each seen better days by the time they hooked up in 1972. But O'Brien and Marino were in their fourth seasons. They were blooming, young, gifted, and each possessed a rocket for an arm. Marino was the top-rated passer in the NFL in 1984, while O'Brien took the honors the following season. O'Brien also had the lowest interception rate in '85 (and '87 and '88) and made the Pro Bowl that season (as well as in '91). This battle wasn't a contrast in types; instead it was two of a kind duking it out in an anything-you-can-do-I-can-do-better-and-I'll-even-throw-it-farther-than-you-too test of wills. Hairs vs. Squares? This one was Maverick vs. Iceman.

O'Brien didn't have to live in the long shadow of one Joe Willie Namath the way Richard Todd had before him, suffering the anger of Jets fans when trying to measure up to all that Broadway Joe had accomplished. But like Todd, O'Brien had his own mythological dragon to slay, for he had to endure constant comparisons to his cross-field rival that day—Dan Marino.

They were both drafted in the vaunted quarterback class of '83. O'Brien, who came out of Division II University of California-Davis, was taken with the 24th pick. Convinced O'Brien was their man, the Jets passed over Marino, who was selected three slots later. Dolphins coach Don Shula famously said, "Who's he?" when the Jets announced their pick. Well, Shula and Marino would surely know the name when the game played on that September Sunday had ended. "Who's he?" would become, "I hate that guy."

It was a perfect 69 degrees in the Meadowlands at game time. For a game that ended with 96 total points being scored,

Jets quarterback Ken O'Brien (7) throws a pass under pressure from the Dolphins' T.J. Turner (95) in the second quarter on September 21, 1986. O'Brien was 29-for-43 and threw for 479 yards and four touchdowns as he outgunned Dan Marino and the Miami Dolphins 51–45. (AP Images)

the contest began as calmly as the weather. Each team scored once in the opening quarter. A harmless 32-yard Pat Leahy field goal put the Jets on the board, while a 6-yard touchdown catch by James Pruitt gave Miami the early lead. There were no signs of the bombardment to come in the first 15 minutes of play, as the explosion would take place in the second quarter with a fireball of rushing touchdowns, short-passing scores, and bombs galore.

Johnny Hector ran for two touchdowns to commence the parade to the end zone, giving the Jets a 17–7 advantage. The lead would change hands seven times over the course of the game, with a sprinkling of ties thrown in for good measure. But the Jets held the lead for the majority of the second quarter. Marino would throw his second and third touchdown passes for a brief Miami advantage, but O'Brien had two answers for him, comprising a pair of words: "Wesley Walker."

Through the Eyes of Wesley Walker

Wesley Walker played his whole career while legally blind in one eye. That handicap didn't stop him from making two Pro Bowls, though. He's tied for fifth place with Mickey Shuler on the Jets' all-time reception list with 438 catches, second in yardage with 8,306, second in touchdown passes caught with 71, and first in yards-per-catch with a 19.0 average.

"I was born with a cataract," Walker said. "Nobody really knew about it. Nobody really checked my eyes, even in college, even in high school. They kind of knew about it. But it wasn't until I had a complete physical where I had to read an eye chart—the Jets didn't even know that. They sent Bob Reese, our trainer at the time, to look at my knee, to examine it to make sure I was fine there. That's how the combines got started. I came in, they were worried about me, but they didn't know I was blind. That bothered Leon Hess, so they started flying in guys and checking them out before, giving pre-physicals. And then they got together with teams and started doing these pre-physicals, and then they started housing guys, and that's how the combines kind of got started.

"I always kept it hid, even as a youngster, because I thought it was going to keep me from playing sports. And I know it scared my mom because I played baseball and I got hit a couple of times in the eye, and that was always a problem for me, figuring I wouldn't be able to play sports. Even when I got here on the Jets I never made a big deal about it, and I probably could have

Walker scored two touchdowns, one a 65-yarder and the other good for 50 yards. "We ran this play-action pass," Walker said. "I remember it was 78 Special. And I was wide open. We had a good run game, and when your run game is working you can do a lot of things with play-action. O'Brien looked off the safety. I was wide open. That was one touchdown. Toward the end of the first half, Kenny O'Brien and I were both on the sideline. I'm pleading with Joe Walton now, we can go do this, we can do this. We wanted to go deep with the ball, and he couldn't make up his mind. Finally he calls this play, we're going to go for it. There's no way I should

helped people who had had disabilities. I was always embarrassed about it. I always got teased as a kid. People made fun of me because my eye drifts a lot. I look like I'm cross eyed.

"A father, who's a teacher, wrote to me when his son was only nine-and-a-half years old. I've been friendly with them from that time on. It's just second nature for me to try to make people happy. But this kid was losing his eyesight. He ultimately lost his eye. And I did nothing but try to encourage him, sent him stuff. His family flew my girlfriend and me out to California, threw this big party. He not only went to Berkeley, but he got two degrees. Sometimes you don't know the impact you may have on an individual. He used to write these things when he was in elementary school and middle school. I have these letters—I'd be with my kids and I'd be crying, just things that he wrote. I just think his mom and dad are something, because they've been an inspiration to me. It's human nature for me to help somebody. They came out to my house. I took them out, we barbecued. I've gone out to California where I did the Jets games, and took them to games, and tried to encourage them. I brought two other people who had lost their eyesight.

"But you never know the impact you have on people. This is going to be one of the things in my life that I'll never, ever forget, this family. And I'm just doing something I'd just naturally do for anybody, since I'm trying to help or encourage somebody who has this disability. But I probably should have made that known when I first got to New York, and I never used it. I always kept it hid because I never wanted it to be a problem or a distraction."

have been open, but Kenny was able just to thread it between the corner and the safety, and I broke a tackle and scored another touchdown."

Forty-two points had now been scored in the second quarter on six touchdowns. It was a bona fide shootout. Namath and Unitas would have been jealous.

O'Brien and Marino had already engaged in a memorable game the previous season, when the Dolphins' Hall of Famer completed a 50-yard touchdown pass to Mark Duper with seconds left to give Miami a 21–17 victory over the Jets. Marino threw for three touchdowns and 362 yards, while O'Brien tossed two touchdown passes and gained 393 yards in the air in a losing cause. That was just one of the rivals' many shootouts during the 1980s, and O'Brien got the best of his draft classmate with a career 8–7 record against Miami. So as O'Brien sat in front of his locker at halftime, he was prepared for what lay ahead.

"It was one of those things where we didn't have much of a choice," O'Brien later told 1240 WGBB's Sports Radio New York. "You either start firing it around and try to catch up and overtake or it's going to be a long day. And it seems like against Miami it always builds up into one of those exciting games."

The second half began with—what else?—an aerial assault, as Marino connected with Duper for a 46-yard score. The Dolphins added a Fuad Reveiz field goal to tie the game and then took the lead on a 1-yard Bruce Hardy touchdown reception. For those keeping score, Miami was winning 38–31, Marino had thrown five touchdown passes, and O'Brien had two under his belt. With the fourth quarter about to get underway, there were still 27 more points to be scored.

Jets running back Dennis Bligen scored one of his three career touchdowns to knot things up once again. If it seemed like no one would win this game, it was only because both teams' defenses were powerless to stop the offensive juggernauts they were facing. When Walker fumbled and the Dolphins marched downfield and capped off the drive with a 4-yard touchdown catch by Mark Clayton, things were looking bleak for the Jets. "Oh my God, I lost the game for us," thought the Jets receiver. And it finally looked like there might be an actual winner to this battle.

The Jets started their last drive in regulation with only 1:04 left on the clock. And they had 80 yards to go. The team didn't have much time, but it didn't take O'Brien & Co. too long to travel 59 yards. The savvy Jets quarterback quickly completed three out of four passes to get the team near midfield. On the penultimate play of the drive, tight end Mickey Shuler caught a 7-yard pass, but instead of accepting the fate of most plays on the football field—getting tackled—he pulled the old hook and lateral and flung the ball to Hector, who raced to the Dolphins' 21-yard line.

With only five ticks remaining on the clock, the Jets had time for one more play, but the hero almost didn't get on the field. Walker explained, "I was on the sidelines for this special play that we always worked on in practice. Kenny O'Brien comes up to me, 'Wesley, get in there.' And that's why I had the utmost respect for him. Here I am on the sidelines, and Joe Walton had so many things on his mind, I guess. And I'm wondering why I'm not in there as they're getting ready to call this special play again. So he tells me to go in."

The Jets set up in an overloaded formation with Hector, Walker, and Al Toon all lining up on the right side. The fateful play was called "Z-short motion, 78 fullback hide." And O'Brien added one caveat to his teammates: "Gimme time." Now the Dolphins' defense had already given up 38 points, so was it realistic to ask them to make one big stop, especially with the Jets lining up in a way they hadn't all day? Of course not. And according to O'Brien, the Jets were at their best when they were in a hurry.

"It seems like whenever we were in a two-minute drill, we always performed pretty well," he said. "It's also the players just making plays when you have to because you can't script them when you're out there. You're just calling plays, going as fast as you can. Guys have to make plays at big times, and for some reason that was always when we had a lot of big catches and big runs. And I was the recipient, fortunately, of a lot of good things in those situations."

As O'Brien took the snap and dropped back, the three receivers ran downfield and the game clock read 00:00. O'Brien scoured the field spying his options. He spotted Walker streaking toward the goal line and threw a bullet up the middle, threading the needle between a handful of Miami defenders. Walker reached up, caught the ball, and tumbled into the end zone for a touchdown. The game would go into overtime, which was its apparent destiny all along.

O'Brien was just as confident when regulation ended. "Just let us win the coin toss," he thought. When the Jets got the ball, they moved to the Dolphins' 43-yard line in four plays. And on the fifth play, on first down, they decided that the game had gone on long enough. After a play-action fake to Hector, O'Brien heaved the ball down the right sideline to a streaking Walker, who was in single coverage. The remarkable receiver capped off his remarkable day by hauling in the pass at the 1-yard line, and as he and defensive back Don McNeal collapsed in the end zone, NBC's Dick Enberg succinctly and unequivocally summed up the whole afternoon: "Oh, my!" The game was exhilarating. It was thrilling. And it was over. Jets 51, Dolphins 45.

Walker set a Jets record with his four touchdown receptions, and he gained 194 yards along the way. But the humble receiver praised his teammates for his performance. "It was a credit to what we did offensively as a team. I could have never done those things or accomplished what I did without my teammates. I mean,

Johnny Hector picked up a blitz on a play, and if he didn't pick up the blitz, we don't execute that last play."

Despite his memorable day, Walker had doubts how it would turn out. "I use this as a motivational tool with kids," he said. "That was a game that I was ready to give up on. I was very angry at Joe Walton. I had strained my groin during the week in practice and had taken off a couple of days, and I wasn't being utilized in the game. And I remember telling Kurt Sohn, who was my backup, 'Hey man, I might as well let you play and save my groin because he's not using me.' I came off the sideline, and I was ready to throw in the towel. I was very frustrated."

But he had fewer uncertainties about his quarterback. "That was another example of Kenny O'Brien and his abilities. He outshined, as far as I'm concerned, Marino that day, not to take anything away from Dan Marino. And this is not anything against Joe Namath. I never had the opportunity to play with Joe, but I said I would take Kenny O'Brien over Joe Namath, over Dan Marino, over John Elway. He was just a pleasure to be around. We worked together—we always could work together anytime we were in the offseason. Just a very personable guy, great work ethic, and just a great athlete."

Both O'Brien and Marino had record-setting days, as well. The Dolphins quarterback finished with six touchdown passes, threw for 448 yards, and completed 30 passes on 50 attempts. Like Unitas 14 years earlier, however, those stats would be the consolation prize. O'Brien chucked his way to 479 yards on 29 of 43 passing with four touchdowns. The combined yardage by the two quarterbacks is still an NFL record.

CHAPTER 13

BAD IDEAS

WHEN LOOKING BACK AT THE 17 head coaches in the history of the New York Jets, Weeb Ewbank stands atop the mountain with his Super Bowl victory. Sonnets and ballads have been penned about the legendary leader for his stunning triumph over the thought-to-be-unbeatable Baltimore Colts, and he remains the king until someone can scale the same heights that he did. He's the lone coach on Mount Jetsmore. Walt Michaels, Bill Parcells, and Rex Ryan have taken the team oh-so-close to the pinnacle, with appearances in the AFC Championship Game. Herm Edwards memorably gave us, "You play to win the game." Joe Walton led the team to the playoffs in back-to-back seasons, while Bruce Coslet and Eric Mangini made it to the postseason, as well.

But the franchise has not always chosen wisely. There were two men whose quirks, deficiencies, and peculiarities added up to less than zero, as the Jets once employed a man who didn't want to be there and a man who shouldn't have been there. That duo of ineffectiveness consisted of Lou Holtz and Rich Kotite. Holtz lasted slightly less than one season, while Kotite somehow made it through two. Their combined record was 7–38, but neither man was fired. The pair recognized as well as anyone that there was no need to stick around any longer. They had already caused enough

Lou Holtz grips a football during the February 10, 1976, news conference where Holtz was introduced as the New York Jets' head coach. Holtz resigned with one game remaining in the 1976 season after his team went 3–10. (AP Images)

misery. History may have shown that they produced woefully poor records, but they at least had the good sense to fire themselves, as they both resigned before the ax could fall.

Lou Holtz was a college coach. He was successful, he was happy, and he was a winner. After making the rounds as an assistant coach in the 1960s, he took the reins of William & Mary for three years beginning in 1969 before moving on to North Carolina State, where he was named the Atlantic Coast Conference Coach of the Year after his first season. There would be no expensive trips overseas to celebrate his achievement. Instead, he would spend his offseason sabbatical tending to his in-laws' grocery store so that they could enjoy some time away from their business.

"Some of the fans wanted to talk football, but I had a job to do," Holtz said. "I sold them groceries from 7 AM to 11 PM. Three nights I accidentally set off the burglar alarm. Then the plumbing broke, but my wife fixed it. We had a littering problem in the parking lot, but I got my kids to clean it up. My biggest complaint was eating nothing but sandwiches all that time. Next year I'm taking my grill and cooking steak in the parking lot."

Lou Holtz was down to earth, and he was a man of the people. He was also quick-witted and could have been named the king of comebacks or the prince of one-liners. He was the Coach in the Wry. What Bob Uecker was to baseball, Holtz was to football. The New York press may have viewed him as a hillbilly who just fell off the turnip truck, but he could have given Rodney Dangerfield or Jerry Seinfeld a run for their money. And he did in fact make numerous guest appearances on *The Tonight Show*. His fallback profession might well have been standup comedy. Holtz had enough wisecracks and bon mots to take his act on the road.

"I always knew I'd had plenty to eat because when I asked for more, my father would say, 'No, you've had plenty.'" Bada-boom. Regarding his home state of West Virginia, "I loved that state. I stayed there until the age of reason." Zing. Said after taking a job as a cemetery plot salesman and his wife insisting he couldn't sell anything, "She was wrong. By the end of the summer, I'd sold our stereo, our car, and our television." He was just getting warmed up. He hated cold weather and was told by Arkansas athletic director Frank Broyles that he wouldn't need a coat in January. "He was right. I needed a parka." And: "The good Lord allows just so much profanity on a team, and I use up our entire quota."

About his clever, playful jocularity, reputation for being a jokester, and his witticisms, he stated, "I think that they come out of the lack of having anything else to say. Sometimes I say something serious and everybody laughs, which doesn't help my self-confidence a lot." But for someone whose self description is, "a guy 5'10", 152 pounds, who wears glasses, talks with a lisp, and has a physique that looks like [he's] had beriberi and scurvy," his wisecracking was a way to get the childhood bullies off his scent.

Holtz may have been one of the best collegiate coaches around, he may have been a droll humorist, and every bone in his body may have been pretentiousness-free, but the one thing he wasn't was a professional coach. Even though he signed on to take over the New York Jets for the 1976 season, Holtz really didn't want the job. After initially rebuffing general manager Al Ward's overtures, he finally caved in and flew to New York to meet owner Leon Hess, who sweet-talked him into accepting the position. "I intended to say 'no,' or at least ask for time to think about it," Holtz said. "But Mr. Hess was a generous and kind man, and I was swayed. I accepted the job right on the spot."

Holtz signed a five-year contract on February 10, 1976, and though he had doubts about moving up to the NFL, he was hopeful about his career move. "We're building a house on Long Island," Holtz said at the time. "Yeah, that's pretty optimistic. It's a little like doing a crossword puzzle with a pen."

In the college ranks, Holtz was a master at taking a struggling program and rebuilding it into a winner. And in the pros, nobody needed rebuilding more than the 1976 Jets. Coming off a 3–11 season, the Jets had a roster filled with unproven or past-their-prime players with not much in between. Joe Namath was in his final season and on his last legs with the team—almost literally. Though he was only 33, he had the knees of an 80-year-old. The fallback at quarterback was rookie Richard Todd. John Riggins was now a Redskin, while Matt Snell and Emerson Boozer were enjoying retirement, leaving rookie Clark Gaines, career-backup Steve Davis, and newcomer Ed Marinaro to carry the rushing load. Rich Caster and Jerome Barkum were the featured pass-catchers.

And first-year linebacker Greg Buttle was the highlight of the defense.

Holtz, never one to shirk hard work or responsibility, took on the job with gusto. He was only 39 years old and had energy to spare. He thrived on long hours and chaos, and he dove headfirst into his new life with the Jets. "I work from dawn to exhaustion. If there's not a crisis, I'll create one," he once said. He often slept on a cot at the team's facilities and joked, "I know the names of three of our four kids."

He discovered right from the beginning that he wasn't on a college campus anymore. On his first day on the job, Holtz attempted to contact Namath but was told that the star quarterback's phone number was classified and that he would have to go through Broadway Joe's lawyer. Another early encounter with one of his players wasn't filled with the old college spirit, either. Buttle excitedly told his new coach, "I want to play so badly I'll play for free." Holtz, impressed with his attitude, replied, "That's commendable, son." Buttle's response? "But if you want me to practice..."

One of Holtz's downfalls with the Jets may have been that he worked too hard. He didn't delegate authority, he treated his players like undergraduates, and he harped on every last detail. He had the players line up by size for the national anthem, demanded they wear their socks and jerseys just so, and in training camp, when Todd and the offense broke out of their first huddle, he emphatically stopped them in their tracks, "No, no, that's not the way you break out of a huddle." Of course, he would also occasionally do magic tricks to entertain his players, so he wasn't all business.

In one preseason game, Holtz's exhaustive accountability didn't account for Namath's brittle knees. Todd was mopping up for Namath, but the rookie kept fumbling the ball. Holtz yanked Todd, and to every Jets player's amazement, he inserted Joe Willie into the game once again. Namath had already taken off his bulky, heavy knee braces, called Lenox Hill Derotation braces, and had unstrapped his shoulder pads. A year earlier, guard Randy Rasmussen said of Namath's protection, "The braces tell a lot about Joe. When they go squeak-squeak-squeak in good rhythm, I know he's okay, but when they go squeak-squeak pause squeaksqueaksqueak, I know he's hurting." With no choice, though, Namath limped back on the field. He eyed the defense, and calmly stated, "Fellas, I'm just going to go down on one knee. Let's not get anybody hurt."

A college atmosphere was all that Holtz knew, and he tried to instill the same zealous, enthusiastic environment to the Jets. After the team's first preseason victory, he said, "I've written a fight song. We're going to sing it after every Jets victory." He handed out sheets of paper with the lyrics written out to his surprised players. The song went to the tune of "The Caissons Go Rolling Along" with Holtz's words:

Win the game, fight like men,
We're together win or lose,
New York Jets go rolling along,
And where e're we go,
We'll let the critics know that
The Jets are here to stay.

When the Jets appeared on *Monday Night Football* against the Patriots on October 18, broadcaster Alex Karras sang the song on the air while he, Howard Cosell, and Frank Gifford set the scene for the game.

The fervor and passion that Holtz projected transferred to the field of play immediately, as his team opened the season on a promising note. They began the year in Cleveland, and when the first quarter ended, the Jets had a 10–0 lead. Maybe this Lou Holtz thing would work out after all. Maybe what the Jets needed was a collegiate, all-for-one attitude. Hey, maybe what the franchise was missing the last half decade was a fight song. Or maybe not. If they had the power to stop the season right there, they should have and just called it a year. For 15 minutes, it was a job well done. Lou Holtz and the Jets were a success. Unfortunately, the second quarter and the rest of the season had to be played out.

Browns quarterback Mike Phipps tossed three consecutive touchdown passes, giving Cleveland a 21–10 advantage at the half. The score jumped to 31–10 after three, and the final damage stood at 38–17. On the bright side, Todd made his NFL debut, scored his first touchdown on an 8-yard rush, and went 4-for-5 through the air. He also threw his first career interception.

If the final three quarters of the opener could be labeled "bad," there may not be a word invented to describe the Jets the following week. In a beat-down of the highest order, the Denver Broncos pulverized the Jets 46–3. Things became slightly better for the defense the next two weeks, as they only allowed 16 and 17 points; but the team's sad-sack offense could only muster up a total of six points in the pair of contests. Holtz had taken the play-calling duties away from Namath, and he also installed a college-option-type offense. Of course, Namath could barely drop back to pass at that point in his career, so the new coach would sporadically insert Todd into the games to run certain plays. That experiment was scrapped as the season went on, though.

In Week 5, the Jets finally found a matchup to their liking—the Buffalo Bills. Buffalo came into the game with a record of 2–2. But it was just a mirage, as they would lose every game for the remainder of the season and be one of three teams to finish with a worse mark than the Jets—the other two were the expansion franchises that had just joined the league, Tampa Bay and Seattle. Against the Bills, Namath was back to playing the whole game and calling the plays, and the Jets responded to the change. Marinaro opened the scoring on a 1-yard touchdown run, and a Namath-to-Richard Osborne touchdown pass gave the Jets a 14–0 advantage. The Bills would ultimately tie the game, but Pat Leahy gave Lou Holtz his first professional victory when he booted a 38-yard field goal in the fourth quarter for the winning points.

After back-to-back losses following the Buffalo game, the Jets took advantage of the Bills once again for their second win of the year. Two weeks later, they would beat the Buccaneers (who finished the season 0–14) for their third and final triumph of the season. The Jets would finish their schedule with four straight losses while giving up 38, 33, 37, and 42 points, respectively. And for the second consecutive season, the Jets ended at 3–11. Only two teams allowed more points over the course of the season, and only two teams scored fewer points than the 1976 Jets. Namath and Todd combined to throw only seven touchdowns while tossing 28 interceptions. Holtz was not around to witness the final game, a 42–3 defeat at the hands of the Bengals, which was coached by Director of Player Personnel Mike Holovak. It was also Namath's last game as a Jet. He went 4-for-15 with only 20 passing yards while having four passes picked off without a touchdown. It was a sad end to the legend's career in green and white.

The good old boy from West Virginia just couldn't take it anymore. While the Jets were tossing interceptions galore and allowing points to rack up at a dizzying pace, Holtz realized professional football just wasn't in his blood. On December 8, 1976, he handed in his resignation, four days before the final game. Arkansas athletic director Frank Broyles came calling, and Holtz went back to college. December was recruiting season, so he bolted the Jets at the first opportunity. "The few talents God gave me are better suited for college. I didn't have the background for that job, and I didn't find that I enjoyed it," he said.

Holtz was always one to look for action, excitement, thrills, and the next challenge ahead. "I don't want anybody to ever do a story of my life and call it *Ruts*," he once said. But ultimately he discovered that the NFL was not the type of jolt that he was craving. "Pro ball was so strange to Lou that he even missed the alums," Broyles stated.

The Jets' decision to hire Holtz was a disaster, and Holtz's judgment in taking the position was also questionable. But the Big City was not an issue for him. "The people in New York were great to me. The only thing wrong with that whole situation was me." The 10-month experiment can be summed up in one pithy sentence uttered by the coach himself: "God did not put Lou Holtz on this earth to coach in the pros."

To get the full, forceful effect of the Rich Kotite Story, we have to go all the way back to November 27, 1994 and the Fake Spike Game. Pete Carroll was the Jets head coach in his single season in New York. The Dolphins and Jets were heading in different directions. After losing two straight, Miami was going south, spiraling downward with their confidence slipping away. The Jets, on the other hand, were on an upward swing. They had won two out of their last three and were coming off an inspired 31–21 victory over the Vikings in which quarterback Boomer Esiason was brilliant with an amazingly accurate 22-for-29, 230-yard, three-touchdown performance. Johnny Mitchell snared 11 passes for 120 yards, and Marcus Turner starred on defense by picking off three Warren Moon passes.

The Dolphins were precariously sitting atop the division with a 7–4 record, while the Jets were knocking on the door at 6–5. First place was on the line, but the stars were aligning in favor of the Jets, and momentum for the rest of the season—and for the franchise going forward—was in the balance.

As the largest crowd in Jets history settled into their seats, there was no reason to think the day wouldn't end with the two teams tied

New York Jets head coach Rich Kotite stands on the sideline during the Jets' 29–10 loss to the Buffalo Bills in 1995. The Jets went 4–28 during Kotite's two seasons as head coach. (Rick Stewart/Allsport/ Getty Images)

for the AFC East lead. Nick Lowery opened up the scoring, booting a 24-yard field goal. Mitchell hauled in a sublime 30-yard spiral from Esiason to extend the lead. Brian Baxter cut and clawed his way into the end zone on a 3-yard run, which was set up by a 69-yard catch and run by Art Monk. The Jets were sitting on a 17-point cushion with visions of first place dancing in their heads. Dolphins receiver Mark Ingram caught a 10-yard touchdown pass from Dan Marino, but the Jets countered quickly with another Mitchell touchdown. The defense had picked off Marino twice, and the offense could do no wrong. The good guys were rolling with a 24–6 third-quarter lead. It was the Jets' day to shine. Unfortunately, the phrase, "Same old Jets" wasn't created for nothing. In fact, it was created for games just like this one.

As it turned out, the Marino-to-Ingram touchdown pass was just the beginning. The quarterback and receiver would seemingly play a simple game of catch for much of the second half. The Dolphins went into their hurry-up offense in the third quarter, and they came storming back on the Jets, who never had an answer. Another Marino-Ingram connection made the score 24–14. And in the final quarter, while Esiason was sacked twice, threw two interceptions, and fumbled the ball on three consecutive plays, Marino was on fire, going 15-for-18 for 164 yards and two touchdowns.

A 28 yard Marino-to-Ingram strike cut the Jets lead to three. The second Esiason pick gave Miami the ball on their own 16-yard line. The Dolphins had 84 yards to go for the winning points. An unflustered Marino marched his team downfield and made it all the way to the New York 8-yard line with 38 seconds left in the game. The breezy Marino stated, "When the last drive started, I was just thinking about taking my best shots. What do you have to lose? Only the game, right?" As the Dolphins ran to the line of scrimmage, the clock wound down. The Dolphins quarterback shouted, "Clock! Clock! Clock!" to his teammates, as he mimicked spiking the ball. It all looked routine; he would slam the ball to the ground, stop the clock, and Miami would try a game-tying field goal. But Dolphin coach Don Shula and Marino had other ideas.

During a training-camp practice, backup quarterback Bernie Kosar faked out his own defense by using "The Clock Play," which went back to his Cleveland Brown days. Shula liked the play, and Kosar suggested using it in a preseason game, but his coach reasoned they could only use it once or the surprise would be lost. Well, that one time to use it arrived on this day against the Jets. But Marino didn't pass that message on to his teammates. While he was at the line yelling and gesticulating, he was also staring down Ingram. "The stare. There's nothing like it," Ingram said. "When he gives you that stare, you know he's coming to you."

So while the other nine Dolphins and most likely all 11 Jets defenders thought the ball would be spiked, Ingram sped into the end zone while rookie cornerback Aaron Glenn hesitated. Marino took the ball from center, faked his spike, and rifled the football to Ingram before Glenn could even turn around. Just like that. Final score 28–24. Jets lose.

The Jets lost more than a football game with Marino's fake-spike chicanery—they were stunned, dazed, confused, and lost in the wilderness. They went on to lose their last four games of the season, Carroll was fired, and the team was at rock bottom. Just like in 1976, they would need a strong hand to guide them through the rebuilding process. They needed a tough taskmaster, a no-nonsense, assertive leader. They needed Vince Lombardi. They needed General Patton. They needed Theodore Roosevelt. They needed Winston Churchill. What they got was Rich Kotite.

Kotite came to the Jets via the Philadelphia Eagles. On the surface, his four-year tenure in Philadelphia was somewhat successful. He led the team to two winning seasons, a .500 campaign, and one losing year. Kotite's Eagles peaked in his second year, 1992, with an 11–5 record. With their playoff hopes teetering uneasily, they finished the season strong with four consecutive victories. Facing the Saints in the wild card round of the postseason in the Superdome, they were behind 20–10 at the end of the third quarter, but a 26-point fourth-quarter explosion shocked New Orleans, and the Eagles won going away 36–20. Kotite's Eagles were resilient, tough, stout, and tenacious. They couldn't keep the momentum going, though, as they fell to the eventual Super Bowl–winning Cowboys in the Divisional round.

The team struggled to an 8–8 record in '93, but the following season they got off to a fast start, winning seven of their first nine games. A new owner, Jeffrey Lurie, was in place, and Kotite was unsure if his contract would be renewed. He stated that he would poke around and keep his options open for the future. His team promptly fell apart, losing their final seven games of the year, and he was canned, his options now totally open.

The Jets—and Kotite, as well—were coming off a disastrous end to the 1994 campaign. Was this really the man to save the Jets? By all accounts, Kotite was no Lou Holtz when it came to a sound, old-fashioned work ethic. He wouldn't be sleeping on a cot at the team's facilities. He wasn't Holtz in the wisecracks department, either. The one thing he had in common with Holtz, though, was that he shouldn't have been the head coach of the New York Jets.

Kotite was a Brooklyn native. He attended college at Wagner in Staten Island, was a tight end for the New York Giants in his short playing career, and served a previous stint with the Jets as their offensive coordinator. So he was coming back home. But he just proved the old adage that you can't go home again. It was his self-proclaimed dream job. But it turned into his worst nightmare, and his two seasons invaded the dreams of Jets fans, also giving them terrifying nightmares—ones that may still be recurring to this day.

The Jets' debut game under the leadership of Kotite came on September 3, 1995, against the Miami Dolphins at Joe Robbie Stadium. It was a disaster. The debacle that was the Kotite era began right then and there and didn't let up until the final game of the following season. It was 32 straight games of catastrophe, calamity, tragedy, mishap, and misfortune—and 32 straight games of torture for Jets fans. The game was tied at 14 in the second quarter. Like Holtz's opener, time should have frozen at that moment so everybody could slowly walk away and rethink the decisions that had just been made that would affect so many people for the next few years.

But time didn't stand still, and Keith Byars caught a 1-yard touchdown pass from Dan Marino to take a 21–14 lead. Then Bernie

Parmalee scored. Then Troy Vincent returned an interception 69 yards for a touchdown. Then Irving Fryar caught a 50-yard touchdown pass. Then Pete Stoyanovich kicked a 29-yard field goal. And even little-used Irving Spikes ran the ball into the end zone. Dolphins 52, Jets 14, Rich Kotite uh-oh. "It's not quite the way I envisioned us to start," said the glum new coach.

Inserted here and there amongst a bushel of losses, the Jets managed a win against expansion Jacksonville, squeezed out a one-point victory over Miami, and defeated mediocre Seattle by six points to go 3–13. The offense was last in the NFL in points scored, while the defense was only slightly better, finishing 26th out of 30 teams in points allowed. In Kotite's first season in Philadelphia, the Eagles were ranked tops in the league in total defense. Where was the Kotite stamp of dominance? Apparently the coach didn't bring it with him to the Jets.

Kotite was the antithesis of what this edition of the Jets needed, but he was friendly with owner Leon Hess, who had handpicked him for the job. "I'm 80 years old. I want results now," said the owner on the day Kotite was hired. "I've waited for 25 years. I'm entitled to some enjoyment out of this team, and that means winning." It was the last time anyone associated with the Jets would use the words "enjoyment" and "winning" in reference to Rich Kotite.

The Jets coach brought in his cronies from Philadelphia to round out his coaching staff. He ran comfortable, painless, easy practices. He didn't hold players accountable. He had almost no motivational skills. And his in-game management ranged from shaky to bad to frightening. Was there any wonder he didn't succeed? And the fans let him hear all about his shortcomings and inadequacies every chance they got, though they didn't go so far as to fly a banner over Giants Stadium as one resourceful, ingenious, yet cold-hearted fan did a few years earlier, which read: "If you put Joe Walton's brain in a bird, the bird would fly backwards."

In year two of the Rich Kotite Experience, the Jets threw money at the problem. Lots of money. The team spent in the neighborhood of $70 million to bring in players such as quarterback Neil O'Donnell, who was just coming off a Super Bowl appearance with Pittsburgh; left tackle Jumbo Elliott; and veteran wide receiver Webster Slaughter. They also added brash rookie Keyshawn Johnson to the mix, who they took with the first overall pick in the draft. Optimism abounded, while bloodcurdlingly nightmarish visions were temporarily set aside.

But on September 1, those hair-raising, horror-movie feelings of dread and fright would return. For it was opening day, and on opening day of 1996, the Jets were demolished again, this time by the Broncos by a score of 31–6. And then they lost again. And again. And so on. Aside from plain old poor play, injuries played a part in all the losing, as well. In the sixth game of the year, against Oakland, O'Donnell separated his shoulder. Later in the season he would return, but during pregame warm-ups, he slipped on the word "JETS" in the end zone and tore a calf muscle. It was one of the most symbolic injuries in NFL history.

After eight straight losses to open the season, the Jets finally won their first game, defeating the Arizona Cardinals 31–21. And they didn't even need overtime to do it. The star of the game was Adrian Murrell, who gained 199 rushing yards. But there would be no carryover, no momentum, no hope, as the team would lose their final seven games. And like Holtz before him, Kotite resigned a few days before the last game. But unlike Holtz, he stuck around to roam the sidelines for the finale, where a fan held up a sign reading, "The End of an Error."

Not all the players disliked Rich Kotite. A fellow small-college longshot to make the NFL named Wayne Chrebet was a Kotite supporter. The coach gave the receiver from Hofstra his big break, after all. When the Jets fell to the Dolphins to end the season,

Chrebet presented Kotite with the ball he caught for the season's final touchdown. Kotite was not a bad man; he was just a bad coach.

While Kotite confounded fans and players alike with his coaching acumen, he also caused confusion during his resignation press conference. "I was not fired. I'm not quitting," he stated. "When

I Have Decided to Resign as HC of the NY Jets

Bill Parcells came in and cleaned up the stain left behind by Kotite. But three years later, when Parcells stepped down as coach, the franchise was thrown into an unexpected tumult of another kind—the Bill Belichick Fiasco. And what a fiasco it was. A routine transfer of power became a convoluted, bizarre non-transaction. A coronation turned into a resignation.

Would the Jets' fortunes have been different if Lou Holtz or Rich Kotite stepped up to the podium during their introductory press conferences and said, "Um, on second thought, I change my mind, I'm outta here!" What would Harry Wismer have given to have Sammy Baugh pull a Holtz or Kotite or Belichick and walk away on his own? And what if Belichick had stayed?

Belichick was actually hired as the head coach of the Jets twice, and neither time did he coach as much as one practice. When Parcells left the Patriots, his contract would not allow him to coach another team. To sidestep that small detail, the Jets employed Belichick as head coach, with Parcells joining the team as an advisor. The Patriots balked at that setup and threatened legal action, but Commissioner Paul Tagliabue stepped in and came up with a solution that satisfied both sides. The Jets gave New England their third- and fourth-round picks in 1997, their second rounder in '98, and their first-round selection in '99.

The dour defensive genius, nicknamed Coach Doom by Giants players when he was an assistant there, signed a six-year contract with the Jets, which stated if Parcells stepped down as head coach, Belichick would succeed him no matter who owned the team. Leon Hess was in ill health at the time, and he passed away on May 7, 1999. After the '99 season, Parcells did in fact quit but remained with the Jets as head of football operations. Belichick accepted his new role as head coach, and on the morning of his introductory press conference, he met with a group of assistant coaches at 10:30 without a hint of the uproar to come.

you're 3–13 and 1–14, a change has to be made. I have no problem saying that. I think you have to hold yourself accountable." He was not fired, nor did he quit. He invented a new way of leaving a job: He was Kotite'd. He went on to say, "I knew the deal coming in. I'm from New York, I live in New York, I love New York. I didn't come

Just before walking to the podium at 2:30 that afternoon, though, he handed team president Steve Gutman a hand-scribbled note. His official resignation letter read: "Due to various uncertainties surrounding my position as it relates to the team's new ownership, I have decided to resign as HC of the NY Jets. I have given this decision every careful consideration. I would like to wish the entire NYJ organization, the players, the coaching staff, and the new ownership, the very best of luck for a prosperous future."

Belichick rambled for 25 minutes with his voice cracking, about family and personal priorities. The Jets were stunned and furious. And they may have thought they were witnessing some sort of nervous breakdown. Gutman said, "I'm not a psychologist, but I think I just listened for an hour to a person who is in some turmoil and deserves our understanding and our consideration."

Whatever the real reasons for not sticking with the Jets, Belichick hotfooted his way to New England as quickly as he could. And he instantly became Public Enemy No. 1 to the Jets and their fans. The Patriots, of course, became a powerhouse under his leadership, and they've had their way with the Jets for the most part, enjoying a 15–9 record during his tenure.

But the Jets have had a few moments of sweet revenge against their old assistant coach, including the infamous Spygate brouhaha. On the field, Eric Mangini bested his teacher in 2006 when the Jets defeated the Pats 17–14, in Foxboro in the "Handshake Game." In 2008, the Jets edged Belichick's crew in a thrilling overtime win. And the most satisfying victory took place after the 2010 season when the Jets knocked the Patriots out of the playoffs with a 28–21 upset win. But whenever or wherever the Jets whip the despised Belichick—the man who spurned the Jets—the team and their fans savor every second of the pleasurable outcome, bringing to mind a line from the TV sitcom *The Office*: "Have you ever tasted a rainbow?"

here so the Jets could lose their fans. I came here to win football games. We didn't win. Sometimes you get to be Joe Torre. And sometimes you end like I did."

Kotite most likely Kotite'd himself to spare Leon Hess from having to do the dirty work himself, but Hess didn't even make an appearance at the coach's resignation press conference. After the final game he did make a statement, though: "I'm as disappointed as anyone could possibly be. This is as disappointed as I have been about the team. I feel badly for the fans. I feel badly for the team. I feel badly for the coaches."

The players themselves acknowledged the pain they and their fans had endured the past two seasons, with Marvin Washington saying, "They say, if [adversity] doesn't kill you, it makes you stronger. Everybody in here should be like Hercules." And they knew that what the team really needed was an anti-Kotite, as Victor Green confessed, "I think everybody respected Richie. Guys just did what they wanted to do. You need to be a little tougher, and we didn't have enough of that. I think any coach they bring in, I don't care if it is a player's coach or whatever, is going to throw his weight around." He would soon get his wish with the oncoming arrival of Bill Parcells.

Did Kotite really have a chance, though, with how the Jets front office was constructed? They had no official general manager, and when queried by a reporter if that setup would change, team president Steve Gutman replied, "The process will have its own life and be reflective of opportunities that present themselves. I'm not acknowledging or in any way commenting upon anything that we're sure about, not sure about, thinking about, talking about. When conditions resolve themselves, they will become apparent." So that cleared that up.

Though Kotite finished his two-year reign with a 4–28 record, amounting to a .125 winning percentage that tied Tampa Bay's

Leeman Bennett for the lowest winning percentage of any coach with at least 30 games at the helm of the same team, he went out with class and dignity. "I've been very fortunate. I'm the only guy who came out of my college who ever played in the NFL. I had two opportunities as a head coach. I'm a very lucky guy, I really am." In the end, Rich Kotite was a failure. But he was a genial and pleasant failure, and just as he was living proof that you can't go home again, he also brought another old saying to life—nice guys finish last.

CHAPTER 14

WASHINGTON SCORED HERE

OVER THE DECADES, there have been a plethora of Jets who have had a swingin' time off the field. There have been unruly, madcap, and exhilarating games on the field, as well. And mixed in among all that swagger, heartbreak, and euphoria, there have been plays that have electrified Jets Nation, stunned the Jets' opponents, and dominated the highlight reels—we're talking about the long line of captivating, thrilling touchdown returns, whether they be on kickoffs, punts, or missed field goals. If somebody boots it, there's a good chance a Jet might be around to run it into the end zone. Some runbacks have won games, some have broken records, and some were just astonishing and awe-inspiring.

Three yards and a cloud of dust is for the Canton Bulldogs. Okay, it's for Rex Ryan, too, as he likes to grind and pound his way to victories. But in their hearts, the Jets live in the fast lane; they have places to go, people to see, broads to pick up. They can't wait interminably while painstakingly marching down the field. They need to get to the end zone fast. They were born to run wild. They have a need for speed. *Talladega Nights: The Legend of Ricky Bobby* is just a metaphor for the return men in New York Jets history.

It all started on September 23, 1960. In the franchise's third game, Leon Burton ran back a kickoff 88 yards for a touchdown, helping New York defeat the Denver Broncos 28–24. And with that return, they were off and running. Burton led the AFL with 30 kickoff returns (most likely the result of the Titans' last-place ranking on defense), two touchdowns, and 862 return yards in the league's initial year. It was also Burton's only season, as he was one and done with the Titans and the AFL (and NFL, for that matter).

The following season, in the home opener, Dick Christy ran back a punt 70 yards for a score. And in the second quarter, he did it again, this time returning one 64 yards in another victory over Denver. Christy led the AFL with two touchdown punt returns in 1961 and '62 and led the league in punt return yardage both seasons. He also topped the league with 38 kickoff returns and 824 yards in '62, earning him a trip to the AFL All-Star Game. He remains the franchise leader with four punts returned for touchdowns.

On September 22, 1963, cornerback Marshall Starks returned a missed field goal 97 yards for a touchdown in the Jets' win over Houston. Bruce Harper led the NFL in kickoff returns and yardage in his first three seasons in the league, 1977 through '79, although he never brought one back for a touchdown in his career. He's the all-time Jets leader in kickoff and punt returns, as well as total yardage in both categories. In a January 2005 playoff game in Pittsburgh, Santana Moss ran back a punt 75 yards for a touchdown. And on it went, with one Jet after another burning rubber, from the Polo Grounds to Shea Stadium to the Meadowlands to the New Meadowlands.

Here are the stories of four classic Jets touchdown returns by four Jets greats: Chad Morton, Leon Washington, Brad Smith, and Aaron Glenn.

Chad Morton

Every team begins their season with a clean slate. They're all tied for first place with a 0–0 record, and they all line up for the opening-day kickoff chock-full of hopes, dreams, and ambitions that this will be their year to hoist the Lombardi Trophy. Even teams who are forecasted for a last-place finish know that numerous Cinderella stories dot the sports history landscape. "Why not us?" is the rallying cry heard 'round the country. But then you get walloped 42–0 in your initial game, your star quarterback tears up his knee, and it's already time to wait until next year. Or you commence your season the way the Jets did in 2002 with a rousing, inspiring finish

Jets kick returner Chad Morton returns the overtime kickoff 96 yards for his second kick return touchdown of the game as the Jets beat the Buffalo Bills 37–31 on September 8, 2002. (Rick Stewart/Getty Images)

keyed by a rousing, inspiring play. Oh yeah, it helps to have Chad Morton on your team, too.

The Jets were coming off a 10–6 season with a playoff appearance to boot, and they certainly held postseason aspirations heading into 2002. They opened in Buffalo on September 8, and for most of the game they looked nothing like a top contender. They lost Curtis Martin in the second quarter when linebacker London Fletcher fell on his ankle. They committed a total of 10 penalties with sloppy play dogging them all afternoon, which had Coach Herm Edwards sighing, "For a spectator, this was probably a fun game to watch. For a coach, it was a nightmare." The Bills were dominating the stat sheet. And the artificial turf in Ralph Wilson Stadium reached a scalding 112 degrees, which made for a long, tiresome day. But the always gutsy Vinny Testaverde made up for the absence of Martin with a splendid game through the air. And Morton dominated on special teams.

The diminutive return man (5'8"—well, if he's standing on a copy of *War and Peace* that is) weaved his first bit of magic in the second quarter. Down 10–0, the Jets needed a spark, but Morton provided more than that. He brought electricity. Fielding the kickoff on the 2-yard line after a Travis Henry touchdown, Morton began the first leg of his record-setting journey. He broke a handful of tackles and was off to the races. He flew 98 yards, leaving Buffalo players eating his dust. Returning a kickoff for a touchdown is certainly thrilling, and in Morton's case important to the context of the game, but it's not that uncommon. It was Morton's second act to come, though, that made history.

The game would go back and forth from the point of Morton's score with the Jets and Bills taking turns with the lead. Finally, with 26 seconds left in regulation, Buffalo quarterback Drew Bledsoe connected with Eric Moulds for a 29-yard touchdown pass (on fourth down no less) to send the game to overtime. There were varying opinions on the Jets' sideline on how the game would turn out. John Abraham plaintively stated, "Oh, no, it's going to be a long overtime." Ray Mickens was more optimistic: "If anyone can bring it back, Chad can." And special teams coach Mike Westhoff was unwaveringly confident, as he predicted, "We'll win it right here."

And win it they did, all thanks to Morton. His second scoring run was a test of stamina, fortitude, and staying power. The heat was unbearable, and he'd already returned five previous kickoffs that afternoon. "I knew it was going to be a foot race," he said, "I didn't know if I had enough gas. At least I had good field position if I got caught." But he didn't have to worry about getting caught on this day. He ran 96 yards and made it all the way to the end zone, where he was mobbed by his joyous teammates. "It was like an endurance run, like the end of a 26-mile marathon," said Edwards, who a month and a half later would famously state, "You play to win the game." Those 96 yards may have been arduous and grueling, but they resulted in a Jets victory that started them on the path to another playoff appearance, where they would make it all the way to the divisional round of the postseason.

For the day, Morton returned six kickoffs for 278 yards. He was only the fifth player in NFL history with two kickoff touchdown returns in one game. And he was the only player to return one in regulation and one in overtime. "Those are the kinds of things you live for," he said. Jets safety Nick Ferguson put Morton's fabulous feat in perspective: "In all my years of football, I've never seen that. Once? Maybe. Twice? Never. It was like a movie. It was like that movie *Varsity Blues*. I'm still blown away by it."

Leon Washington

Justin Miller set the franchise record (three) for career kickoff touchdown returns in his two-plus seasons with the Jets. But his record didn't last long. That's because a man named Leon

Washington came along. Washington was as breathtaking and hair-raising a player as you'll find. He could do it all—take a handoff and cut and slash his way through the line of scrimmage with defensive players reaching in vain to tackle him as if he were a ghost; catch a screen pass and turn it into a track meet; and field a kickoff and dash through 11 opponents while making them look like the Keystone Kops.

Unfortunately, Washington broke his leg in the seventh game of the 2009 season, which ended his Jets career. But he was much more than a blip in franchise history; he was a rousing all-around package of excitement. He was a ball of fire who was galvanizing with a football in his hands.

Washington returned three kicks for scores in his sophomore season of 2007, and the record-breaker came the following year. It was November 13, 2008, a Thursday night game at Gillette Stadium against the despised New England Patriots. Washington stated the obvious when he said winning the game "would mean a lot. If you think about all the games they've beaten us in the past and all the divisions they've won the last 10 years..." The Jets were tired of being New England's patsies. They needed to win this game, not only because it was a division-rival game and meant a little extra in the standings—they needed to win this game for their own sanity.

Washington himself opened the scoring when he caught a 7-yard touchdown pass from Brett Favre. The two teams then alternated field goals, first the Patriots, then the Jets, and the Pats once again. In the second quarter, with the Jets holding a 10–6 lead, Stephen Gostkowski kicked off after nailing his second field goal. Taking the ball at the 8-yard line, on the right side of the field, Washington cut diagonally through a seam that opened up in the middle, flew past a diving Gostkowski, and scampered untouched down the left side of the field to extend the Jets' lead. And he broke a team record in the process. It was his fourth career touchdown return as a Jet, smashing the mark set by Miller in 2006.

A Jerricho Cotchery 15-yard touchdown catch gave the Jets a seemingly comfortable 24–6 cushion in the second quarter. But New England chipped away at the lead with a couple of touchdowns and a field goal to tie the score 24–24. The unthinkable was not only happening—Jets fans everywhere were thinking, *Here we go again. Another Jets loss to the loathsome Patriots.*

Thomas Jones ran the ball into the end zone, giving Gang Green a lead once again. But with not a moment to spare—1 second in fact—New England tied the game in regulation on a Randy Moss touchdown catch. The Patriots wouldn't be able to put their usual evil spell on the Jets that evening, though, as Gang Green had too much pluck, grit, and just a pinch of Leon Washington. Jay Feely booted a 34-yard field goal in overtime, sending the fans of Foxboro home unhappily but sending Jets Nation into a state of jubilation.

The loss was a crushing blow to the Pats, who missed the playoffs by a tiebreaker. Before the game, tackle Damien Woody claimed, "This has got to be the biggest game in a long time for the Jets." They came through in the clutch, and it was another scintillating return by one of those speedy Jets special teamers that helped set it all up.

Brad Smith

When Washington fractured his leg halfway through the 2009 season, the brunt of the kickoff return duties was handed to Brad Smith. And on December 27 of that year, Smith's agility, acuteness, and velocity inspired Gang Green to victory in their second-to-last regular-season game. However, much of the attention that day was shining on their opponent.

The Indianapolis Colts spit in the face of fate. They sneered at the gods of football. They belittled the significance of history. Gods and history were not on the minds of the Jets, though; all they cared about was winning the game. The Colts started the day with a spotless 14–0 record, their position in the playoffs secure and a perfect season in their grasp. The Jets, on the other hand, needed help—lots of help—along with a victory to keep their postseason hopes alive. As it turned out, those same football gods that would eventually smite the Colts were discovered to be New York Jets fans. Gang Green needed the Dolphins, Ravens, and Jaguars all to lose that day. And the gods saw to it that it happened. Now the Jets needed to win themselves.

Both offenses could get little going in the first half, with the high-powered Colts only mustering up nine points on a Joseph Addai 21-yard touchdown run (the extra point attempt was blocked) and

Brad Smith (16) sets a Jets record with a 106-yard kickoff return against the Indianapolis Colts on December 27, 2009. The Jets won 29–15, handing the Colts their first loss of the 2009 season. (Al Pereira/Getty Images)

a 22-yard field goal by Adam Vinatieri, while the Jets could only scrape together a 35-yard Jay Feely kick. No matter what took place in the first half, though, Indianapolis still had Peyton Manning behind center, and if his team was anywhere near sniffing distance of a victory, he would pull it out, somehow, someway.

There were two crucial turning points in the game, both in the Jets' favor. The impetus for one came from a decision by Colts coach Jim Caldwell, and the other was all the doing of the Jets… or Brad Smith, to be more specific. On Indianapolis' two kickoffs in the first half, Smith downed both in the end zone. He had the green light from special teams coach Mike Westhoff, though, to run one back even if the next kickoff was once again booted into the end zone. And as Vinatieri's kick to open the second half sailed deep past the Jets' goal line, Westhoff let out a little "uh oh," remembering that he gave Smith the okay to attempt a return.

Westhoff had nothing to worry about. Smith caught the kick standing on the "L" in "COLTS," 6 yards deep in the end zone. He went straight up the middle, following the impeccable, by-the-book blocking by the Jets' special teams unit. He cut to the right at the 25-yard line and turned on the burners. Vinatieri tried to track down Smith, but he didn't have a chance. And the last man to beat, defensive back Tim Jennings, desperately dove for Smith, but it was all in vain. Smith was gone. One end zone to the other. He would race 106 yards, not only giving the Jets a 10–9 lead but also setting a franchise record. It was the longest play in Jets history. Safety Jim Leonhard felt it was just what the team needed. "It was huge. For Brad to come out and do that, it gave everyone life. He really jump-started our offense and our defense."

Smith himself said of the play, "Catching the ball six deep you try to get the wedge as soon as possible. Rob Turner and Mike DeVito were the two wedge guys, and they did a great job of setting up the block and making the read definite. When you go back and see that film and see the blocking on that play, it was textbook. I can't tell you how easy they made it. We had a couple of guys double teamed, and I tried to break to the outside and break it up the sideline."

"It was a big burst, a big boost for the team, something we needed. It was one of the most exciting plays of my life, knowing the situation in the game and seeing how happy the guys were on the sideline. It got the team going a little bit, so that meant a lot."

Of course there were still almost 30 minutes left to play. Later in the third quarter, Hall-of-Famer-to-be Manning led his team downfield with Donald Brown running the ball into the end zone from the 1-yard line, giving the Colts a 15–10 bulge. And then Caldwell tempted fate, decreeing by his actions that going for history—an undefeated season—would take a backseat to resting his star quarterback (and other starting players) for the playoffs. It was a bad decision for two reasons. One, the Jets feasted on Manning's rookie replacement. On Curtis Painter's second possession, Calvin Pace stripped him of the ball and defensive end Marques Douglas recovered it and had all of 1 yard to go for a touchdown. The Jets never looked back and cruised to a 29–15 victory. The second reason Caldwell's decision would backfire was that the well-rested Colts would lose this game and their last, spoiling their pristine record, and they would go on to be defeated in the Super Bowl, as well.

The football gods had been angered, and the Jets were the beneficiaries. Gang Green would destroy Cincinnati in the season finale and become the Cinderella story of 2009, making it all the way to the AFC Championship Game, ultimately falling to these same Colts. The talking points after Gang Green's upset of Indianapolis in the penultimate game of the season revolved around the idea that the Jets won by happenstance. Rex Ryan wasn't buying it, though. "[The Colts] don't have to apologize to anybody about anything and neither do we. We won the game, ended up doing what we had to do whoever was in Colts' jerseys. There's very little credit that our football team has been given, and that's unfortunate."

Aaron Glenn

Who held the franchise record broken by Brad Smith with his 106-yard touchdown return? Longtime Jets cornerback Aaron Glenn. The Texas native almost didn't get a chance to set the record, however. The Jets were battling the Colts in Indianapolis on November 15, 1998. With the clock winding down in the first half, Peyton Manning scrambled his way out of bounds as time expired. Jets coach Bill Parcells and most of his players were halfway to the locker room when they were called back on the field. The refs had decided to put one more second on the clock, which sent Parcells into a rage. But the zebras held their ground.

The Colts decided to go for a what-the-heck 63-yard field goal. As kicker Mike Vanderjagt lined up for his attempt, a furious Parcells sent Glenn to stand deep in Jets' territory. The kick fell short, and Glenn caught the ball and headed up field. The first 50 yards were easy—mainly because the 11 Colts players on the field didn't even realize Glenn had the ball or that he was even back near the goal line. Once he passed the 50-yard line, Indianapolis made futile attempts to corral him, but it was too late. Glenn dashed 104 yards, setting a new Jets record that would last 11 years until Smith bested it by two yards.

Unfortunately, the Colts would come back and win the game, but Glenn had his moment in the sun. "I had the easy part," Glenn said. "Everyone else did all the work with the blocking. I looked for all the openings, and I found the end zone. But it doesn't matter if I broke an NFL record or not. When you lose it takes away from the excitement." Glenn would play eight seasons for the Jets, intercepting 24 passes and making two Pro Bowls in his time with the team. And the 104-yarder wasn't his only big play. He intercepted a pass and returned it 100 yards for a touchdown in 1996.

From Leon Burton and Dick Christy to Leon Washington and Brad Smith, the Jets have sprinted, bolted, scampered, slashed, and dashed their way to the end zone and into Jets fans' hearts. And those speed demons helped win a few games along the way, as well. Shake and bake.

CHAPTER 15

A FISTFUL OF SWAGGER

JETS COACHES HAVE COME in all shapes and sizes, be they large, medium, small, skinny, roly-poly, husky, hefty, and fit. And they've possessed an array of personalities, too. There have been loud ones, quiet ones, confident ones, tight-lipped ones, enthusiastic ones, stoic ones, gruff ones, overwhelmed ones, overmatched ones, understated ones, and underrated ones. But there's been no leader in franchise history quite like Rex Ryan.

When he came to town in January 2009, Ryan was more than the latest coaching hire by Gang Green—he brought the circus along with him. And the circus that's followed him to New York has been one chock-full of swagger, hyperbole, controversy, and braggadocio. Like the Bronx Zoo Yankees or 1986 Mets, the Rex Ryan Jets are an outrageous conglomeration of strutting, pleased-with-themselves rebels who couldn't give a hoot what others think of their act.

Unlike Richard Todd replacing Joe Namath, Ryan didn't have to live in the shadow of his predecessor. Eric Mangini may have been a competent, smart football man, but he didn't leave a legacy of winning, nor did he light up a room. He was the Art Howe of the Jets. Comparing Ryan to Mangini is like comparing someone who wrestles bears in his spare time to a mild-mannered stamp

Rex Ryan addresses the media during the January 2009 press conference where Ryan was introduced as the Jets' new head coach. (Andy Marlin/Getty Images)

collector. When lining up the coaches of Jets past—cuddly, grandfather-figure Weeb Ewbank, stern yet quiet Walt Michaels, and the preacher-like Herm Edwards all there for juxtaposition's sake—it's Bill Parcells who Ryan most resembles.

When Parcells came back to New York in 1997, he not only changed the culture of the Jets—destroying the stamp of losing that was put on the franchise by Rich Kotite—he took a team that was 1–15 in 1996 and in two short years had them playing in an AFC Championship Game. Parcells was confident, successful, and didn't suffer fools gladly. He was the Godfather of Swagger, though he intimidated and bullied the media rather than entertain them the way Ryan does.

When Ryan was hired, Parcells spotted a younger version of himself. "That's what I was," the former Jets coach said. "I could see it. I've been in this business a long time now. Some guys are football guys. Some guys are in the football business, but they're not football guys. They act like their job says football, but they are in it for a paycheck. This guy's a football guy, and I could smell that."

On January 21, 2009, Rex Ryan was unveiled to the world as the 17th head coach of the New York Jets. It was immediately apparent to all onlookers that Gang Green now had a confident, unwavering general at the helm...or maybe carnival barker would be more appropriate. Like Parcells, Ryan set out to change the culture of the team he inherited, but he didn't change it as much as blow it up with a dozen sticks of dynamite. Ryan made sure these weren't your father's Jets. But he wanted to make them your grandfather's Jets—the Super Bowl–winning Jets.

He began his speech on that fateful afternoon in the winter of 2009 not with humility or any sign of tentativeness, but with a bold, cocksure vision of the future. "First off, with all the cameras and all that, I was looking for our new president back there," Ryan said, referring to Barack Obama. "I think we'll get to meet him the next couple of years anyway." And Ryan wasn't going to settle for a second-term visit. "In his first term, there's no question. You give me four years, we should win the championship. I know it's been 40 years since the Jets won one, but with the abilities of the people here in place in this organization, I think it should be expected."

It just may be in the franchise's DNA to make guarantees and prognostications. The Jets' most memorable and significant moment in time is Joe Namath's Super Bowl boast, after all. And the first person ever associated with the team, original owner Harry Wismer, was the king of bluster. Ryan's chatter is nothing new. He's just carrying on a Jets tradition.

But coaching is surely in Ryan's genes, as his dad, Buddy, was a defensive genius with the Jets, Minnesota, and Chicago, as well as head coach of Philadelphia and Arizona. Rex's twin brother, Rob, is the defensive coordinator in Dallas. The Ryans know coaching, and the Ryans know defense. Their family crest might as well be a defensive tackle stuffing a running back behind the line of scrimmage.

"I'm not blessed with a silver tongue, but I know one thing. I know how to coach this game," Ryan stated on that first day. "We want to be known as the most physical football team in the NFL... the players will have each others' backs, and if you take a swipe at one of ours, we'll take a swipe at two of yours." He vowed that the Jets would play like Pete Rose but "without the gambling." It was the most stirring, brash speech since the opening scene of *Patton*.

In the tradition of Wahoo McDaniel claiming New York wasn't big enough for him and Sam Huff, Ryan made a similar statement about his rival. Ryan boldly proclaimed that he did not come to New York to kiss Bill Belichick's rings. The Northeast wasn't big enough for Ryan and anybody else, Belichick included. The new

Jets coach may have been selling himself short with his statement referencing a lack of a silver tongue, for he knows how to turn a phrase and can banter and jab with the best of them.

Before coaching his first game with the Jets, Ryan described his ultimate team: "When I picture the team I want, it's tough and physical, it can stop the run and it can run the ball. If it turns out the strength of our team is defense and we're not throwing the ball all over the place, that's great. That means we'll be in every game."

He covered every base when preparing his team to play the brand of tenacious, rock-'em, sock-'em football he envisioned. During his first training camp he not only encouraged his players to fight each other and, of course, the opponent, but he gave his charges rules and guidelines on how to act when a scuffle ensues, with the most important directive being not to pull a teammate off the pile as that may give an opponent an opportunity to get in a free shot at a defenseless Jet.

Of course, it was love at first sight for the players once they started working with Ryan. After Ryan's initial meeting with the offense on the first day of training camp, Jerricho Cotchery excitedly said, "When he talked to us in that meeting, you could just feel his passion. I looked around the room, and it was like, 'We want to go out and practice right now.' We're juiced to play for this guy."

Over the course of his two seasons with the Jets, Ryan's players have gushed over him. Veteran Tony Richardson, who's seen it all, explained Ryan's magic. "He just has this unique ability to make people around him feel very comfortable," Richardson said. "And it's funny, too, 'cause I don't think he goes out of his way to do it. I just think that it's his personality. Many guys I talk to around the league just say, 'Man I wish I had a chance to play for Rex Ryan.' And I tell 'em, 'You don't even understand. Everything you guys see from afar, you don't even understand how great we really have it here.'"

Trevor Pryce concurred with Richardson's assessment. "He's kind of like a teammate to us instead of a boss. Every team has a great cause they play for, and this is one of the few teams that play *for* our head coach, not in spite of him." And Pryce appreciates the fact that Ryan doesn't put on any airs or pretend to be anyone other than who he is. "It makes you play well, it makes you play for him, it makes you appreciative of what you have. He keeps it loose and has a smile on his face, and that exudes confidence from his players. If the head coach has confidence, you should have confidence. Rex is not going to change who he is just because this is a big game. He was like this as a coordinator, he was like that as a D-line coach, he was like that in college." In a November 2010 *Sports Illustrated* poll of 279 NFL players asking which coach they would most like to play for, Ryan came out on top with 21 percent of the vote.

The big-talking coach's players love to play for him, and they've also taken on his personality. Ryan's puffery and crowing have become contagious. Not only would the players run through a brick wall for their coach, but they would insult the wall and brag how they would smash it to pieces first. Ryan doesn't stand out all alone in his trash-talking; he's just become the ring leader of a confident gang of bullies who boast, chatter, talk, and chide, even if that means suffering embarrassment or having to eat crow— which they never do, because they don't regret one word they say. These are Rex Ryan's Jets, love 'em or hate 'em. Ryan's simple philosophy: "We're not hiding. We never hide. It's on."

Even the quiet, understated players are relishing the atmosphere that Ryan has fostered, as D'Brickashaw Ferguson said, "It's enjoyable to see the hams on the team, like your Bart Scotts, your Kris Jenkinses. We're the type of team that's like, 'Hey, this is what we're going to do. If you don't like it, screw you.'"

A Fistful of Swagger

The 2009 season got off to a roaring start, when Ryan began his Jets career with a 3-0 record, including a gratifying 16-9 victory over New England in Ryan's debut matchup with Belichick. There was no reason to give the Patriots coach's rings a smooch on that day. The Jets would stumble to a 4-6 record but would recover to win five of their last six games to qualify for the playoffs. Ryan established his "ground and pound" philosophy as Thomas Jones led the team with 1,402 yards, while rookie Shonn Greene added 540. Unfortunately, sparkplug Leon Washington broke his leg midseason. But Ryan's pride and joy, the defense, was ranked No. 1 in the NFL. The key piece to that defense was Darrelle Revis, who Ryan called the best defensive player in the game.

The highlight of the season came in the second round of the playoffs with a victory over the favored Chargers. All the chatter concerning the Jets' qualifications for the postseason centered on the word "luck." They were lucky to be there. They were lucky the Colts rested their starters in the 15th game of the season. They were lucky the Bengals had already clinched their playoff spot when they met on the final day of the year. That the Jets didn't earn their status was the all-too-common theme running through the end of the 2009 season. All that did was put a chip on the shoulder of the always-confident Jets, who had already played all season with a chip as big as Rex Ryan himself on their shoulder.

In the wild card round, Gang Green didn't need any luck as they easily handled the Bengals again 24-14. But when they reached the next round, San Diego jumped on the just-lucky-to-be-there bandwagon, as linebacker Bart Scott explained: "We were a little agitated because when we came out, a lot of those guys on their sideline were saying we didn't deserve to be here. Coming out in pregame, a lot of guys were saying we didn't belong. That kind of put us on edge coming out."

San Diego got on the board first when Kris Wilson hauled in a 13-yard touchdown pass from Philip Rivers. After the Jets closed the gap to 7–3 on a third-quarter, 46-yard Jay Feely field goal, safety Jim Leonhard made a crucial interception in the fourth quarter with the Chargers backed up deep in their own territory. That turnover set up a Dustin Keller 2-yard touchdown catch, giving the Jets the lead.

While Rivers would throw 40 passes in the game, Mark Sanchez would only air it out 23 times. The Jets were sticking to what got them this far: ground and pound. With starter Jones battling knee issues, it was up to Greene to shoulder the load. The rookie proved he was up to the task the previous week when he mauled the Bengals for 135 yards and scored the game-tying points on a 39-yard touchdown ramble. And he would come through on this day, too.

With 7:17 remaining in the game, and with one of the NFL's top quarterbacks in Rivers watching on the sidelines just waiting for his chance, Greene made the run that would propel the Jets to the AFC Championship Game. The New Jersey native took a handoff from Sanchez at the Jets' 47-yard line and started up the middle on what looked to be an innocuous short-gain play. The Jets' powerful offensive line moved to the right after the snap, and a giant hole—like the parting of the Red Sea—opened up in the middle. Greene, slightly cutting back to his left, shot through the gap between Ferguson and tight end Ben Hartsock, bounced off Charger safety Eric Weddle, and was home free, 53 yards for the eventual game-winning points.

The Chargers would score one more touchdown on a Rivers 1-yard run, and the Jets would convert a critical fourth-and-1 with 1:09 left to put the game away, but it was Greene's long bolt that would prove to be the decisive play of the game. The University of Iowa product gained 128 yards for the day and, combined with his previous week's total, his 263 rushing yards were the second most by a rookie in his first two playoff games in NFL history, bested only by the Cowboys' Duane Thomas' 278 yards in 1970. And with this victory, it gave the Jets two playoff wins for the first time since 1982.

Even though Ryan had the chutzpah to include plans for a Super Bowl parade in his team's playoff itinerary, they fell just a little short. After taking a 17–6 lead in the second quarter of the AFC Championship Game against the Colts, heartbreak won out again when Indianapolis scored 24 unanswered points to defeat the Jets 30–17. It was wait-until-next-year time once again.

The 2009 season was just a warm-up for 2010. Ryan and his Jets turned up the volume on the bombastic pronouncements, and it was Super Bowl or bust for this group. But what happens when swagger goes bad? When bravado turns to buffoonery? Rex Ryan is a mixed bag; with the good, you get the bad. When Ryan took the reins of the Jets, he created a culture of confidence, but he also produced a breeding ground of bad behavior, with some viewing his team as a band of hooligans and troublemakers with a boorishness that exemplified the crassness of modern America. Sure, there are delinquents throughout the NFL, but Gang Green was a polarizing force in a league run amok by lawbreakers and other questionably comported personalities.

The first chink in the armor came on January 30, 2010. A picture popped up on the Internet of Ryan giving the finger to a group of Dolphins fans in Miami at a Mixed Martial Arts event. He was certainly prodded, as he was allegedly spat on and verbally abused by a Miami rooter, but as he said himself after the incident, he "wouldn't accept that type of behavior from one of the coaches or players." But he did just that a little less than a year later when an unprovoked Antonio Cromartie called Tom Brady "an asshole." Ryan was fined $50,000 by the Jets for his peccadillo, while Cromartie got off scot-free. The cornerback was just following his coach's lead, after all.

Ryan singlehandedly made August 2010 "Obscenity Celebration Month" with his performance on HBO's *Hard Knocks*. In the opening episode, during one 80-second span, Ryan cursed nine times. Even his own mother was offended, as she chastised her foul-mouthed son. Another highlight (or is it lowlight?) of the series was Cromartie attempting to name all nine of his kids (by eight different women). The miscreant, F-bombing Jets made for a ratings bonanza, though. This was the highest-rated season in the series' history. HBO president Ross Greenburg stated, "As we're preparing to do *Hard Knocks*, I look at the head coach as the lead actor in a series. We've had Brian Billick, Herm Edwards, guys like that. Rex has just captured the lead actor award for the history of the series, and we knew that would happen." And Ryan uttered a new catchphrase that may yet sweep America: "Let's go eat a goddamned snack."

Just before the 2010 season got underway, TV Azteca reporter Ines Sainz, who was named the Sexiest Reporter in Mexico, appeared at a Jets practice to conduct an interview with Sanchez. And the Ryan zoo was in full force. The head coach, defensive backs coach Dennis Thurman, and a few of the players tossed footballs in her direction as an excuse to sidle up to her and give her the once-over. In the locker room, catcalls, whistles, and rude remarks flew her way. Sainz tweeted that she was "dying of embarrassment." Sanchez himself was polite and pleasant, but a group of reporters witnessing the scene dragged her out of the humiliating, awkward situation.

"In my opinion, I never felt attacked, nor that they reacted grossly toward me. I arrived in the locker room, and there were comments and games. One of the other reporters came up to me and apologized for what was happening, but I thought [the players] were joking around," she later said. The Jets' ironically named owner Woody Johnson apologized on behalf of the franchise.

There was no punishment from the commissioner's office, but a league-wide media training program was instituted. It was another Rex's-boys-will-be-Rex's-boys moment.

The hits kept on coming. In September, Braylon Edwards, who previously had been sent packing by the Browns due to his selfish antics, was arrested for drunk driving. At the same time, newly acquired receiver Santonio Holmes was sitting out the first four games of the season with a suspension for violating the league's substance-abuse policy. Three months later it was Ryan who was making headlines when an Internet video surfaced of a couple acting out a foot-fetish scenario. The woman was a dead-ringer for Ryan's wife, while the man's voice sounded eerily like Ryan's. That breaking news quieted the talkative coach for the first and only time. "This is a personal issue, and I'm not going to discuss it," was all he would say about the matter.

The downside of swagger also reared its ugly head in a December 12 loss to Miami. While covering a punt, Nolan Carroll ran out of bounds onto the Jets' sideline, wherein strength and conditioning coach Sal Alosi stuck out his knee and tripped the Dolphin. Carroll went down in a heap but wasn't seriously injured. It came to light that Alosi ordered a handful of injured players and other personnel to form a wall, impeding the opposing team's gunner. Ryan and special teams coach Mike Westhoff denied any knowledge of the dangerous tactic, and Westhoff went so far as to cryptically accuse the Patriots of the same wrongdoing. Alosi was not fired by the team; instead, he was suspended without pay for the remainder of the season and fined $25,000. The team itself was fined $100,000 by the league.

Alosi even attempted to disguise himself that day. He was wearing a green hat when the incident occurred, switched to a black hat, and finally wore no hat at all. His ruse did not work, though, as he was caught red-handed. Why did he do it? "You're asking me to give you a logical explanation for an illogical act," he said. "I can't explain it. I wasn't thinking. If I could go back and do it again, I sure as heck would take a step back. That's the problem. Nothing went through my head. I wasn't thinking." On January 31, 2011, Alosi resigned from the Jets.

Though many players around the league have expressed an interest in playing for Ryan, there are just as many who are not enamored with the Jets. Miami's Channing Crowder explained, "They're cocky for no reason. They haven't won anything. They act tough, but they're not tough. They're a good team, but they're not what they come off as they are. I hate fake people and I hate posers, and a lot of them are."

Even controversy that Ryan had nothing to do with came to light during his tenure. In 2008, Brett Favre swooped into the Jets' world as a savior with fanfare, trumpets, and the warm welcome of a soon-to-be hero. He led the team to an 8–3 record, including a six-touchdown-pass game against Arizona, and he brought some lighthearted locker-room shenanigans with him when he left a present in Eric Barton's locker—a bag filled with blood and guts, which turned out to be a dead wild turkey. The season ended in disaster, though, as the team lost four out of their last five games, missed the playoffs, and Mangini was fired.

After Favre was long gone in 2010, Jets employee Jenn Sterger accused the then-Vikings quarterback of having left her salacious voicemail messages and texts, along with sending her photos of his private parts. On top of that, the Jets and their former quarterback were sued by a pair of massage therapists after they were let go by the team when they blew the whistle on even more inappropriate behavior by Favre. Sterger didn't come forward in 2008 because she felt nothing would have been done. The whole situation devolved into he-said, she-said ugliness. Favre was ultimately given a $50,000 slap-on-the-wrist fine for not cooperating with the league. "The reason I didn't come forward two years ago is because the results would have been the same," Sterger said, "except now I have representation who has my back and protects me."

Owner Woody Johnson does not have a problem with the perception of the Jets as a team that others love to hate. "I think it's great," he said. "Whatever feeling they have, as long as it's a vivid feeling. I think it's more positive than having apathy or any of that. I'm glad they feel strongly about us." He went on to say, "People are gonna like us. People aren't gonna like us. But we're gonna be who we are." And Johnson certainly has no regrets about his bombastic coach. "I hired him because of his personality, not in spite of it."

A day after the 2010 season ended, Ryan even acknowledged that his players may be a little too out of control; he felt the need to warn his team about behaving themselves in the offseason. "I told them to hold each other accountable and you represent yourself, [but] you also represent this organization on and off the field," Ryan said. "I have to be mindful of that as well, obviously, with my past history. Be proud to be a Jet because I know I am." But with the owner and head coach giving a wink and a smile to the degenerate actions of the team, the players and employees have just been falling in line behind their leaders.

With all those self-inflicted issues swirling around the Jets, they still had a season to play in 2010. After a memorable offseason—which included lap-band surgery for the coach; the *Hard Knocks* television series; the additions of LaDainian Tomlinson, Jason Taylor, Cromartie, and Holmes; the losses of Jones, Washington, and guard Alan Faneca; and the training camp holdout of Revis, who signed a new contract only after Ryan flew down to the cornerback's home in Florida along with Johnson to help mediate, the Jets opened up 2010 in their new stadium with a loss to Baltimore. They quickly recovered and won five consecutive games, which included a rainy Monday night game dubbed the Favre Bowl when his Vikings visited the New Meadowlands shortly after his 2008 sexting became publicly known, plus a thriller in Denver highlighted by a pass-interference call against the Broncos on a desperation heave by Sanchez in the waning seconds of the game. The Jets pushed across the winning points and headed into their bye week in the conversation as one of the top teams in the NFL.

While the Jets' 9–0 loss to Green Bay in Week 8 was an omen of offensive struggles that would haunt the team in their two most crushing losses of the regular season, the exciting, lucky-to-get-out-of-Denver-alive victory over the Broncos foreshadowed more pulsating, edge-of-your-seat wins to come, as the Jets would go on a wild ride filled with electrifying finishes in three straight games in the month of November.

Although the Jets' opponents—the Lions, Browns, and Texans—were a trio of mediocrity, and although Gang Green came out on top in all three contests, they had to do so using every second of the game clock. Nick Folk booted an overtime field goal to edge Detroit; Holmes weaved and scampered his way 37 yards to put away Cleveland, again in overtime; and Sanchez threw a perfect pass to the corner of the end zone to Holmes, who made a just-as-perfect catch in the final seconds of regulation to defeat Houston.

Before the Cleveland game, Ryan proved why he's the funniest Jets coach since Lou Holtz when, during a midweek press conference, he donned a costume, long blond wig and all, to resemble his twin brother, who was the defensive coordinator of the Browns. It was the greatest disguise in New York sports since Mets manager Bobby Valentine was ejected from a 1999 game and snuck back into the dugout sporting a fake mustache and sunglasses.

The fun and games continued into Thanksgiving night when the Jets finally won the easy way with a 26–10 romp over the Bengals. Brad Smith was the star, scoring on a 53-yard end-around to open up the second half and later returning a kickoff 89 yards for a touchdown, which was impressive enough, but he also lost one of his shoes along the way.

Next up was a Monday night showdown for first place between the 9–2 Jets and the 9–2 Patriots. The Jets had already beaten New England 28–14 in Week 2, and the team was wholly confident they would defeat their arch rivals once again. In true Rex Ryan style, Gang Green announced to the world that they would whip the Patriots and that they were the best team in football. But once again, swagger was given a cold hard slap in the face. After quickly falling behind 17–0 the Jets put three points on the board with a 39-yard Folk field goal, and that was the grand sum of the team's scoring for the night. Meanwhile, the Patriots' offense ran right over, through, and around Gang Green's defense for four more touchdowns and embarrassed the Jets with a 45–3 win.

Ryan reached down into his bag of tricks and came up with a unique reaction to the devastating loss, as Revis explained, "He told us to go outside and we were all saying, 'What are we doing? Going on a field trip or something?' The hole was right there, already dug there with the dirt on the side, and he threw the ball in the hole. It was a funeral for a game ball. That might be the best I ever saw. I've never seen a coach do that. You usually hear a coach say, 'Let's bury this game.' Rex actually buried it. Everybody was in shock. Nobody said anything."

The Tripgate loss to the Dolphins came next, and again the offense couldn't find their way into the end zone as Miami won 10–6. The team finally got back on track with an impressive win over the Steelers, with the key scores being a naked bootleg run by Sanchez and another kickoff return for a touchdown by Smith.

It was the first win ever for the Jets in Pittsburgh. The next week saw the Jets lose a tough one to Chicago, but they did score 34 points as their offense started producing again. And in the season finale, with a spot in the playoffs already clinched, they rolled all over the Bills 38–7.

The 2010 Jets improved their record by two wins from the previous season, finishing in second place with an 11–5 mark. Their defensive showing and ground-and-pound running game were not quite as effective, though. But that didn't stop the Jets from entering the postseason thinking they were on the road to Dallas to play in—and win—the Super Bowl. What stood in the Jets' way were three superstar quarterbacks who had been thorns in the team's side for years—Peyton Manning, Tom Brady, and Ben Roethlisberger.

First up were Manning and the Colts in a rematch of the 2009 AFC Championship Game. The game seesawed back and forth well into the fourth quarter with the Jets holding a late 14–13 lead. With the game heading toward the 2-minute warning, Manning, a game-winning-drive machine, took control of the ball. And looming on the sidelines was one of the greatest clutch kickers in NFL history, Adam Vinatieri. The legendary quarterback did his part and swiftly drove his team into field-goal range, and Vinatieri booted a no-doubt-about-it 50-yard field goal, that looked like the winning points.

But the Colts made two mistakes. Gang Green's defense stopped Manning from reaching the end zone, and Indianapolis scored a little too quickly. Cromartie, filling in for the injured Smith, gave the Jets' offense a great head start with a 47-yard kickoff return. And it took Sanchez only five plays to move the Jets into field-goal range with an improvised 18-yard completion to Edwards being the crucial play of the drive. Folk came in and repeated his heroics from the Lions game, kicking a 32-yard field goal as time expired to give his team a 17–16 victory, which set up another clash with New England.

The Jets and Patriots had been on a collision course all season long. New York wanted to exorcise their Bill Belichick demons, while New England looked to put the big-mouthed Jets in their place. The week leading up to the game was a trash-talking extravaganza. Ryan had gotten the ball rolling the previous week when he praised Manning while insulting Brady along the way. Cromartie hurled expletives at the Patriots quarterback. Even New England receiver Wes Welker broke his coach's rules with a stone-faced speech referencing any and every phrase having to do with feet, rubbing Ryan's face in his December controversy. For his transgression, Belichick pulled Welker from the starting lineup. Ryan, of course, had no such rules.

Among all the classless pronouncements and insults, the Jets and Ryan did one thing right. The coach brought in former Jet Dennis Byrd to give the team an inspirational speech. In 1992, Byrd was temporarily paralyzed in a collision with teammate Scott Mersereau. While he eventually learned to walk again, he never played another down of football, and he told the present edition of the Jets that he would give anything to be involved in just one more play. Not one Super Bowl. Not one game. Just one play.

Even though New England jumped out to a 3–0 lead, it was all Jets for the remainder of the game. Tomlinson and Edwards scored second-quarter touchdowns, and Holmes and Greene crossed the goal line in the second half. The defense sacked, intercepted, knocked down, and punished Brady, with the Tasmanian devil–like Sean Ellis in his face all day long. Both the game plan and execution were brilliant. The Jets upset the Patriots 28–21, and to a man Byrd's speech was given as a key reason for the victory. Ryan may have overstated things when he announced this would be the second biggest game in franchise history, but it was certainly one

Jets quarterback Mark Sanchez and head coach Rex Ryan celebrate after the Jets upset the New England Patriots 28–21 in the Divisional Playoffs on January 16, 2011. (Al Pereira/Getty Images)

of the most satisfying victories the team has ever experienced. The Rex Ryan Jets were now 3–2 against Belichick's Patriots.

The Jets reached the AFC Championship Game for the second consecutive season, the first time that feat had been accomplished in team history. But their Super Bowl dream came to a crashing halt yet again. This time, there wasn't too much mud, nor did the Jets lose an early lead. This one was all too similar to the playoff game against Buffalo in 1981. The Jets dug themselves a 24–0 hole, thanks to some startlingly poor tackling, mounted a heroic comeback, but fell just short, losing 24–19 with Roethlisberger making just enough clutch plays to keep the Jets at bay.

If Richard Todd's late-game interception was the rueful moment of the heartbreaking loss three decades prior, Pittsburgh's fourth-quarter goal-line stand was the regretful sequence in this contest. With a first down on the Steelers' 2-yard line, the Jets had four chances to cross the goal line but ultimately failed. Greene rushed for 1 yard on first down, which was followed by two incomplete Sanchez passes, and Tomlinson was stuffed for no gain on their final try. The radio in Sanchez's helmet malfunctioned (what was the call-his-own-plays Joe Namath thinking as he watched this?), and the whole set of downs seemed off-kilter and out of whack. In fact, the Jets seemed off-kilter and out of whack for most of the first half. The trash talking, fire, and intensity all seemed to have been left behind in New England.

Close but no cigar isn't good enough anymore for these Jets. One by one, the players acknowledged the new losing-is-not-acceptable attitude that had been instituted by Ryan. "I'd like to say it was a good year," Revis said, "but around here, we believe a good year would mean playing football for two more weeks." Calvin Pace added, "I'm proud of what we did, but we have higher expectations." Ferguson agreed with his teammates. "The bar here is very high. It's a very high standard."

In only two short seasons, Ryan has won more playoff games than any coach in Jets history, while Sanchez has more postseason victories than any franchise quarterback. Ryan's tactics and techniques for achieving success don't always come with class and sportsmanship. Some despise him for what he stands for. His Super Bowl predictions are now met with a roll of the eyes. And embarrassing moments have become part of the Rex Ryan package.

But Ryan is not accepting the "same old Jets." He's not accepting the same old losing. And he's not accepting a Super Bowl–less season. Though his cockiness is often nothing but hot air, he's taking that stormy bluster and doing all he can to blow away the ghosts of the incompetent 1970s, the Mud Bowl, roughing-the-passer in Cleveland, the Fake Spike, 1–15, and the failed Brett Favre experiment.

The Rex Ryan Jets aren't just pursuing a Super Bowl victory for themselves. Their quest is also for Jerome Barkum. And Rich Caster. And Pat Leahy. And Richard Todd. And Wesley Walker. And Joe Fields. And Joe Klecko. And Marty Lyons. And Greg Buttle. And Al Toon. And Ken O'Brien. And Mickey Shuler. And Freeman McNeil. And Dennis Byrd. And Mo Lewis. And Wayne Chrebet. And Curtis Martin. And Vinny Testaverde. And Chad Pennington. And all the Jets who have never won a Super Bowl.

Losing "cuts your heart out," Ryan said. But his vision and tenacity will not be altered. "Our goal for next year—I got news for you, it won't change. And it'll never change. We're gonna chase that Super Bowl. We're gonna chase it 'til we get it. And then we'll chase it after that again."

SOURCES

Chapter One: Hustlin' Harry, Slingin' Sammy, and the Birth of the Titans

Berger, Phil. *More Championship Teams of the NFL*. New York: Random House, 1974.

Boyle, Robert. "AFL Verdict: Not Quite a Hit." *Sports Illustrated*, September 19, 1960.

———. "Horatio Harry." *Sports Illustrated*, October 31, 1960.

———. "The Underdogs Have Made It." *Sports Illustrated*, November 12, 1962.

Chastain, Bill. *100 Things Jets Fans Should Know and Do Before They Die*. Chicago: Triumph Books, 2010.

Felser, Larry. *The Birth of the NFL: How the 1966 NFL/AFL Merger Transformed Pro Football*. Guilford, CT: The Lyons Press, 2008.

Kroll, Alex. "The Last of the Titans." *Sports Illustrated*, September 22, 1969.

Maynard, Don. *You Can't Catch Sunshine*. Chicago: Triumph Books, 2010.

Miller, Jeff. *Going Long: The Wild Ten-Year Saga of the Renegade American Football League in the Words of Those Who Lived It*. New York: McGraw-Hill, 2004.

Chapter Two: Portrait of a Cowboy in a Strange Land

Brown, Gwilym S. "Oh, How Gently Flows This Don." *Sports Illustrated*, July 23, 1973.

Crichton, Andrew. "They Said It." *Sports Illustrated*, July 16, 1974.

Devaney, John. *Star Pass Receivers of the NFL*. New York: Random House, 1972.

Jones, Robert F. "Eub Weebank's Mother Hens." *Sports Illustrated*, November 10, 1969.

Kroll, Alex. "The Last of the Titans." *Sports Illustrated*, September 22, 1969.

Lemire, Joe. "Don Maynard." *Sports Illustrated*, July 14, 2008.

Maynard, Don. *You Can't Catch Sunshine*. Chicago: Triumph Books, 2010.

Namath, Joe Willie, and Dick Schaap. *I Can't Wait Until Tomorrow...'Cause I Get Better Looking Every Day*. New York: Signet, 1970.

Chapter Three: Just Watch *Heidi*, Baby

Crowe, Jerry. "The 'Heidi Game' Remembered, November 17, 1968." *Los Angeles Times*, November 18, 2008.

Miller, Stuart. *The 100 Greatest Days in New York Sports*. New York: Houghton Mifflin, 2006.

Namath, Joe Willie, and Dick Schaap. *I Can't Wait Until Tomorrow...'Cause I Get Better Looking Every Day*. New York: Signet, 1970.

Shrake, Edwin. "Joe Passes the Big Test in a Breeze." *Sports Illustrated*, January 6, 1969.

Zimmerman, Paul. "Hold the Phone! Here Come the Jets." *Sports Illustrated*, January 24, 1983.

Chapter Four: Chief Wahoo
Creamer, Robert W. "Scorecard." *Sports Illustrated*, July 26, 1976.
Freemantle, Tony. "'Wahoo' McDaniel, wrestling giant, dead at 63." *Houston Chronicle,* April 22, 2002.
Jenkins, Dan. "How They Do Run On." *Sports Illustrated*, November 1, 1971.
Kinkhabwala, Aditi. "Ed Marinaro, Heisman Hopeful." *Sports Illustrated*, November 29, 1999.
Plimpton, George. "Yesterday Is Not Far Away." *Sports Illustrated*, September 8, 1975.
Shrake, Edwin. "Wahoo! Wahoo! Wahoo!" *Sports Illustrated*, October 26, 1964.
Shropshire, Mike. "Wahoo McDaniel." *Sports Illustrated*, July 2, 2001.
WrestlingMuseum.com

Chapter Five: They Might (Not) Be Giants
Jones, Robert F. "Eub Weebank's Mother Hens." *Sports Illustrated,* November 10, 1969.
Kriegel, Mark. *Namath: A Biography*. New York: Penguin, 2005.
Miller, Stuart. *The 100 Greatest Days in New York Sports*. New York: Houghton Mifflin, 2006.
Taylor, Lawrence, and David Falkner. *LT: Living on the Edge*. New York: Penguin, 2005.
Zimmerman, Paul. "Reaching for Respect." *Sports Illustrated*, September 29, 1986.

Chapter Six: It's Good to Be Joe Namath
Beech, Mark. "John Riggins, Running Back." *Sports Illustrated*, May 20, 2002.
Boyle, Robert H. "The Return of a Couple of Old Sticks-in-the-Pocket." *Sports Illustrated*, December 13, 1971.
Bruns, Bill. "Different Strokes for a Different Joe." *Sport*, November 1977.
Cimini, Rich. "Jets Leave Plenty of Stories Behind in Hempstead." *New York Daily News*, August 16, 2008.
IMDB.com
Jenkins, Dan. "The Sweet Life of Swinging Joe." *Sports Illustrated*, October 31, 1994.
Johnson, William. "Mod Man Out." *Sports Illustrated*, June 16, 1969.
Kirshenbaum, Jerry. "Scorecard." *Sports Illustrated*, April 28, 1975.
Kriegel, Mark. *Namath: A Biography*. New York: Penguin, 2005.
Marshall, Joe. "Hollywood or Bust for Off-Broadway Joe." *Sports Illustrated*, April 25, 1977.
Montville, Leigh. "Off Broadway Joe." *Sports Illustrated*, July 14, 1997.
Maule, Tex. "Joe Bits the Astrodust." *Sports Illustrated*, October 9, 1972.
Namath, Joe Willie, and Dick Schaap. *I Can't Wait Until Tomorrow...'Cause I Get Better Looking Every Day*. New York: Signet, 1970.
Reid, Ron. "He's Free, But Not Cheap." *Sports Illustrated*, June 7, 1976.
TheGregBradyProject.com
WayneCochranandtheCCRiders.com
Zimmerman, Paul. "Guaranteed Cool." *Sports Illustrated*, January 28, 1991.

Chapter Seven: The New York Sack Exchange
Anderson, Dave. "It's Time for the Jets to Sack Mark Gastineau." *New York Times*, October 4, 1987.
———. "Time Has Come for Klecko to go to Hall of Fame." *New York Times*, November 7, 2008.
———. "Was it a 'Cheap Shot,' or Was it Clean?" *New York Times*, December 9, 1987.
Anderson, Lars. "The 'Bama Defense." *Sports Illustrated*, July 13, 2009.
Arias, Ron. "Five-Year-Old Rocky Lyons, Son of Jets Star, Thought He Could Save His Mom's Life—and He Did." *People*, December 14, 1987.

Sources

Cimini, Rich. "Jets Leave Plenty of Stories Behind in Hempstead." *New York Daily News*, August 16, 2008.

Chick, Bob. "Tampa Bay's All-Century Team, No. 23 Marty Lyons." *Tampabayonline.net*. http://tampabayonline.net/reports/top100/no23.htm.

Garber, Greg. "Gastineau Ready to Put His (Track) Record Behind Him." *ESPN.com*, January 4, 2001. http://static.espn.go.com/nfl/columns/garber_greg/1305782.html

Kennedy, Kostya. "Click This." *Sports Illustrated*, December 3, 2007.

Lieber, Jill. "Extra Points." *Sports Illustrated*, September 16, 1985.

Miller, Stuart. *The 100 Greatest Days in New York Sports*. New York: Houghton Mifflin, 2006.

Newman, Bruce. "No! No! No! Gastineau." *Sports Illustrated*, September 5, 1984.

Ottum, Bob. "Killer With a Baby Face." *Sports Illustrated*, September 24, 1979.

Zimmerman, Paul. "The Sackers." *Sports Illustrated*, September 1, 1982.

———. "The Verdict Is in on Practice." *Sports Illustrated*, September 3, 1984.

———. "Dr. Z's Alltime Great Pass Rushers." *Sports Illustrated*, August 28, 2000.

Chapter Eight: Just Give Me the Damn Flashlight

Bradley, John Ed. "Blue Plate Special." *Sports Illustrated*, May 12, 1997.

Cimini, Rich. "Wayne Wins it in a Flash: Lights Way for Jets to Silence Keyshawn." *New York Daily News*, September 25, 2000.

———. "In Defeat, Keyshawn Hardly at Loss for Words." *New York Daily News*, September 26, 2000.

———. "Crossing the Finish Line: From Jets Bust to Drug Addict to Sex Offender, Johnny (Lam) Jones Has Turned His Life Around." *New York Daily News*, April 24, 2005.

Elliott, Josh. "Key Figure." *Sports Illustrated*, April 24, 2000.

Gola, Hank. "Curtis Throws Bucs for Loss." *New York Daily News*, September 25, 2000.

Johnson, Keyshawn and Shelley Smith. *Just Give Me the Damn Ball!: The Fast Times and Hard Knocks of an NFL Rookie*. New York: Grand Central Publishing, 1997.

King, Peter. "Vinny Vidi, Vici." *Sports Illustrated*, January 18, 1999.

MacGregor, Jeff. "Muddied But Unbowed." *Sports Illustrated*, November 8, 1999.

Murphy, Austin. "The Stupor Bowl." *Sports Illustrated*, September 30, 1996.

———. "Down for the Count." *Sports Illustrated*, December 30, 1996.

Myers, Gary. "Just Get Johnson the Damn Excuses." *New York Daily News*, September 25, 2000.

O'Brien, Richard and Hank Hersch. "Scorecard." *Sports Illustrated*, May 5, 1997.

Silver, Michael. "Guiding Light." *Sports Illustrated*, October 2, 2000.

———. "Class of '96." *Sports Illustrated*, December 5, 2005.

Stroud, Rick. "Keyshawn Johnson." *St. Petersburg Times*, September 1, 2000.

Walters, John. "Wayne Chrebet." *Sports Illustrated*, November 25, 1996

Chapter Nine: Monday Night Madness

Cimini, Rich. "Jets Pull Out Win With Wild Finish; Rally Makes Green History." *New York Daily News*, October 24, 2000.

———. "Al Tirade Makes Jet Miracle; Groh Gang Gives Credit to Halftime Rant." *New York Daily News*, October 25, 2000.

———. "Jumbo Jet Flying High After TD Grab." *New York Daily News*, October 25, 2000.

McCarron, Anthony, Rich Cimini, and Gary Myers. "Miller Gives Roger a Little Comic Relief." *New York Daily News*, October 24, 2000.

Myers, Gary. "File This Jets Comeback as Miracle at the Meadowlands." *New York Daily News*, October 24, 2000.

Sandomir, Richard. "One Night in 1970, the Revolution Was Televised." *New York Times*, November 23, 2005.

Chapter 10: Richard Todd and the Battle of the Mud People
Cannizzaro, Mark. "Woe-for-Three." *New York Post*, January 21, 2011.
Cimini, Richard. "Jets Leave Plenty of Stories Behind in Hempstead." *New York Daily News*, August 16, 2008.
Horowitz, Jamie. "New York Jets Quarterback Richard Todd." *Sports Illustrated*, January 12, 1998.
Kirshenbaum, Jerry. "Scorecard." *Sports Illustrated*, November 30, 1981.
Looney, Douglas S. "Wall Street Richard." *Sports Illustrated*, August 1, 1983.
Marshall, Joe. "They Jetted Back to Earth." *Sports Illustrated*, September 25, 1978.
Miller, Stuart. *The 100 Greatest Days in New York Sports*. New York: Houghton Mifflin, 2006.
Reid, Ron. "Getting Chilled by a Very Slight Draft." *Sports Illustrated*, April 19, 1976.
Zimmerman, Paul. "In Todd They Trust." *Sports Illustrated*, November 30, 1981.
———. "What's New? New York, New York." *Sports Illustrated*, December 28, 1981.
———. "Miami Was One Tough Mudder." *Sports Illustrated*, January 31, 1983.

Chapter 11: I Ain't Got No Home
Lowry, Philip J. *Green Cathedrals*. Boston: Addison-Wesley, 1992.
Maynard, Don. *You Can't Catch Sunshine*. Chicago: Triumph Books, 2010.
Namath, Joe Willie, and Dick Schaap. *I Can't Wait Until Tomorrow...'Cause I Get Better Looking Every Day*. New York: Signet, 1970.
Powers, Ian. "Die-hard New York Jets Supporter Bruce 'The Base' Gregor Is the Man Beneath J-E-T-S Chant." *New York Daily News*, January 24, 2010.

Chapter 12: The Wild, Wild West
Maule, Tex. "Say It's So, Joe." *Sports Illustrated*, January 20, 1969.
———. "Joe Bites the Astrodust." *Sports Illustrated*, October 9, 1972.
Namath, Joe Willie, and Dick Schaap. *I Can't Wait Until Tomorrow...'Cause I Get Better Looking Every Day*. New York: Signet, 1970.
Zimmerman, Paul. "Reaching for Respect." *Sports Illustrated*, September 29, 1986.

Chapter 13: Bad Ideas
Bondy, Filip. "Kraft-y Move by Belichick: Forget Speech, Bill Wants Deal." *New York Daily News*, January 5, 2000.
Cimini, Rich. "Rich Ducks Line of Fire: Calls it Quits to Beat Jets to the Punch." *New York Daily News*, December 21, 1996.
———. "One & 15 'Tis the Season: Kotite's Sendoff Is Coal in Jets Stocking." *New York Daily News*, December 23, 1996.
———. "Belichick Bails Out After Just One Day." *New York Daily News*, January 5, 2000.
Creamer, Robert W. "They Said It." *Sports Illustrated*, June 7, 1976.
Eskenazi, Gerald. "The Spike Was Fake, But the Damage to Jets' Season Is Real." *New York Times*, November 28, 1994.
———. "New York Jets Go Rolling Along." *New York Times*, November 24, 1996.
Gola, Hank. "Departure's Timing Stuns Watchful Jets." *New York Daily News*, December 21, 1996.
King, Peter. "Roasted Turkeys." *Sports Illustrated*, December 5, 1994.
Loony, Douglas S. "Lou, You're a Lulu." *Sports Illustrated*, September 11, 1978.

Lupica, Mike. "Rich Ducks Line of Fire: Kotite Stands Tall." *New York Daily News*, December 21, 1996.

Mulvoy, Mark. "No Roses for Garden City Joe." *Sports Illustrated*, September 29, 1975.

Murphy, Austin. "Down for the Count." *Sports Illustrated*, December 30, 1996.

———. "Heeeeeere's Lou!" *Sports Illustrated*, September 25, 2006.

Myers, Gary. "For a Start, 0 and Awful This Is Not What Leon Had in Mind." *New York Daily News*, September 4, 1995.

Myers, Gary. "Jets Prez Says Coach in Chaos." *New York Daily News*, January 5, 2000.

O'Connor, Ian. "One & 15 'Tis the Season: If Hess Wants Success, It's Time He Step on Gas." *New York Daily News*, December 23, 1996.

O'Keeffe, Michael. "The Score. Holtz Still Haunted by His Jets Fiasco." *New York Daily News*, September 3, 2006.

"People." *Sports Illustrated*, July 23, 1973.

Chapter 14: Washington Scored Here

Cannizzaro, Mark. "Wacky Scoring Run Is Only Bright Spot." *New York Post*, November 16, 1998.

———. "Jets Due to Pay Back Bill; Pats' Defense is 'Slow' and 'Old.'" *New York Post*, November 13, 2008.

———. "'Gift' Talk Doesn't Fly With Jets." *New York Post*. December 30, 2009.

———. "Smith's Kickoff Return Makes Jets History." *New York Post*, December 30, 2009.

Cimini, Rich. "Chad Returns For Seconds; Saves Jets With OT Kickoff TD." *New York Daily News*, September 9, 2002.

Chapter 15: A Fistful of Swagger

Bontemps, Tim. "Jets Owner Will Pay for Media Training After 'Unprofessional Conduct' in Locker Room." *New York Post*, September 17, 2010.

———. "Cro to Union, Owners: Get Your Bleep Together." *New York Post*, January 25, 2011.

Cannizzaro, Mark. "Jets Upset Chargers, Will Face Colts in AFC Championship." *New York Post*, January 18, 2010.

———. "Coach's Attitude Inspires His Jets." *New York Post*, December 5, 2010.

———. "Bury the Blowout: Rex Says R.I.P. to 45-4 Defeat With Game-Ball Funeral." *New York Post*. December 9, 2010.

———. "Suddenly 'O'Ful Jets Trip & Fall: Assistant Pulls Dirty Trick as Offense Goes MIA Again." *New York Post*, December 13, 2010.

———. "Trip Coach Apologizes; Jets Suspend Him for Rest of Season." *New York Post*, December 13, 2010.

———. "Gang Loves Playing for Rex." *New York Post*, January 19, 2011.

———. "Ryan to Gang: Behave Yourself." *New York Post*, January 25, 2011.

Cherner, Reid. "Brett Favre, a Dead Animal and a Teammate's Locker." *USA TODAY*, October 8, 2008.

"For the Record." *Sports Illustrated*, February 15, 2010.

Fox, Ashley. "Rookie Helps Jets' 'Ground and Pound' Game." *Philadelphia Inquirer*, January 23, 2010.

Gregorian, Dareh, and Dan Mangan. "Jet Harass-Flap Gals Sacked." *New York Post*, January 4, 2011.

Hack, Damon. "Jets Defense Is Ready to Rise." *Sports Illustrated,* June 18, 2010.

Hale, Mark. "Greene's Late Run Ices Jets' Win." *New York Post*, January 19, 2010.

Jenkins, Lee. "Open and Shut." *Sports Illustrated*, January 18, 2010.

"Jets Coach Ryan Dodges Questions Regarding Foot-Fetish Videos, Calls it a 'Personal Issue.'" *New York Post*, December 22, 2010.

King, Peter. "Why We Fight." *Sports Illustrated*, August 17, 2009.

Lewis, Brian. "Jets Strength Coach Trips Dolphins CB." *New York Post*, December 12, 2010.

Mangan, Dan. "Reporter Claims She 'Never Felt Attacked' by Jets Players During Practice." *New York Post*, September 13, 2010.

———. "Sterger Had Secret Meeting With NFL Commissioner." *New York Post*, January 5, 2011.

Perloff, Andrew. "3 New York Jets." *Sports Illustrated*, September 7, 2009.

Reiter, Ben. "1 New York Jets." *Sports Illustrated*, September 6, 2010.

Rushin, Steve. "The Summer's Best @#$%! Comedy." *Sports Illustrated*, August 23, 2010.

Serby, Steve. "Move Over Broadway Joe, Ryan Brings New Attitude." *New York Post*, January 22, 2009.

———. "Parcells: Rex Has What it Takes, Just Like I Did." *New York Post,* January 24, 2009.

———. "Gung-ho Green: We're Gonna Win," *New York Post*, November 30, 2010.

———. "For Woody, It's a Love-Hate Deal: Bold Is Beautiful for Jets Owner." *New York Post*, January 6, 2011.

———. "Serby's Title Game Q&A With Tony Richardson." *New York Post*, January 21, 2011.

———. "Rex's Title Boast Winds Up Toast." *New York Post*, January 24, 2011.

"SI Players NFL Poll." *Sports Illustrated*, November 29, 2010.

Vaccaro, Mike. "Same Old Jets? No Way." *New York Post*, January 18, 2010.

———. "Standard Answer: Rex's Expectations Rub Off on Unsatisfied Jets." *New York Post*, January 25, 2011.

Web site Sources:

IMDB.com

NewYorkJets.com

NewYorkJetsBlog.com

Pro-football-reference.com

Sportsecyclopedia.com

SportsRadioNewYork.com

TheGregBradyProject.com

WayneCochranandtheCCRiders.com

Wikipedia.com

WrestlingMuseum.com

YouTube.com